PROFESSOR BARK'S AMAZING DIGITAL ADVENTURE

PROFESSOR BARK'S AMAZING DIGITAL ADVENTURE

FIVE FACES OF THE INTERNET

DENNIS L. BARK

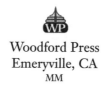

Woodford Press
Emeryville, CA
MM

4

Design: Jim Santore, Woodford Press

Printed in the United States.

ISBN: 0-942627-75-x
Library of Congress Card Number: 00-104026

Distributed in the United States and Canada by Andrews McMeel Universal, Kansas City, Missouri.

Woodford Press
5900 Hollis Street, Suite K
Emeryville, California 94608
www.woodfordpub.com

For

Nalini Indorf Kaplan

and

Gaku Sato.

Both deserve all the credit, but
none of the responsibility.

That's mine!

And for *France,*
who has put up with all this in
real time …

CONTENTS

INTRODUCTION

Stand to your work and be wise —
Certain of Sword and Pen.

[Rudyard Kipling, 1865-1936]

I

NALINI & GAKU

It was a certainty by early 1995. My world was disappearing. I couldn't do anything about it. I hadn't been able to buy a slide rule since the early 1970s. No one used fountain pens anymore. And I felt like an eccentric when I signed letters with real ink. But I did it anyway because my father, who was a professor of medieval history at Stanford University, had brought me up that way. I also liked it. I still do.

When this story began, I was living in the middle of Silicon Valley on the Stanford campus, in an academic world full of new technology I didn't understand. "Laptop computers," which people talked about all the time at Stanford, was a term that was Greek to me. Three years earlier, in 1992, an Apple personal computer had been installed in my office at the Hoover Institution. Our computer experts called it a PC. But all it really was, as far as I could tell, was a glorified typewriter, otherwise known as a word processing machine. And that's what I used it for.

Until I found myself on a United Airlines flight from Washington, D.C., to San Francisco, in January 1995.

Shortly after takeoff an attractive young woman sitting in the seat next to mine unpacked a laptop computer and turned it on. She told me it was IBM's newest, and her company had bought it for her. It cost more than $6,000. It was called a 755 CE and it had an active matrix. I didn't have a clue what that was, but she made a convincing argument that it was the next best thing to sliced bread (my phrase, not hers).

The colors on the screen were dazzling. She started moving a lot of boxes and columns around with what she described as her Track Point II. She was, she told me, a senior principal at American Management Systems in San Mateo, California. She explained she had a presentation at nine o'clock the next morning for a bank, and she needed to review the presentation before the flight attendants served dinner. The review itself didn't interest me, it turned out, because she was moving an arrow around the screen so fast I couldn't keep up. But the colors! There was an elegance and force in their brilliance that I had never seen anywhere before — Elizabethan yellows and greens, and deep blues and reds. I was captivated.

By the time the plane landed she had written down all of the specific things I should order if I decided to get a laptop. I assured her I wanted to do that. But, to be honest, I didn't know what I was talking about, and I wasn't entirely convinced she did either. She was, I could tell, at least twenty years younger than I — in other words, about the age of my eldest son. It was hard for me to admit that anyone that young could know more about anything than I did.

She had the extraordinary name of Nalini Chimene Indorf Kaplan. Thirty-one years old when I met her, she convinced me during that plane ride that I should try the 755 CE. "If money is no object," she said, "it will change your life." She was right, but I didn't know it then.

I had listened to Nalini very carefully during that flight because a close friend of mine in California, Henry "Hank" Kuechler, and I had spent a fair amount of time at lunch in the autumn of 1994 talking about computers and the Internet. We really didn't know what the Internet was, but we knew it was there: the word kept cropping up in newspaper articles. Hank had a computer in his office that his staff used. He knew how to operate his better than I did the one in my office. But both of us felt we really didn't understand what computers and all the fancy software could do, or why. We just knew that a lot of people in the Bay Area were doing a lot of things with both, because articles in the business section of the *San Francisco Chronicle* said so.

We had both grown up on the San Francisco peninsula. Hank had gone to college at the University of California at Berkeley and I at Stanford. We had a lot of friends who were involved in venture capital. One of them, Bill Davidow, had been a major player in the development of Intel Corporation, the computer-processor maker in Santa Clara, California. Another one, Mario Rosati, had joined a fledgling law practice in Palo Alto in 1971; by the 1990s, Wilson, Sonsini, Goodrich & Rosati had become the leading firm in Silicon Valley.

A third friend had a decisive role in raising money to start what became known as Sun Microsystems. The idea for the company came from several students at the Stanford Graduate School of Business who created a network called SU Net.

In a geographical sense, we were in the middle of the high-tech world, but understood nothing about it.

More important, we felt we were, somehow, at the station platform in Palo Alto, watching the Silicon Valley train pull out while we stood by, never figuring out where it was going, or why. To make matters worse, we both felt that because we were only in our mid-fifties, we still had a few years or so of productive professional life ahead of us. It seemed pretty clear to us that if we didn't get on the train soon, time and technology would pass us by. We didn't know how many of our friends felt that way, but we knew we did. We just weren't sure what to do about it.

So when I met Nalini, several months later, I went home directly from the airport to explain to my wife what I wanted to do. She agreed it was a good idea. The next week I ordered a 755 CE at the Stanford Bookstore. I gave Nalini's list of specifications to the salesman, a Stanford student who couldn't have been more than twenty years old. He nonetheless seemed to understand terms like modem, megahertz, bytes, M-wave, RAM and Windows 3.1. I didn't.

My laptop arrived seven weeks later, at the end of March 1995, just two days before I was to leave on a three-week research trip to Germany. I took it with me on the airplane. As I looked around the cabin I noticed several people using *their* laptops. Well, what can I say to explain the following behavior, except that I was flying business class and I wanted everyone to know that I was an up-to-date businessman who had a laptop too. So, very proudly and ostentatiously, I stowed mine in the overhead luggage rack. No one knew I didn't know how to use it.

* * *

On April 14 I checked into the Hotel Kempinski in Berlin. The first thing I did was to plug in the laptop. Then I got out all the manuals that came with it. I plugged the telephone wire from the laptop into the telephone outlet in the wall. Then I tried to send a fax to my office. Nothing happened! I couldn't figure out from the manuals which buttons to press. And, as I would be told the next day, I had wired the computer into the wrong telephone jack.

I went to dinner in the hotel, came back upstairs, looked at my manuals, pressed more buttons, and ordered a Jack Daniel's and soda from room service. Everything went downhill from there. By one o'clock in the morning, nothing, and I mean nothing, made any sense on the computer. I thought I had done something terrible to my laptop. Each time I pressed a button numbers and directions came up on the screen that were even more confusing than the ones a minute before. I ordered another Jack Daniel's and soda — at least I got that part right — and things got worse. By two o'clock in the morning the screen on the laptop looked like a war zone. There were little boxes and messages everywhere about *general protection faults*. What the hell were *general protection faults*? My mood was terrible. Room service knew I was "wired." And, my laptop was broken.

The next day I had lunch with a longtime Berlin friend, Eberhard Hoene, at *Leysieffer*, a *Konditorei* (pastry shop) on the *Kurfürstendamm*, founded in 1909.

The date and tradition comforted me. I explained everything, including the part about this new and unknown term, *general protection fault*. Eberhard didn't know how to work a laptop, either, but he told me his eldest son, Matthias, did. So he suggested we propose a bargain. I called Matthias and invited him to take a taxi to the restaurant for *Baumkuchen* — a German dessert that, according to his father, Matthias loved. The *quid pro quo* was that he would accompany me back to my hotel room to take a look at my laptop.

Matthias, who was twenty-two, hid his amusement pretty well as he entered the hotel room. Without a word he turned on the laptop. In about thirty seconds he had everything back where it was supposed to be. The *general protection faults* had disappeared (and I didn't have the nerve to ask him what they were). He explained that the laptop operated like a tree, and if I could understand *that* principle, I would have no more problems. That was very helpful, I thought, except I didn't know what trees and computers had in common. So I did what any man would do when talking to a child. I thanked him profusely, said how pleased I was that he had enjoyed the *Baumkuchen*, and assured him that everything was now perfectly clear!

* * *

I RETURNED TO CALIFORNIA IN EARLY MAY, AND STRUGGLED WITH MY LAPTOP FOR THE remainder of the spring and summer. The laptop won. I made little significant progress.

My wife and I left for Paris at the end of August. During September and October everyone to whom I showed my laptop marveled at the state-of-the-art hardware and software. The laptop operated at 100 megahertz, with Windows 3.1. It had 16 DRAM, and 340 megabytes of space. Wow! And that's exactly what my brother in New York City said when I called him — "Wow!" I had also bought WordPerfect 6.1 and QuatroPro, a big deal in September 1995. But I couldn't operate the thing any better that autumn than I could during April in Berlin. In the meantime I had learned some of the language, which helped my conversation with admiring Frenchmen; but it was all a fraud, because I couldn't translate my command of computer terms into laptop practice. I authoritatively told my friends, like Bertrand and Roselyne in Paris, and Hank and Hodge in Palo Alto, that the 755 CE was on the cutting edge of communication technology. But I still didn't know why.

When I returned from Europe in November I was still proud of my laptop, but that didn't make it work. Then, a few days before Thanksgiving, I was sitting in the Senior Commons of the Hoover Institution, when in came John McCarthy, whom I had known for some time. John was a professor of computer science at Stanford, and he had developed time-sharing technology, which permits many people to work independently — or interactively — on one computer. I explained the whole story and told him I really wanted to learn how to operate my $6,500 investment.

I was ignorant because there was no educational program at Stanford for teaching scholars, in a systematic way, how to use a computer. It is impossible to learn how to operate a computer by reading a manual, unless you're a real glutton for punishment and have limitless quantities of time. I thought this was ironic in the extreme, and not at all funny. There I was, in the middle of Silicon Valley, which had been spawned by Bill Hewlett and David Packard. I had known them both since I was a little boy. They were graduates of Stanford University, and I had gone to school with their children. But, unlike them, I couldn't operate my computer.

Professor McCarthy suggested I place an advertisement on the Internet. That seemed to me like a good idea, but I didn't know what the Internet was or how to use it. So he did it for me in my office. I sat on a chair next to him, watching. I couldn't have repeated what he had done if my life had depended on it, but I could see that he had put an ad on some kind of electronic bulletin board that computer-literate Stanford students were likely to read. The ad itself requested the tutelage of a student who would be willing to come to my office each week, for as many weeks as it took, to teach me from the ground up how to operate my laptop. I should add that by this time I had finally come to the conclusion college students understood a lot more about computers than most of my colleagues and I did. They still do.

The next day I went to my office and anxiously "turned on" my electronic mail. (I hadn't yet learned that the proper term is to *check* e-mail, but at least I had figured out how to read it.) There was only one response, sent at 2:59 A.M. that morning, from one Gaku Sato. He was interested and asked me to give him the details. But I couldn't, because I didn't know how to answer his e-mail — I hadn't mastered that part yet. Then I noticed that Gaku, who, as I would come to discover, is a master of anticipation, had written a postscript at the bottom of his message: "P.S. Ah, I forgot, you probably don't know how to reply to my e-mail, so here is my telephone number ..."

I called him. He wasn't a Stanford student, but he was a graduate of Princeton, and his wife was getting her Ph.D. in the Department of Education at Stanford. I decided that was good enough. Moreover, I thought anyone who was using his computer at 2:59 in the morning was probably just what I needed at that point. I didn't know how right I was.

Things were not the same after that. What I have learned during the past five years about computer networks, the wired world, and the Internet Generation is a result of the teaching of Gaku Sato and the initiative of Nalini Indorf Kaplan. Gaku, by the way, was thirty years old when I met him. Today, as we exchange e-mail messages about this book, I address him as The Professor, and sign my name as The Student. He earned the distinction.

* * *

FROM THANKSGIVING 1995 TO CHRISTMAS 1999, GAKU TOOK ME STEP BY STEP through the integrated circuits of the computer, to the World Wide Web and beyond, into the universe of cyberspace. Nalini was right! Meeting the computer, at age fifty-three, opened up a new, wired and wireless world of networks that operate in real time. Meeting the computer introduced me to the Information Age. Meeting the computer has made me part of the Internet. Most important, the silicon train, which long ago pulled out of the Palo Alto station, has a new passenger.

II

REVELATIONS

Once I had purchased my laptop, and Gaku had taught me how to work it, I began to understand what the revolution was made of. It became clear that it was about a lot more than just communication. It is about how the use of networks changes what we do, how we do it, and where we do it. It is about how electronic communication redefines the marketplaces of the world. It is about how the freedom of networks is altering the nature of political power. It is about why the Internet will be one of the most important factors affecting change in the future, as computing and telecommunications converge to become a wired and wireless world of information technology.

The revolution is about the death of the knowledge monopoly. It is about how governments are losing control over information. It is about why this loss weakens political rule and decentralizes government power. It is about the force of the written and spoken word. It is about why governments fear the freedom to exchange information. It is about how networks are bypassing intellectual elites and the knowledge class. It is about how networks are remaking economic and social relationships. It is about language — the common language of the Internet is, and always will be, English — a fact that can be frustrating and not easy to accept.

The revolution is about why geographical borders are losing their traditional, sovereign meaning, as companies conduct e-business internationally, without having to open new offices around the globe. It is about why a world of telephone wires, fiber-optic cables, satellites, and real-time communication has produced the Information Age. It is about the fax revolution in central Europe and in the former Soviet Union in the 1980s, about the end of communist regimes in the 1990s, and about how they are being replaced by democracy and free markets in the 2000s. The communication revolution, in short, is about what we are becoming!

* * *

As I was getting to know the computer, I thought about the communication revolution — if it was about all these things, then the implications must be enormous. I became convinced I had to become part of this network tidal wave, or be swept away by it. That's why it was so important that Nalini and Gaku were able to show me that, even for a person hidebound and over fifty, it was not too late to enter the wired world of real-time data networks. It was not too late to become connected.

During 1996 and 1997, with Gaku teaching me more and more each week, I became overwhelmed by what I was seeing. As I learned how to make my laptop work, I discovered what most people half my age now take for granted. I could write things anywhere — whether I was on a boat dock at Lake Tahoe, or leaning against the wall of a barn in central France on a Saturday afternoon. And I didn't need my pen. In fact, in mid-1997 I even sent a fax from an airplane, without paper, just to see if I could do it (and to impress a young woman sitting next to me).

That I could communicate without paper was a revelation — at least that's how it seemed to me. It began to affect my professional as well as my private life. I was becoming more productive, and I was using my laptop everywhere, and all the time: in the library of my house in Stanford, in my kitchen in France, on the airplane to Washington, D.C., in my hotel room in Berlin, and in the train from Paris to Brussels.

In other words, I discovered what every computer-literate person knows — that by using a computer and the Internet effectively, one's productivity increases. I was working with a very sophisticated device, and I felt a responsibility to explain it to anyone who would listen, especially my friends in their early fifties and older. But I found it hard to convey my feeling that I had been given a new life. The whole idea sounded silly, and my friends didn't understand. None of them knew how to use a computer, and they didn't understand the terminology. So while they responded to my excitement with patient amusement, the message I wanted to send went in one ear and out the other. My friends did, however, all have something in common. They were, without exception, curious. "Why are you so excited?" they wanted to know. Since I wasn't very good at telling them, I started to write my thoughts down.

So what has happened to me? To begin with, my world isn't disappearing anymore. It's expanding! I send e-mail to Berlin and Paris and I get it from London, Ann

Arbor, New York, and Copenhagen. (I still use fountain pens, by the way; in fact, I bought my last Mont Blanc pen on the Web.) And I don't go to music stores anymore. For the past three years I've purchased all my CDs on the Internet, and most of my books, too. I do still feel like an eccentric character, but I've got a lot more eccentric company than I had before. Moreover, I feel as though I were twenty years old (except I'm bald!).

My emotional reaction of excitement and wonder at learning how to use my laptop led me to this obvious conclusion: To be part of the communication revolution you have to understand it. So, as Gaku's teaching took me on my new, electronic journey, I decided I would start asking my colleagues to explain to me what this world was all about. I assumed that they all knew how it worked, and furthermore, I was sure they would be able to answer all my questions. But that, as it turned out, wasn't the case. I was not prepared at all for the discovery that many of my colleagues, in addition to my friends over fifty, didn't know any more about the revolution than I did.

* * *

I AM A SENIOR FELLOW AT THE HOOVER INSTITUTION, LOCATED IN THE MIDDLE OF Stanford University's campus of Spanish-style sandstone buildings with red tile roofs built in the 1890s. Any way you look at it, the setting is a national treasure. As *The Economist* put it in a 1992 article headlined "The Good Think-Tank Guide: The Joys of Detached Involvement," the Hoover is "hard to match for sheer intellectual firepower…. [M]oney, location and a superb library and archives largely detach Hoover from the hurly-burly of everyday politics and make it an extremely congenial hangout for disputatious academics, untroubled by liberal thoughts."

To understand what this means you have to picture the life we lead there. We have what we call a Senior Commons, where coffee and tea are served at 3:30 each afternoon. The idea is to provide a place where we, as scholars, can gather and talk about what we are working on, or just exchange views and information about anything. It's open to any professor on the campus who wants to come; that's why John McCarthy came there that afternoon in November 1995. We sit at a round table. It's an ideal intellectual environment.

For the past thirty years I have specialized in European affairs. I took my Ph.D. degree in 1970 at the Freie Universität Berlin, in the city behind the Iron Curtain that was the lighthouse of the Cold War. Europe, the way I look at the world, is important because it is the cradle of western civilization. I thought it was natural, as my laptop was introducing me to the Information Age, to begin thinking about how the new wired world of real time would affect the conduct of foreign policy, and by implication, how it would affect Europe.

On a late autumn afternoon in 1995, I started, very tentatively, to ask my colleagues what they thought about the communication revolution, and whether it would change political and economic relations with Europe.

It was the right idea, but the wrong question.

The response was fascinating, but surprising at the same time. The majority of my colleagues didn't understand why I was asking the question. One of them even said to me, "it's all smoke and mirrors." Indeed, it would have gratified the editors at *The Economist* to know that the disputatious nature of my colleagues was intact, untroubled by real-time technology. But the world they were living in was changing under their scholarly feet and many didn't recognize it. One of the Hoover's senior administrators — they are welcome at the round table, too — told me, "the Internet's fine, but it has no future." I countered, although I wasn't at all sure I could prove it, that the Internet will change the nature, scope, and exercise of political, economic, and military power in fundamental ways. As governments and businesses lose their monopolies on information of all kinds, my theory went, and as ambassadors seek to conduct diplomacy in a world where geographical boundaries are in many ways becoming irrelevant, new power will reside in the ability to find information quickly, to distribute it widely, to exchange it instantaneously, and to act on it.

This line of argument didn't get me very far that afternoon, so I gave it up. Instead, more out of desperation than anything else, I turned to Annelise Anderson and Tom Moore, colleagues who, to their everlasting credit, had been patiently teaching me some of the mysteries of Microsoft's Windows 3.1 software. Still trying to recover from my loss of face, I asked them about the time-saving advantages of electronic mail. We observed that there were some people at our round table who, quite clearly, hadn't gotten "the message." One scholar had arrogantly declared, "I don't have time to use electronic mail." All my life I had heard the phrase about someone's eyes "glazing over," but I had always thought it was a figure of speech. Well, that afternoon in the Senior Commons, it happened right in front of me as we talked about baud rates and modems. Their eyes got a faraway, cloudy look and glistened, as if nobody were at home.

The message was clear, and you didn't have to be a Nobel Prize winner to figure it out. (Some of my colleagues *are* Nobel Prize winners!) The round table was witnessing a real-time information gap, as well as a generation gap. Many of my colleagues my age and older simply didn't understand what the communication revolution was all about. Some, to cover their ignorance, even argued that the whole thing was a flash in the pan. It came as such a shock I still haven't fully recovered from it. But it really shouldn't have surprised me, because just a year earlier I had been asking myself, "What would I use a computer for?" I had been answering my own question with the words, "Nothing! It takes too much time to use one, and moreover, I'm a scholar, not a scientist." That response, of course, was a rationalization to justify my refusal to learn how computers worked. I had no idea there existed a communication revolution that was changing the world in profound ways, and that would shortly change mine, too. The advantages of a fax machine were obvious to me, but that was really all I knew.

These two gaps, as I now know, are very real. The information gap separates those who know from those who don't. The generation gap exists because most of the people who don't know are the elders of those who do. Neither gap, obviously, will last forever. But they will be with us for a long time, because it's not possible to introduce computers tomorrow to everyone on earth who is older than age fifty. The generation gap is defined primarily by age and ignorance, not intelligence. My friends and colleagues *are* intelligent. We know we're living in the Information Age, but are just beginning to learn how to use the new communication technologies of the wired world. More and more of us can send and receive electronic mail. But many of us still don't know how to send faxes without paper, nor has it occurred to us that one day the fax machine will be obsolete.

We hear about the Internet, about e-commerce, about e-business, and about the Web almost daily; but most of us can't really explain what these things are. Most of us don't speak the technical language of those, like Nalini and Gaku, who do understand. And, by consequence, the two generations — those who understand what the Internet is and those who don't — have a tough time carrying on a rational conversation about it with each other. In June 1997 the mean age of those who used the Internet was thirty-one years! Two years later, in June 1999, the mean age was approaching forty years. In March 2000 about 14 million adults in the United States fifty years old and older were on-line (about 15 percent of all U.S. users). So, for those in their seventies and eighties, with some exceptions, the wired world still remained a foreign one. I tried to explain to my wife's aunt in October 1999, for example, that I could send a fax without paper. At the age of eighty-seven she is a lady striking in appearance, intelligent, and delightful. But I was talking about a world that, for most of her generation, is simply incomprehensible.

The generation gap is illustrated best by the results of a public opinion poll released in April 1999, financed by Microsoft Corporation and the American Society on Aging. Not surprisingly, computer usage and ownership decreased with age: while 37 percent of those surveyed between fifty and fifty-nine owned a personal computer, less than 4 percent of those over the age of eighty owned one. Indeed, in one 1999 study 82 percent of those polled between seventy and seventy-nine were

18

"not at all interested" in finding out what a computer could offer them.

As I began to write down my reactions to meeting the computer I recognized two things. First, I was a Johnny-come-lately to the wired world; there was no point in trying to reinvent the wheel by impressing my friends with a lot of profound observations. The second thing, however, was different: my late arrival didn't make my reactions any less important. And, in fact, because I did arrive late, and because I was a generation older than the mean age of Internet users, my sense of awe and amazement might be just what my friends and colleagues could understand.

We have several things in common besides being over fifty. One is we can still recognize that age doesn't always mean we are more knowledgeable than the younger generation. So some of us, the older we get, grudgingly admit that in spite of our advancing years there are some things we still have to learn. The Internet is an example par excellence. The other thing most of us possess is historical perspective, which our children, because of their youth, cannot share. That's just another way of saying that this new world of network communication isn't, merely by definition, as strange and overwhelming as it may seem. In the United States, the future wonders of communication were introduced to my generation more than half a century ago in a famous comic strip.

Recall Dick Tracy's two-way wrist radio? It allowed police officers at headquarters and out in the field not only to talk to one another, but eventually, as the two-way wrist television, to see each other. The radio first appeared in the hands of a cartoon fugitive from the law, B.O. Plenty, on January 13, 1946. In 1964 the two-way wrist radio was followed by the two-way wrist television. And finally, in 1986, the comic strip introduced the two-way wrist computer. It seems electronic networks have been with us in our imagination for some time.

Members of my generation, I suspect, may understand the value and importance of the communication revolution better than we think. In many ways, it is the younger generation that must teach the older how all the fancy network hardware and software work. But when my friends and colleagues finally learn what computers can do and recognize what networks make possible, they will bring with them the valuable tool of experience, historical perspective, and what wisdom we can muster, to help interpret and design this new world.

The communication revolution gives added value to information. And in this sense, the revolution is about what happens when "closely held" information becomes easily available, via electronic computer networks, to huge numbers of people who never had access to it before. When that happens, "power changes hands," in the words of former Citibank chairman Walter Wriston. The hierarchical "old boy network" is thus being replaced by the wired world of electronic networks. It is accessible to anyone with a computer, a modem, and a telephone line. It's as simple as that, but many of the old boys still don't know it! Political leaders today, in Asia, in Europe, and in the United States, love to visit computer expositions and have their pictures taken standing next to the newest, state-of-the-art technology hardware. But don't make the mistake of asking them to explain what it does and why it changes things. Most of them can't.

Don't conclude from this, however, that they don't want to learn. Politicians will have to learn, because everyone who has been making a living by monopolizing information is being forced to change how they do business — stockbrokers, writers, bankers, journalists, car dealers, librarians, insurance salesmen, lawyers, teachers, doctors, booksellers, newscasters, as well as politicians. Information monopolies are dying. Anyone can access the Internet and find whatever information they seek. We don't have to pay the stockbroker for information about companies, and we don't have to depend on newscasters to get the news. We can verify their accuracy and we can analyze their value, and we don't need anyone's permission. We are communicating, comparing, and conducting the affairs of business, education, and politics with computers and the Internet. It will not be so easy to befog the general public anymore.

Information networks are setting millions of people free. This freedom is bringing with it both opportunities and challenges. Youth alone is not sufficient to meet the challenges. And the wisdom that comes with age alone is not sufficient to grasp the opportunities. But together all of us have a vested interest in understanding how the wired world of real time works, and what we can do with it when we are connected. If this book sheds light on these areas, then it is written for any age.

III

THE INTERNET GENERATION

The wired world of real time, I am convinced, will transform our lives in more dramatic ways than the Industrial Revolution did with its dynamo and electricity. The Internet already allows electronic commerce, banking, messaging, and research.

Much of the information in this book, for instance, was found on the Internet: I found *International Herald Tribune* articles on the newspaper's Web site, and didn't have to see the actual paper. Magazines also are available electronically, such as Microsoft's *Slate* (a magazine, incidentally, you can't buy at a newsstand). What are the implications? There are no printing costs, paper costs, or postage costs. That means, in turn, that bankers, stockbrokers, publishers, booksellers, librarians — in short, all of us — will change our ways of doing business, or go out of business. The marketplace is no longer confined to main streets and town squares, nor to shopping malls and mail-order catalogs. It is now also electronic. It is something very real on a computer screen, that you can see, but which has no physical address, though it does have e-mail addresses and Web sites.

The design of domestic policies and the conduct of foreign ones are being affected, too. Politicians and political groups have Web sites, as do the White House and government offices in the capitals of Asia and Europe. Censorship is becoming much more difficult. Satellite photographs, once available only from government intelligence agencies, can be downloaded from the Internet. It's not easy anymore for governments to control access to information and keep secrets. Concepts of sovereignty are changing as well. The Internet doesn't recognize tax jurisdictions, passports, time zones, or customs barriers.

The debate in the United States about encryption and its private use is a superb illustration of government officials still trying to play the role of Big Brother. Complicated ciphers, impossible to break, used to be classified by the government as "munitions." Today, anyone who wants to encrypt an e-mail message can do it by using free software available on the Internet. Yet some governments have declared unbreakable encryption illegal. But it's a futile gesture, made by ignorant politicians who believe they can control the Internet. They can't.

Long-held concepts of loyalty and patriotism are changing, also. For example, ask one hundred American college students at Harvard University, or one hundred French students at the Sorbonne, to answer the following two questions: (1) Are you loyal to your country? and (2) Are you a patriot? If you ask me, I would say "yes" to both questions. But what if you ask our children? The Information Age is redefining traditional definitions of loyalty and patriotism, just as the conventional significance of geographical borders is vanishing. Internet travelers can go everywhere via the information highway, without passing border controls. Never have so many people been able to travel to so many houses, towns, and marketplaces, using just one kind of transportation.

Conducting business in the Information Age raises new questions about how governments will be financed in the next century. Electronic commerce will not only change how governments collect taxes, but how much money they will collect. The nation-state and the commercial marketplace of the twenty-first century aren't going to bear a lot of resemblance to the last one. What this means in both financial and political terms was summarized in 1992 (when few were listening), by the former chairman of the Citibank of New York, Walter B. Wriston, in his 1992 book *The Twilight of Sovereignty:*

> The marriage of the computer with telecommunications, resulting in movement of information at the speed of light and to enormous audiences, tends to decentralize power as it decentralizes knowledge. When a system of national currencies run by central banks is transformed into a global electronic marketplace driven by private currency traders, power changes hands.... When an international telecommunications system, incorporating technologies from mobile phones to communications satellites, deprives governments of the ability to keep secrets from the world, or from their own people, power changes hands.

The chapters of this book are reflections on the marriage of the computer with telecommunication. The result of that union, the Internet, is a world of electronic networks created initially, and ironically, as a product of the Cold War — a conflict brought to a peaceful conclusion, thanks in large part to the economic, political, and diplomatic roles played by people now in their sixties, seventies, and eighties. That includes a number of my older colleagues now or formerly at the Hoover Institution, such as Milton Friedman, James Stockdale, Henry Rowen, F.A. Hayek, Charles Wolf, Sidney Hook, Bertram Wolfe, Ronald Reagan, Robert Conquest, George Shultz, Glenn Campbell, and Edward Teller. In turn, this new world has given birth to the Internet Generation. Nalini and Gaku, members of this generation in good standing, are the beneficiaries of this Cold War product. They understand how the Internet is setting the world free. But many of my colleagues are still frustrated by this wired world, even though the responsibilities they discharged as scholars or government officials on leave from the Hoover Institution during the 1960s, the 1970s,

22

and the '80s influenced, in one way or another, the post-Cold War world of freedom of communication.

The Internet Generation has inherited, from those who fought and won the Cold War, a civilization built on the values of classical liberalism, of freedom, truth, and moral decency. This political inheritance is a legacy of liberty. The colleagues of my generation at the Hoover Institution know this. But many of them don't yet recognize that the communication technologies now available to all of us are creating a new world of freedom never imagined by Benjamin Franklin, George Washington, or Thomas Jefferson. Instead, they wonder if the Internet Generation really understands that the legacy of liberty is *the idea of freedom,* and is the consequence of the will to defend the values of classical liberalism. Conventional wisdom suggests that the answer to this question requires a knowledge of history. The story of the Cold War teaches us, after all, that the idea of freedom has both friends and enemies. It follows that the newfound freedom of the Internet will also have friends and enemies. So logical questions arise: Does the Internet Generation understand that threats to freedom, truth, and moral decency still exist? Does it care? Does it consider these questions relevant? Does any of this matter? Will the Internet Generation feel any commitment to defend freedom, truth, and moral decency, as stewards of the liberty it has inherited?

I raise the questions because some of my colleagues and contemporaries doubt the responsibility of the younger generation. "Look at how these people dress," they say. "Can they spell the word civilization? Have they ever heard of a coat and tie? Can they tell you the difference between the beauty of French savoir faire, and the vulgarity of 'Hey dude, whassup?' Do they give a damn?"

My colleagues, as former players in the Cold War, know that freedom, truth, and moral decency can always be attacked, just as they have been under siege since time immemorial. Will the Internet Generation defend these values successfully? The outcome may produce a clash of civilizations, as some, such as Samuel Huntington at Harvard University, argue. Or the outcome may produce a new world of greater freedom and prosperity than any civilization has ever known. What concerns my colleagues is the certainty that civility, decency, freedom, and prosperity are all, once again, hanging in the balance of what we call the historical process. How the balance is weighed and measured will be influenced by the imagination, by the creativity, and by the courage of the Internet Generation. What that courage is made of and who the members of the generation are I had never thought to ask five years ago. But I have asked these questions since.

I've talked to Nalini about it as well as with others of her generation, including my three sons. Nalini understands very clearly that the credibility of the

Introduction

users of electronic networks is of decisive importance. She values honesty, freedom of expression, and moral decency, because without them the wired world won't work. And for those of my generation who remain ignorant of how the Internet works — how can they possibly understand what happens when computing and telecommunication converge? How can they possibly grasp what the end of the information monopoly really means? They are unaware that electronic networks, to have any real and lasting value, must be based on a respect for freedom, trust, and moral decency. A dramatic illustration of why this is true is grippingly described in a book called *The Cuckoo's Egg*, by Cliff Stoll. I didn't know that the book, first published in 1989, existed until April 1997. (When I read it I was so impressed I sent an e-mail message to my colleague Annelise Anderson, and urged her to read the book. She replied, "I read it five years ago!" But most of my colleagues have never heard of it.)

Reading *The Cuckoo's Egg* was the result of my introduction to a remarkable individual. He, like Nalini and Gaku, has helped shape my perception of the Internet Generation. In March 1997 the computer system manager at the United States Institute of Peace in Washington, D.C., spent the better part of an afternoon trying to educate me about the world of "remote sensing and foreign policy" — in other words, satellite photography. He told me about a conference he had attended on satellite imagery the previous week, and said there had been an expert there who worked for Sandia National Laboratories in Berkeley, California.

This expert's name is Vipin Gupta, and he was twenty-nine years old in 1997. I contacted him and asked him if he would read my draft — at that time about ninety pages — and he said he would. At the end of April he had a business meeting at Stanford, so we met at the Hoover Institution. We started off by going over this introduction, and I became quickly embarrassed because it was taking a fair amount of time. But he proceeded to go through every page of the manuscript, staying for more than two hours as I sat there asking questions and taking notes. He is one of the sharpest people I have ever met.

That afternoon I was especially interested in how he would answer my questions about freedom, trust, and moral decency on the Internet. He told me that the value of networks is only as strong as the integrity and decency of the people who use them. And it was he who told me to read *The Cuckoo's Egg*, a true story about tracking a spy through the maze of computer espionage. In the conclusion the author, an astronomer at the University of California at Berkeley named Cliff Stoll, writes:

> I learned what our networks are. I had thought of them as a complicated technical device, a tangle of wires and circuits. But they're much more than that — a fragile community of people, bonded

together by trust and cooperation. If that trust is broken, the community will vanish forever.

My meeting with Vipin was unforgettable. He was wearing, if I remember rightly, Levis and sandals, and his hair was in a ponytail. I had on a coat and tie. When he was about to go, he said, "I'm amazed you had the courage, at your age, to write this introduction." That was a compliment tough to match, and I thanked him for it. But what he didn't know, and what I couldn't have explained then if I'd tried, was that it wasn't a question of age. It was, on the contrary, a question of having the good fortune to meet Nalini and Gaku, the wit to admit my ignorance, and the common sense to do something about it. It was also clear that what we wear isn't always a sign of what we're made of; I hadn't thought enough about that before, either.

What we do, and how well we do it, has always been affected by how we communicate. If we want other people to recognize the value of what we think, it is critically important how we express it, how we say it, and in the world of the Internet, also how we send it and how we protect it. How this is done is the difference between freedom and dictatorship. Lest there be any misunderstanding, here it is *not* the medium that is the message. If that were true, I would be making a technological determinist argument. That's a concept I reject. A computer, after all, is nothing more than a little black box. Technology doesn't determine its value. People do, by how they use it. The value of a message is what's in it. But if a message can be transmitted at the speed of light in the world of the Internet, then obviously the medium enhances the value of the information, depending on what we do with it.

So what am I trying to say? In the world of the Internet, the medium serves as a new dimension in which the message is delivered in real time — at once. The immediacy creates new relationships. The medium of the computer network gives the message additional value, above and beyond its content. Neither the dictator nor the benevolent bureaucrat can censor it, stop it, or even read it — if you know what you're doing. That, at the height of the Cold War, was the value of the fax machine. It was also the beginning of wired sovereignty.

At the center of the Cold War was the struggle for the hearts and minds of twentieth-century man. It was a conflict about freedom and truth, over the right to express values and ideas, to communicate them, to give them real life, and to defend them. The conclusion of that war, in 1989-1990, liberated tens of millions of people in Central Europe and the Soviet Union from the yoke of political and economic oppression. For the first time in half a century Europeans were free to communicate, to say what they thought, and to exercise the right of freedom of speech. Europe would never be the same again.

How important that was, and is, was put poignantly during an interview my former colleague at the Hoover Institution, David Gress, and I conducted with an East German in February 1991, several months after the unification of Germany. His name was Heinrich Fink, a professor of theology and the new president of the University of Berlin. We met him in his office on Berlin's most famous street, Unter den Linden, in what had been the Soviet Sector of that city, and recorded the experience in our 1993 book, *A History of West Germany, Democracy and Its Discontents 1963-1991 (Volume II)*:

> We ... asked him to tell us something of the problems that needed solving. They seemed almost endless, and we listened to his recitation for over an hour. Just before going we asked him if there was anything positive he could tell us. He thought for almost twenty seconds, and said: 'That one can express a different opinion, without having to be afraid.'

In a fundamental way the revolution in communication technology is about the freedom to express opinions, to exchange ideas, and to trade information, without fear of punishment by government. It is about the freedom and power of speech. From that freedom and power flows initiative, innovation, invention, and imagination. The Internet Generation lives in this new world, where slide rules are the stuff of museums and rotary dial telephones have been replaced with wireless ones, e-mail, and electronic networks.

But is it, or will it be, more productive? I argue in this book that it is vastly more productive. What does that really mean?

We already know that the revolution is changing the arena in which ideas compete and the marketplaces in which commerce thrives. It is changing how we conduct foreign affairs. It is changing how we think about things, and how we imagine things. It is changing where we work, and how we work. The world of communication is no longer reactive or passive. It is *interactive*. The linear world of television is being transformed by the geometric world of the World Wide Web. What the Internet will eventually become is still taking shape. But out of this world is walking a new class of entrepreneur, for whom using networks and the Internet will be as natural as using electric light. Ten years from now we will still be turning off the light, but we will leaving our computers on.

"Real time" is, indeed, a symbol for the Internet Generation. But that generation itself is anything but symbolic. How this generation will interpret and defend the classical values of "the sacredness of truth ... the ordinary rules of moral decency ... a common belief in the value of human freedom ... an affirmative action towards democracy ... [and] opposition to all forms of totalitarianism," to use R.M.

Hartwell's words from his book *A History of the Mont Pelerin Society*, is a challenge it is already meeting — with, moreover, the same courage and conviction with which its Cold War forefathers defended the same values of classical liberalism in the struggle between freedom and tyranny. The Internet Generation has no gender, just independence and imagination. It includes Tim Berners-Lee, who started a revolution in 1989 with a proposal called the World Wide Web (he is discussed in Chapter One), and Phil Zimmerman, who in 1990 created something called Pretty Good Privacy (you'll meet him, too). It includes Jeff Bezos, founder of the on-line retailer Amazon.com, and Marc Andreessen who in 1992-93 developed a "portal to the Web" that became Netscape. And it includes Bill Gates of Microsoft, the company that gave new meaning to an old word, windows.

For the first time in the history of civilization, technology has given mankind the tools for unlimited freedom of speech, via the computer, the mobile telephone, the fax, e-mail, and the World Wide Web. You can call it an accidental empire, if you like, but whatever we call it, there is no arbitrary barrier to entry. The Internet has no address and levies no taxes. No government owns it (although a French defense official visiting me at the Hoover Institution in 1997 asserted with Gallic certainty that "the Americans control it"). The Internet doesn't know the difference between man and woman, black and white, college student and professor, or between Asian and African, American or European. It belongs to no one, and to everyone.

So, will the values of classical liberalism define the Information Age, or will they become the victims of real time? This question, to quote *The Detroit News* editorial-page editor Thomas J. Bray, another friend who has read this manuscript, "is of significant concern, given the fundamentally libertarian and entrepreneurial nature of the Internet."

But it's not fair to leave it at that. Where's the bottom line? The answer is, it's at your fingertips. The wired world is producing the real certainties of electronic networks, electronic commerce, and electronic politics. It is this same world of virtual certainties that will protect classical values, because the Internet Generation must protect the world in which it lives. And so belongs to the Internet Generation the future of freedom.

IV

THE LAST WORD

There is one final matter. How did this book get here? When I began I had no publisher. I had thought about it, but I wasn't sure how to approach it. I knew I needed help, but I didn't know what kind, until my brother read the Introduction and said, "Dennis, what you need is an agent!" I said, "Fine. But I want someone who is more or less my age, who is as captivated by the communication revolution as I am, and who believes in this with the same excitement and conviction that I do."

Jed's response was, "No problem. My company, Bark Frameworks, works with a public relations agency. I will ask the lady we work with to give me some suggestions — because you will never break into the world of book agents without some help." So it was that I wrote a letter to a well-known literary agent in New York City in October 1997.

The agent returned the manuscript several weeks later, and had written the following note on the bottom of my letter to her:

28 October 1997

Dear Dennis Bark,

Thanks so much for the proposal. I think it's not for me. Truthfully I see the Internet as an intrusion and an unfortunate necessity. I do wish you the best w/ this project elsewhere. I am sure it will be a splendid book ...
Don't give up. There's someone out there just waiting ...

I think I'll send her a complimentary copy.

———

Dennis L. Bark
The Hoover Institution – Stanford University
16 August 2000

Part I

REAL CERTAINTIES

*Thus in the beginning the world was so made
that certain signs come before
certain events.*

[Cicero, 106-43 B.C.]

CHAPTER ONE

UNINTENDED CONSEQUENCES

*What is going on in the world today is not a
new Industrial Revolution.
It is the birth of a new civilization with corre-
sponding changes in every facet of our existence, changes that are an order of magnitude
greater than those that affected the factories
and workers of an
Industrial Revolution.
What is happening today may, by an oversim-
plification, be thought of as
a consequence of the sudden interaction of science and society.
But the effects of this interaction transcend
both science and society.*

{B.D. Thomas, November 12, 1964}

1.

Two Generations in the Information Age

Pictured at left:
Different Generations Using Time Differently

One, whose family founded the *San Francisco Chronicle* in 1865, was born
in 1942, the year that Hedy Lamarr and George Antheil were, without
knowing it, laying the foundation for the Internet.
He is whittling away his time.
The other, whose family founded the *Dallas Morning News* in 1885, was
born in 1987. In that year there were only 28,000 host computers in the
United States. By 2000 there were more than 100 million. She is traveling
through the time of cyberspace, a word that
didn't exist when she was born.
Peter and Audrey come from two great newspaper families. It is appropriate
that theirs is the only photograph in this book, which is about
communication without paper.
Audrey brought her laptop with her to the mountains of the Sierra Nevada in
August of 1997, when this picture was taken. Peter has a laptop, too, but he
didn't bring it with him. In fact, one evening several months later, when he
was having problems sending e-mail (which he hadn't mastered), he threw his
laptop across the room and stomped on it.
Different generations communicate with their computers differently.

2.

AN IDEA IN HOLLYWOOD?

Toto, something tells me we're not in Kansas anymore.

{from the 1939 film *The Wizard of Oz*}

On an evening in 1940 an American expatriate piano player from Paris was at a dinner party in Hollywood. There, at the home of Janet Gaynor, he met a young actress from Vienna. She was in her mid-twenties and had studied theater in Berlin. It was said her teacher, the famous Max Reinhardt, called her "the most beautiful girl in Europe," and by all accounts she was.

At the age of nineteen she had married Fritz Mandl, an Austrian arms dealer.

In the Vienna of the mid-1930s everyone with name and reputation in the war industry was, sooner or later, Mandl's dinner guest. While Mandl worked out his sales to the Nazis at one end of the dining table, his strikingly beautiful wife was on exhibition on the other end, or so his guests thought. On these evenings, as she joined the conversations, she was also getting a first-class education on the effort to build a torpedo guidance system that couldn't be jammed by the enemy. In fact, she even joined her husband when he reviewed films of field tests for torpedo systems. Most people would have struggled to stay awake, but for some reason this woman concentrated on what she was hearing. Perhaps she remembered out of spite, because she resented being treated by her husband as a virtual prisoner. As she later put it, she was "a kind of slave. I couldn't even go swimming without him."

So, she made plans to escape.

On a dark night in 1937, after allegedly drugging the maid, she climbed out the window of her house and fled to London. From there she took the *Normandie* for

New York City. While on board — or perhaps in London; it's not clear — she met a man who would change her life. He offered her a job in Hollywood. His name was Louis B. Mayer, one of the cofounders of MGM. She was already well known for a film in Europe called *Ecstasy*, but would become even more so as the leading lady for actors such as Charles Boyer and Gene Lockhart, Robert Young and Bob Hope, Basil Rathbone and Spencer Tracy, Clark Gable and Jimmy Stewart. Her real name was Hedwig Eva Maria Kiesler. But in Hollywood no one knew that. Neither did anybody know that she wasn't only interested in movies. The way she put it, no doubt recalling the Viennese dinner table, "'Any woman can be bewitchingly beautiful. She only has to keep her mouth shut, and look dumb.'"

The piano player she met in Hollywood was named George Antheil. He was an avant-garde composer, born in Trenton, New Jersey, but well known in Europe as "the bad boy of music." In Paris he had written the *Ballet Mecanique* in 1926, a piece for sixteen synchronized player pianos, two electronically driven airplane propellers, four bass drums, four xylophones, and a siren. It was said he considered machines to be more predictable than people. But in 1940 he found himself working in Hollywood, at the beginning of World War II, writing music for films. When Kiesler and Antheil met each other that night, Hitler's Third Reich was conversation number one, as it was for everyone in America. As a European living in California, the war touched Kiesler in a special way. She felt at home, but also far from home. So it couldn't have come as a great surprise to Antheil when Kiesler, in her Austrian accent, started explaining why she wanted to help the war effort against Germany.

When she left that evening, she wrote her telephone number in lipstick on the windshield of his car. The next day he called, and she invited him to dinner. What she told him at home in Benedict Canyon, however, must have shocked him. On that evening the twenty-six-year-old actress outlined a concept for a torpedo guidance system that would work even if the enemy tried to interfere with it — so that the target would always be hit. The torpedo would be guided by a radio signal which, in the form of little signal packets, could hop rapidly, and seemingly accidentally, from frequency to frequency, in a way that couldn't be jammed or monitored. The only thing missing, she explained, was a mechanism to synchronize the changing radio frequency between the ship and the torpedo after it had been fired.

Antheil recognized in her idea the same principle he had employed to synchronize his player pianos, using slotted paper cylinders similar to piano rolls. Lying on the living room rug, he sketched out the concept in a spiral notebook while she spoke. Shortly before Christmas they had figured out in detail how to make it work; or so they thought. Six months later, on June 10, 1941, they formally submitted it to the U.S. patent office. Granted on August 11, 1942, patent number 2,292,387 was called "Secret Communication System." The invention was designed to synchronize

An Idea in Hollywood?

eighty-eight radio frequencies, exactly the number of keys on a piano. But nothing came of it. Said Antheil much later: "The revered, tin-helmeted gentlemen in Washington who reviewed our invention, only read as far as the word *player piano*. I hear them saying, 'My God, we're supposed to pack a piano in our torpedoes!'"

Their patent, for technical reasons, gathered dust during World War II as one of Washington's military secrets, although *The New York Times* reported in October 1942 that "so vital is her discovery to national defense that government officials will not allow publication of its details." But twenty years later, by the time of the Cuban missile crisis of 1962, the technology had been developed into something called frequency hopping. It was used for the first time when Sylvania Corporation installed it in electronic systems on ships that President John F. Kennedy sent to blockade Cuba.

How could Kiesler and Antheil have known — how could anybody have known — that from signal packets hopping from frequency to frequency would emerge wireless communication for pagers, faxes, e-mail, voice mail, cellular phones, and other types of hand-held communicators and organizers? It is a world of tones and pulses and bandwidths, of spread-spectrum communication, digital telephone systems, mobile data networks and wireless messaging systems, and of modems — some with wires and some without — with names like *Ricochet*. It is an interconnected world of webs and nets. Today, we call this wired and wireless world of virtual freedom the Internet. And the Hollywood actress? Well, the patent, which lapsed in 1959, had been taken out under the names of Antheil and Hedwig Kiesler Markey. Only a few figured out, until recently, that her stage name was Hedy Lamarr.

In 1997, more than half a century later, Lamarr and Antheil were given the recognition they deserved. In March of that year Lamarr, then eighty-two and living in Florida, and Antheil, who died in 1959, received the Pioneer Award for their invention from the Electronic Frontier Foundation (EFF). The award was presented at the seventh annual "Computers, Freedom and Privacy Conference" in Burlingame, California. Their concept, conference organizers noted, had become "the basis for the spread-spectrum radio systems used in the products of over forty companies manufacturing items ranging from cell phones to wireless networking systems." EFF's staff counsel, Mike Godwin, put the award's significance in the following perspective: "Ironically this tool they developed to defend democracy half a century ago promises to extend democracy in the twenty-first century." Lamarr's response to the award: "It was about time!" When she died two years later, in January 2000, her obituaries made scant reference to the invention.

In 1962 — more than two decades after Lamarr and Antheil's patent — the RAND Corporation, in Santa Monica, California, was giving life to another modest proposal. It was based on work by Paul Baran, one of RAND's research fellows. He called his research, commissioned by the U.S. Air Force, "On Distributed Communications Networks." The report was the reflection of a concern, held by U.S. leaders in the early 1960s, about how to assure the integrity of government communication in the event of a world war. The Cuban missile crisis had underscored the seriousness of the issue, because for the first time since World War II the United States government had come eyeball to eyeball with the Soviet Union. It was a potential nuclear confrontation. What, namely, would happen if there was a "decapitating" attack?

This question raised an all-important issue: How would the U.S. maintain command and control if a preemptive nuclear strike destroyed the government's communication system and, therefore, its ability to respond with nuclear weapons? The dilemma, in layman's terms, was simple: if you can't communicate through the chain of command because the telephone system has been knocked out, how can you respond?

In practical terms such a possibility put the credibility of U.S. nuclear forces at risk. The president of the United States always had a military officer with him carrying what was euphemistically referred to as the "football." It was a briefcase with the codes necessary for the president to authorize a nuclear attack. If a first strike against the U.S. cut off communication between the president and his commanders, the president, in military terms, would be "decapitated." The "football" would be useless. Moreover, if a potential enemy knew that "decapitation" might be possible, the value of a nuclear response, as a deterrent to a first strike, would be seriously weakened. All of these concerns were directly related to the U.S. government communication system.

That system, in the early 1960s, was a telephone network. It connected the White House with the Strategic Air Command, for example, and with Naval ships in the Pacific, and with NATO forces in Europe, and so on. But this communication link was vulnerable as long as it could be cut. So, senior government analysts went in search of a solution, to make the link secure. It took the form of the idea sketched out by the RAND Corporation's Paul Baran. The project was funded and carried out under five successive directors of the Advanced Research Projects Agency (ARPA): Jack Ruina, Bob Sproull, Charles Herzfeld, Ed Rechtin, and Steve Lukasik. Starting in 1967 and continuing until 1974, Lukasik served first as deputy and then as director. It was during this period that the major investment in networking research bore fruit. The result was creation of an electronic network. It came to be called the ARPANET.

Was the purpose strictly military? Initially, in June 1961, ARPA was assigned development of a program called Command and Control, whose charter was "to support research on the conceptual aspects of command and control and to provide

An Idea in Hollywood?

a better understanding of organizational, informational, and man-machine relationships." Between 1962 and 1964 an unusually perceptive and thoughtful man was in charge of what was called Command and Control Research and Behavioral Sciences. His name was Joseph Carl Robnett Licklider. He was on leave from Bolt Beranek and Newman (BBN) in Cambridge, Massachusetts, a company founded in 1948 by two Massachusetts Institute of Technology faculty members with engineering and physics backgrounds, but with practical work in acoustics, and by one of Bolt's students, Newman, an architect with experience in engineering. Bolt had been approached to design the acoustics for the new United Nations building, to be located in Manhattan on the East River. But the project was overwhelming, so he consulted his colleague Beranek, and out of that BBN was born. By the late 1950s BBN had become well known for work in the areas of information systems, human information systems, acoustics, and psycho-acoustics. So it wasn't surprising that the company had a first-rate group of scientists.

Bolt had enticed one of the best, J.C.R. Licklider, to BBN in 1957 from MIT. He brought with him knowledge in mathematics, engineering, and psychology, a highly unusual background for anyone. He also had an intense interest in the relationships between human beings and machines. One year after his arrival he convinced Beranek to purchase BBN's first computer, an LGP-30 manufactured by a subsidiary of the Royal Typewriter Company, Royal-McBee, for $25,000. It didn't use IBM cards, but "modern" paper tape. Licklider, in turn, was given the freedom to hire promising young computer scientists, and did so. They included, from MIT, the very young Marvin Minsky and John McCarthy, both of whom would go on to play major roles in the development of artificial intelligence in the 1960s.

Licklider's reputation had preceded him at ARPA with the publication in 1960 of a paper entitled "Man-Computer Symbiosis." Its central thesis was described as follows in 1996 in Kate Hafner and Matthew Lyon's *Where Wizards Stay Up Late* (Simon & Schuster), a colorful history about the origins of the Internet:

> A close coupling between humans and 'the electronic members of the partnership' would eventually result in cooperative decision- making.... Together ... man and machine would perform far more competently than either could alone. Moreover, attacking problems in partnership with computers could save *the most valuable of postmodern resources: time* [the italics are mine]. 'The hope ... is that in not too many years, human brains and computing machines will be coupled ... tightly, and that the

resulting partnership will think as no human brain has ever thought and process data in a way not approached by the information-handling machines we know today.'

"Lick," as he apparently preferred to be called, turned out to be the perfect choice to head the ARPA project. It was his view that "the problems of command and control ... were essentially problems of human-computer interaction." He had a vision of an "intergalactic computer network," and he also had a $14 million budget to work with. When he arrived at ARPA in October 1962, at the age of forty-seven, he gathered together computer scientists in a group and called it Intergalactic Computer Network. Its principal charge was explained in a remarkable ten-page memorandum on using data and programs interactively, written on April 23, 1963.

Licklider left ARPA after two years, in 1964. By the time he departed, note Hafner and Lyon, "... he had succeeded in shifting the agency's emphasis in computing R&D from a command systems laboratory playing out war-game scenarios to advanced research in time-sharing systems, computer graphics, and improved computer languages." In the same year the program's name was changed and the Information Processing Techniques Office (IPTO) was born. It was located in the third-floor D-ring of the Pentagon. The office of ARPA was located in the E-ring (and had a view). The original focus now became a dual one, combining both defense and civilian interests. Defense analyst Stephen J. Lukasik explained to me that the ARPA project supported, in a straightforward way, the development of computer and information technology,

> ... because those subjects are central to military command and control.... They also happen, functionally, to be virtually identical to the requirements of 'command and control' as required by non-military people and organizations. Hence the brilliant success of the ARPANET and the rapid application of its component concepts and technologies into the Internet.

Like many great inventions, what we now call the Internet was based on a simple idea: try to create a communication network that couldn't be deliberately destroyed by a targeted attack. A more reliable communication network was clearly in the national interest, whether it concerned defense, education, business, or government. The concept consisted of two principles: (1) the communication network would have no central authority, therefore making it impossible to pinpoint and destroy, and (2) it would be designed from the beginning to operate while "in tatters." The basic idea was similar to Hedy Lamarr's vision of a torpedo guidance system that couldn't be jammed. But, if you mention the name of Hedy Lamarr to anyone today in their late thirties — the approximate mean age of Internet users in early 2000 was thirty-nine — more than likely you'll hear, "Hedy whooo ...?" And this is exactly what happened on a Saturday night in June 1999. I read the beginning of this chapter to one of my thirty-one-year-old twin sons. When I finished, he looked blank, so I asked him, "Have you ever heard of Hedy Lamarr?" His answer: "Hedy whooo?"

3.

INVENTING THE INTERNET

It's hard to understand computers
unless you understand that the whole thing is
just a bunch of charged particles called
zeros and ones.

{From my notes taken while Annelise Anderson was trying to explain to me "The Glitch of the Millennium" in the Senior Commons of the Hoover Institution, April 14, 1998. I thought to myself, when I heard this, "That's really helpful, Annelise. What the hell happens?"}

It took twenty-five years to move from Lamarr's frequency-hopping to Paul Baran's distributed communications. And, when computer and information technology finally did get there, the RAND Corporation's modest proposal represented a milestone. Baran imagined a network without a center. What was being created in the mid- to late 1960s was, for all practical purposes, a new way to use Alexander Graham Bell's invention, but with computers and telephone lines. We're all familiar with Bell's idea. The point is especially well illustrated in the example of command and control: the president of the United States picks up the telephone, dials a number, waits, and expects somebody to pick up the receiver on the other end of the line. But he can't do that if a bomb has destroyed the direct link between the White House and the Strategic Air Command. If the link no longer exists, the White House telephone network is in "tatters." A direct call is not possible. But suppose the call could be made in a nondirect way, using computers, each of which would pass the call (the message) on to another computer, and on to another one, and so on, until the call finally gets to its destination. In other words, suppose a computer network existed that would allow computers to connect, one to another, in a roundabout way.

Baran wasn't the only one thinking about this question. So, among others, was Leonard Kleinrock at MIT, as he worked on a theory of distributed routing and packet-switching in the early 1960s. It was the same basic idea of how computers could be used to send a message from one computer to another over telephone lines. Stephen J. Lukasik, the ARPANET director, explained that the collective result was a focus on

> ... the idea of packet-switching as an alternative to the message-switching and circuit-switching technologies that formed the basis of the ... communications practice [in the early 1960s].... Studies ... suggested that dividing digital traffic into packets perhaps several hundred bits in length and routing them through a multiply connected network of 'packet switches' could achieve high reliability despite the loss of multiple links.

The approach, in computer language, was to divide up a message into little digital packets of weightless zeros and ones moving almost at the speed of light. They would then be routed to their destination, from what we call one computer node to another computer node, thereby creating a network. The average size of the packet would be about 1,000 bits — large enough to write *Dennis L. Bark* about ten times. To make it difficult to knock out the network, each computer would have to be able to connect to other computers via many different pathways — so that if the packet couldn't be routed and switched from node 1 to node 2, it could be routed randomly to another, like node 3. If node 3 was busy or destroyed, the packet could be routed to node 4, or to node 6, or to node 14, and so on, moving the packet closer and closer to where it was being sent, until it finally arrived. It stands to reason that the more nodes you have, the more difficult it becomes to destroy the network, even if the network is "in tatters." In other words, even if some nodes are knocked out, the packet can still make a connection by following another path. The following three diagrams illustrate the point:

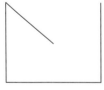

A Weak Network

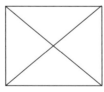

A Strong Network

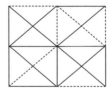

A Network "in Tatters"

The foregoing is straightforward enough, but it doesn't answer the question — what is actually going on here? What is it the computer nodes and packets are doing? An article in a 1995 issue of *The Economist* provides part of the answer:

> Imagine you wanted to make a telephone call from New York to Los Angeles without paying the long-distance charge. If you had the right kind of telephone and knew enough people across the country, you might call someone at the western limit of your local zone, who would call someone at the western edge of their local zone and patch you through, and so on across the country. This may be an impractical method of making telephone calls, but it hints at the way the Internet uses the telephone networks without being controlled by them.
>
> All the content on the Internet is held in computers known as 'servers' at the edges of the network, usually owned and operated by the companies and organizations that want to distribute the information. Microsoft has servers; so do thousands of other companies [including *The Economist* and Stanford University]. In response to a request, the machines parcel up data in a lot of packets with an address on each one, and send them blindly down the nearest connection to the Internet [the network]
>
> When they arrive on the network, they are read by a computer (called a 'router') that has a rough idea of where things are on the Internet. It reads the addresses [which are numbers, not names] and sends the packets in the right general direction, using the best path [the best telephone line] available at that moment. The same thing happens at the next intersection, and so on until the packets reach their destination. The network's best path from A to B at any one time may bear no relation to real-world geography. At the moment this paragraph was written, for example, the best path from London to Amsterdam, using one Internet provider, was via New Jersey. Other providers might have used different routes.
>
> None of the routers has a map of the whole Internet [because there isn't any]; it just knows the best way to the next router at that time. That makes it impossible to predict what path a particular packet

will take. It all depends on what is available at that moment; the individual packets making up a single message may end up taking different routes, only to be sewn back together again at their destination.

How the packets get to where they have been sent, however, is a different matter. That's where Lamarr's concept of moving from place to place gets to be important. When we use mobile telephones, we don't call it frequency hopping any more, we call it spread-spectrum communication. When distributing information via computers over a telephone line, while the idea is the same in concept, it's called packet-switching. Our message, broken up into packets, is sent from one computer node to another, and to another, and to another, and so on, until all the packets finally arrive and are put back together again. It reminds me of the still popular child's poem "Humpty Dumpty." He was a man made out of a hollow eggshell. In the poem he had a great fall. All the King's horses and all the King's men couldn't put Humpty Dumpty back together again (have you ever tried gluing the pieces of a broken eggshell together?). But in this case the packets *are* put back together again as they arrive at their destination. The beauty and strength of this design is that, unless the entire network of computer nodes is shut down, it continues to work.

What we are talking about is not a new kind of telephone network. It's a different kind of network altogether, that rides on top of a common telephone line, built for example, by AT&T, or France Telecom, or Deutsche Telekom. If you want to use this network, you need someone to provide the service for you — in other words, to provide "access" to the network. We call this someone an Internet service provider (ISP). An academic ISP, for example, is Stanford University.

The best known commercial ISP is America Online (AOL), founded in 1985. But there are thousands of them, including Wanadoo in France and Compuserve (now owned by AOL) in Europe and the United States. The ISP rents usage of the line from its owner — AT&T, perhaps, or some other phone-service network. Figuratively the ISP rides "on top" of the line, using the bandwidth of the line it has rented to route and switch the digital messages, whether that line is an optic fiber, a radio spectrum, or a copper wire. The bandwidth is simply another word for the size of the "pipe" your ISP is using. The size of bandwidth therefore determines how quickly information, or data, can be moved.

The ISP sends us a monthly bill that covers the cost of connecting us to the Internet whenever we want to, and also for improving technical capability, such as increasing the size of the "pipe." The ISP's investment is the purchase and maintenance of the equipment that allows the technology to work, as well as the cost of leasing use of the lines. We aren't replacing telephone network A with telephone network B. We are just putting telephone network B on top of, or parallel to, telephone network A. Network B doesn't operate the way our normal telephone network does, even though it uses lines and connections. It needs switches and Internet routers, so that the information packets of a message can be routed (the packets are routed via one computer node to another node), and switched (the signals are switched at each computer node), and reassembled at the final destination in a readable form.

What was the real purpose of this strange way of communication? The idea, as ARPA itself, was a child of the Cold War. There's no question about that. So it isn't surprising that it has been asserted more than once that the Pentagon developed the Internet to withstand the effects of a nuclear attack. But this isn't entirely true, because almost from the beginning it was clear that not only defense purposes would be served. Stephen Lukasik, who signed the checks to pay for the research, explained it to me this way:

> ... The ARPANET was *specifically* developed as a central experiment in packet-switching. Packet-switching was important because the technology offered critical new capabilities to provide flexible, reliable, and survivable communications to military users, users in fixed facilities, on mobile platforms, and, yes, for survivable strategic command and control. The ARPANET itself was not designed to do any of these.... The ARPANET *never* carried messages involved in the command and control of America's nuclear forces.

Lukasik's description of all this took place on the telephone, and because I'd never heard it before, he had my full attention. He saw two things of major significance in packet-switching. On the one hand it represented a vital technology that would support the credibility of America's strategic forces. On the other hand it was an adventure — as is all research — whose purpose was to improve significantly the creativity and productivity of computer science. And that, in some ways almost by accident, is exactly what happened. As the work went forward computer scientists recognized "the need for flexible access to a variety of research machines and developmental software, ... resources that could be shared through the widest access possible if research sites were connected via a computer network." It sounds so simple. But it was a revolution.

In 1968, a Network Working Group (NWG) was formed to discuss the multitude of emerging questions. These included designing the protocols (the codes) for computers so they could communicate with each other. (Without protocols to encode the digital zeros and ones, and without a way for computers to understand their order and relationship, they have no meaning.) In March 1969, the NWG's participants decided they should start keeping a record of their meetings in some kind of consistent way. This task fell to a young University of California at Los Angeles graduate student, Steve Crocker, who acted as recorder. He later described his trepidation as follows:

> I remember having great fear that we would offend whomever the official protocol designers were, and I spent a sleepless night composing humble words for our notes. The basic ground rules were that anyone could say anything and that nothing was official. And to emphasize the point, I labeled the notes 'Request for Comments' [RFCs]. I never dreamed these notes would be distributed through the very medium we were discussing in these notes. Talk about Sorcerer's Apprentice!

The idea was elementary and, in practice, very effective. The RFCs served as a means to promote frank discussion and a free-flowing exchange of information. The vehicle of the RFC established an operating principle of openness among those doing the work, so that they could exchange ideas and comments without worrying about offending a senior colleague. The result was to encourage both collaboration as well as competition. Vinton Cerf (known as "Vint") was another graduate student from UCLA involved with the project (he had been an undergraduate of Stanford). The poem he later wrote about the "early days," entitled "Requiem for the ARPANET," captures a creative spirit of excitement and naïveté, but also of sadness and respect:

> Like distant islands sundered by the sea,
> We had no sense of one community.
> We lived and worked apart and rarely knew
> That others searched with us for knowledge, too.
>
> Distant ARPA spurred us in our quest
> And for our part we worked and put to test
> New thoughts and theories of computing art;
> We deemed it science not, but made a start.
>
> Each time a new machine was built and sold,
> We'd add it to our list of needs and told
> Our source of funds 'Alas! Our knowledge loom
> Will halt till it's in our computer room.'
> Even ARPA with its vast resources

Unintended Consequences

Could not buy us all new teams of horses
Every year with which to run the race.
Not even ARPA could keep up that pace!

But, could these new resources not be shared?
Let links be built; machines and men be paired!
Let distance be no barrier! They set
That goal: design and build the ARPANET!

The RFCs were both the vehicle and the symbol for people using computer systems, learning how to work together. Although geographically separated by long distances, included in the joint undertaking were systems and scientists at the Massachusetts Institute of Technology in Cambridge, the Stanford Research Institute in Menlo Park, California, the University of Illinois in Urbana, and Carnegie Mellon University in Pittsburgh, Pennsylvania. What this development meant was that computers were no longer merely number-crunching machines that consumed punch cards and spools of magnetic tape. They were being transformed into something different, into a new means for people to communicate with each other in real time. Lukasik describes what was unfolding this way:

> The computer-science community sensed that the pace of research could be enhanced if results from one group could be shared widely and easily by a larger body of researchers, both to establish the limits of the results as well as to build on them to progress further. … It was expected that connecting software, data, and computers would provide major synergy to other ARPA programs.

> This, then, was the origin of the ARPANET. Beyond the appeal of this new concept in communications technology, equally important is the innovation in the management of research. Because a sufficiently large body of researchers from different research communities all were funded by ARPA, there were economies of scale and breadth of technical capability to develop the idea of a nationwide computer communications network and to exploit its facilities for a diverse set of purposes.

While few people outside of university science departments recognized it in those days, a new and legitimate academic discipline was being formed. Unlike departments for traditional subjects of the humanities and sciences, departments of computer science were the creation of the Information Age.

By 1969, ARPA had overcome numerous technical issues, described as link capacity, routing strategies, balanced-switch speed, construction and installation of packet switches, and establishment of flow-control algorithms. The network was ready. So ARPA, in December of that year, created the first four-node network of computer-science research sites at University of California campuses in Los Angeles and Santa Barbara, at the University of Utah, and at the Stanford Research Institute. Five additional organizations were added within six months: RAND Corporation and the System Development Corporation on the West Coast, and on the East Coast Harvard University, MIT, and Bolt Beranek and Newman. By September 1971, eight more had joined, bringing the total to seventeen. They included Stanford University, next to Palo Alto, California, the National Aeronautic and Space Administration (NASA) in Sunnyvale, California, the Lincoln Laboratory and MITRE Corp., both in Bedford, Massachusetts, as well as the University of Illinois, Carnegie Mellon University in Pittsburgh, Pennsylvania, and Case Western Reserve University in Cleveland, Ohio.

By August 1972 the University of Southern California became the eighteenth node, followed by ten government facilities. They included the National Atmospheric and Oceanographic Administration in Boulder, Colorado, the National Bureau of Standards, McClellan and Tinker Air Force Bases, and the Seismic Array Analysis Center in Alexandria, Virginia, and ARPA itself.

The expansion of the network in just a little more than two years from four to twenty-eight nodes represented an increase of 700 percent. No aspects were classified, so while under the direction of ARPA, increasing numbers of computer scientists began giving form and substance to the basic network. The leadership was provided by, among others, Robert Taylor, who at the age of thirty-four was appointed the third director of the Information Processing Techniques Office in 1966 by ARPA's then director, Charles Herzfeld. At this juncture, Larry Roberts, who as a twenty-nine-year-old at the Lincoln Laboratory in Massachusetts had joined IPTO in 1966, believed that the time had come for a public demonstration. As the program manager who had overseen in detail the network's development, Roberts in 1971 enlisted the help of Robert Kahn, formerly a professor of electrical engineering at MIT and, in 1971, part of the consulting group at BBN.

Kahn was charged with organizing what would be the first public demonstration of the ARPA network as the sole exhibit at the First International Conference on Computer Communications (ICCC). It was held in Washington, D.C., in October 1972 and included participants from Great Britain, Canada, France, Japan, Norway, Sweden, and the United States. In the basement of the Washington Hilton Hotel, the

ARPANET was introduced to the world, with forty computers connected to one node. The conference agenda included a discussion of the need for network communication protocols. What emerged from the discussion was a proposal to develop a system for interconnecting independent computer networks. As described by Henry Edward Hardy in an academic thesis on the subject, the system would be based on "the architectural principles for an international interconnection of networks, ... 'a mess of independent, autonomous networks interconnected by gateways, just as independent circuits of ARPANET are interconnected by IMPs'" (interface message processors; otherwise known as packet switches). In understandable English the proposal entailed developing a "network of networks" — namely, an inter-net.

The conference produced the InterNetwork Working Group (INWG) to coordinate discussion on the development of a common Internet protocol. Its first chairman was the young Vint Cerf. There was no argument over the need for a common protocol. It was clear that the primary challenge to developing a broader network was how to connect computers so they could understand each other. By 1973 there were several efforts under way. One network was being designed by Donald Davies in the National Physical Laboratory in England. Another, a version of the ARPANET called Cyclades, was being developed in France by computer scientist Louis Pouzin. Davies and Pouzin, along with colleagues such as Cerf and Kahn, all shared the same concerns.

In the United States it was Cerf and Kahn who designed the conceptual framework. It started with a rough outline drawn by Cerf in the lobby of a San Francisco hotel in 1973. As Katie Hafner and Matthew Lyon note in their 1996 book *Where Wizards Stay Up Late*, Kahn that summer joined Cerf and his graduate students at Stanford University in modifying and refining "the details of developing the host-to-host [computer-to-computer] protocol into a standard allowing data traffic to flow across networks." By May of 1974, Cerf and Kahn had authored a paper titled "A Protocol for Packet Network Intercommunication" and had also flipped a coin to determine whose name would appear first under the title. Cerf won. Years later journalists gave him the title "Father of the Internet," but in reality the honor belonged to many, including Robert Kahn.

Cerf and Kahn had produced the Internet Protocol (IP) and Transfer Control Protocol (TCP). One determined how information was sent, and the other how information was put into packets. Both protocols worked together. What they did, in a sense, was to allow computers to *connect* to one another. The protocols represented a common way to transfer data and files from one computer on one network to another computer on a different network. It meant that, for the first time, it was technically possible to bring the loose connection of networks into an "internetwork." Authors Hafner and Lyon observe in their book that "it was now obvious that networking had a future well beyond the experimental ARPANET. The potential power and reach of what not only Cerf and Kahn, but Louis Pouzin in France and others, were inventing was beginning to occur to people. If they could work out all the details, TCP might be the mechanism that would open up worlds."

Kahn served at ARPA from 1972 to 1985. His last position there was director of the Information Processing Techniques Office. In 1997, he and Cerf were awarded the Alexander Graham Bell Medal by the Institute of Electrical and Electronic Engineers "for conceiving the Internet architecture and protocols, and for the vision and sustained leadership that led to the current Internet." In the same year they also both received the National Medal of Technology from the president of the United States. In 1999 the medal was awarded to Robert Taylor, who later retired to his home in Woodside, California. Describing Taylor's contributions to development of the Internet and the evolution of the information economy, *Scientific American* wrote in April 2000 that "few innovators can claim to have left so great a mark on the fortunes of the world."

The first demonstration of the ARPA network, in October 1972, was an unreserved success, and it sent a powerful message. Kahn had recognized it during the two-and-a-half-day ICCC meeting:

> The ICCC demonstration did more to establish the viability of packet-switching than anything else before it. As a result, the ARPANET community gained a much larger sense of itself, its technology, and the resources at its disposal. For computer makers, there was the realization that a market might emerge.... Bob Kahn had just devoted a year of his life to demonstrating that resource-sharing over a network could really work. But at some point in the course of the event, he turned to a colleague and remarked, 'You know, everyone really uses this thing for electronic mail.'

Among computer scientists connected to ARPANET, a by-product, e-mail, was proving enormously popular. The initial delivery system between two machines was developed in 1972 at BBN. It represented the first *interconnectivity*, and by the following year three-quarters of all traffic on the ARPANET was e-mail. The principal devotee, wrote Licklider in 1978, proved to be Steve Lukasik, "who soon had most of his office directors and program managers communicating with him and with their colleagues and their contractors via the network." Lukasik recognized the potential of e-mail as a new way to communicate, so he used that network to manage ARPA. In 1973, no one had yet thought of calling e-mail "an earth-circling message-handling system." But that is, indeed, what it would become, as the use of e-mail within ARPA served also to give a real push to further growth and expansion of the ARPANET:

> E-mail was to the ARPANET what the Louisiana Purchase was to the young United States. Things only got better as the network grew and technology converged with the torrential human tendency to talk.

At the same time, computer scientists began working on ways to make the network itself more useful. The Royal Radar Establishment in Norway and University College in London were added to the network by mid-1973. Satellite links were added to provide connections with overseas nodes; that meant potential worldwide connectivity. New communication protocols were devised for the packet-switching network for the transmission of speech. Encryption capabilities were added for secure communications. Packet-radio technology was also developed to permit operation in a mobile environment.

It was, however, still an experiment. To become a proven tool of communication, the experiment had to be transformed into a large-scale operating network of nodes and users. So ARPA dramatically increased the size, making it available to its contractors, and to affiliated organizations. At that point the network proved itself. What had been once just an idea became reality, and in turn, it was time for the experiment to end. ARPA was, after all, not in the communication business, but in the research business. And for the requiem, of which Vint Cerf had written in his poem? There wasn't any. The network of nodes remained, unscathed. For almost twenty-five years — until the 1990s — the world at large wouldn't recognize the full significance of what a little-known government agency had actually done.

What had been created was an extraordinary information and communication structure. The ARPANET was, for lack of a better term, *virtual freedom* of communication. As Bruce Sterling writes in an article headline "A Short History of the Internet," "as long as individual machines could speak the packet-switching lingua franca of the new anarchic network, their brand names, and their content, and even their ownership, were irrelevant." But ARPA's charter did not envision permanent operation. So in the mid-1970s ARPANET was turned over to the Defense Communication Agency to provide packet-switched service for defense users, defense contractors, and other government agencies.

By the late 1970s networks had been created by the National Science Foundation and by NASA, and additional networks had been developed by IBM, Hewlett-

52

Packard, Xerox, and Digital Equipment Corporation for their own research and internal communication. As the network rapidly reproduced itself, new networks were born. They were given names like TELNET (the first commercial version of ARPANET), created in 1974 by BBN, and USENET (Unix User Network), created by graduate students at the University of North Carolina and Duke University in 1979, originally just as a way to send messages to each other. It would prove to be of special value, for it became the primary vehicle for people to exchange views and opinions in newsgroups on the Internet, first in the United States and Europe, and then around the globe. Thus, EUnet (EUROPENET) began in 1982 to provide e-mail and USENET services between the Netherlands, Denmark, Sweden, and the UK. In was followed by EARN (European Academic and Research Network) in 1983, and the next year saw creation of JUNET (Japan Unix Network).

By 2000 USENET was the "old boy" of the network, even though a majority of Internet users are unaware of its role today. It is made up of thousands of news servers on which millions of messages are published every day. These are then divided up into categories, called newsgroups, where millions of users from all over the world can discuss politics or pornography, polygamy or physics, routers or religion — you name it.

Networks were created everywhere in the 1980s. In 1981, BITNET (originally called "Because It's There NETwork," it later became "Because It's Time NETwork") came into being as a cooperative network at the City University of New York. CSNET (Computer Science Research Network) became fully operational in 1983. The Whole Earth 'Lectronic Link (The WELL) was started in Sausalito, California, in 1985. BARRNET (Bay Area Regional Research Network) was begun in 1986. In 1989 European Internet service providers formally established RIPE (*Réseaux IP Européens*) to assure administrative and technical coordination for the operation of a pan-European network. Finally, in the midst of this expansion, administrators of USENET refused to host newsgroups discussing drugs and recreational sex, an event known as the "Breaking of the Backbone Cabal." Thereupon, creative young users with more respect for self-indulgence than for responsibility "devised" new electronic paths and created an anarchic network. It was, and is, known as where the bizarre, the fetish, and the erotic world of binaries resides. It is the ether of the "alt.binaries" hierarchy, informally and anonymously christened "the alter-net." Some of the alternet's users address more conventional subjects, ranging from architecture to music to tennis. Others focus on more prurient areas, like pornography, thanks to the right of free speech, or provide a platform for discussion of the immoral, the decadent, and the fake.

By 1983, fourteen years after the first experiment with four computers, hundreds of host computers were connected to networks, operating primarily at American military laboratories or at academic computer-science departments. Although many of the networks were already using the TCP/IP protocols, ARPANET did not do so until this same year. At the same time the Defense Communications Agency concluded that the ARPANET had become so large that security issues were a legitimate concern. So it split the ARPANET into two networks. The new MILNET, for non-classified military information, was integrated into the Defense Data Network, which had been created in 1982. The ARPANET, with forty-five nodes, scaled down from 113, continued serving the computer-research community; "the switch" was overseen by Robert Kahn. The result was the Internet.

What had occurred was the birth of many networks, all using the TCP and IP protocols. The old ARPANET, Hafner and Lyon wrote in *Where Wizards Stay Up Late*, had become a full-fledged Internet. And Cerf observed: "Now it could go where no network had gone before." MILNET would become eventually just one of hundreds of networks catering to specific interests. A United States government network for secure, secret defense communication — the *raison d'être* for the creation of ARPA in the first place — finally emerged. This was, in other words, a line that couldn't be cut. In turn, other networks were developed to serve government — the Department of State, for example, has two separate networks, one for classified and one for unclassified information — and to serve business, where old companies such as IBM and new ones such as Cisco Systems, Intel, Microsoft, and Oracle would become communication-technology leaders.

Between 1977 and 1983, the number of computers connected to the Internet increased from 111 to 4,000. By the mid-1980s, the main protocol (SMTP, for simple mail transfer protocol) used to send electronic mail on the Internet had existed for some time. Another protocol had also been developed. Called NNTP (network news transfer protocol), it made it infinitely easier to use USENET's rapidly growing network of newsgroups. In 1985, the National Science Foundation created NSFNET, a computer backbone crossing the country to support research and education. By 1987, the number of host computers had increased to more than 28,000 in the United States. Originally NSFNET used systems called gateways, developed at the University of Delaware, to route traffic. But by 1988, demand was expanding so rapidly that NSF selected the University of Michigan in Ann Arbor to develop and administer a faster network, in cooperation with IBM and MCI Corp. The result was a thirty-fold increase in speed. By 1989, the number of host computers exceeded 100,000. Four years later, in 1993, NSFNET included members throughout the world from Europe, Asia, the Middle East, India, South America, Africa, Central Europe, Southeast Asia, the Russian Federation, and the Newly Independent States (of the former Soviet Union).

By the beginning of the 1990s, hundreds of networks had emerged, and more were coming into digital being. ARPANET, which remained in service throughout the 1980s, was discontinued in 1990 and its network backbone became part of NSFNET. Two years later, in 1992, following the decision by NSF to lift its restriction on for-profit use, commercial Internet service providers began operation. In 2000, there were more than 8,500 ISPs selling access to the Net, with names like Bluelight, Vulcan Communications, America Online, EarthLink, MindSpring, Juno Web, Spire, CompuServe, Silicon Connections, Brigadoon.Com, and Global Crossing.

In April 1995 the National Science Foundation, as the government agency closest to being the relevant federal authority, formally relinquished all responsibilities for the Internet's operation to private industry and academia. Therewith, the Internet was privatized. By July 1996, the Internet had grown to more than 12.8 million computers — a quarter-century earlier there had been only four. And, by the year 2000 millions and millions of computers were serving as the soldiers of the revolution in computing and communication technology. It is these soldiers that allow me to send my e-mails flying over continents and oceans, as I communicate in ways I had never imagined in 1995, when Gaku began teaching me about packets and nodes.

4.

A WORLD OF WEBS

*It's the wired decade. It's the Internet,
connecting, globalism, a little bit of millennial fever,
a quickening of pace.
The zeitgeist of the '90s is all about the Web:
the Webbing of the planet, the global teenager, wiring up the youth culture.*

{Kevin Kelly, executive editor of *Wired*, from an interview with Bob Jones, titled
"It's the Wired Decade," *World*, July 12-19, 1997}

In the early 1990s, working with computers linked together on a network still presented formidable obstacles. Most of us didn't use computers at all. It took forever to find files "on-line" if we didn't know where they were — and I didn't. First, we had to know, or somehow find, the name of the server (the computer) where the files were stored. We also needed to know how to "log in" to that server, and we needed a password that the server would accept. Then, we needed to "connect" to the server using a program that would allow us to retrieve a file. The best known *client* programs (we were the clients) were called GOPHER and FTP (file transfer protocol). And that wasn't all.

Available connections were limited, and often connection was possible only during certain hours. And, once we were "connected," we were faced with a long list of folders and files. Sometimes the contents were clear from the names, and sometimes they weren't.

Searching information stored on databases was not only frustrating, it took too much time. A great deal of information had to be typed into the computer, the ensuing search was an exercise in trial and error, and the entire process gave the word patience real meaning. Many of us at the Hoover Institution had heard these horror stories and concluded that computers were made for scientists. The invention that would change all of this did not come from ARPA or the National Science Foundation. The idea was conceived, if that is the right way to put it, at CERN, the *Organisation Européenne pour la Recherche Nucléaire*, founded as one of Europe's first joint ventures in 1954. Research is conducted at CERN's European Laboratory for Particle Physics, just outside Geneva on the border between Switzerland and France. The laboratory houses the world's largest scientific instrument, the LEP (Large Electron Positron Collider), in a twenty-seven-kilometer circular tunnel one hundred meters below the ground. To provide a flavor of what goes on there, CERN maintains a list of "Approved Experiments" at its Web site. Three of them, although totally incomprehensible to a historian like me, give an idea of what modern science is looking at. They are (1) CPLEAR: Measurements of CP and T violation in the neutral kaon system and tests of CPT, (2) NA 50: Study of muon pairs and vector mesons produced in high energy Pb-Pb interactions at SPS, and (3) WA 97: An experiment based on a silicon pixel telescope for measuring hyperon and anti-hyperon spectra to probe the onset of a Quark-Gluon Plasma.

In 1989, a simpler experiment was proposed to CERN's administrators. Its title was "World Wide Web: Proposal for a HyperText Project," and the estimated cost was about $80,000. Suggested by Tim Berners-Lee, an Englishman in his early thirties, and by Robert Cailliau, a forty-two-year-old Belgian, the experiment was based on a concept of "non-sequential writing" developed by Theodor Holm Nelson in the 1960s. The phrase was coined by Nelson in a paper written in 1965, entitled "A File Structure for the Complex, the Changing, and the Indeterminate." He later developed a system for electronic publishing, called Xanadu, its name drawn from Samuel Taylor Coleridge's poem *Kubla Khan*, "to suggest 'the magic place of literary memory where nothing is forgotten.'" In 1980, he wrote a good deal more about this subject in a book titled *Literary Machines*; the 1981 edition was dedicated to Eric Blair, whose nom de plume was George Orwell, and the 1987 edition to his friend Douglas Engelbart, the inventor of the computer mouse. Nelson also authored a series of newsletters, in one of which he concluded:

> … The future of humanity is at the interactive computer screen.…
> The new writing and movies will be interactive and interlinked. It
> will be united by bridges of transclusion and we need a worldwide
> network to deliver it with royalty.

Berners-Lee and Cailliau embraced Nelson's idea in their proposal to CERN, but described it like this:

HyperText is a way to link and access information of various kinds as a web of nodes in which the user can browse at will. Potentially, HyperText provides a single-user interface to many large classes of stored information, such as reports, notes, databases, computer documentation and on-line systems help.

… The current incompatibilities of the platforms and tools make it impossible to access existing information through a common interface, leading to waste of time, frustration, and obsolete answers to simple data lookup. There is a potential large benefit from the integration of a variety of systems in a way which allows a user to follow links pointing from one piece of information to another one. This forming of a web of information nodes rather than a hierarchical tree or an ordered list is the basic concept behind HyperText.

… The texts [the documents] are linked together in a way that one can go from one concept to another to find the information one wants. The network of links is called a web.

What this means is that I can travel from document to document on the Web. For example, from a Web page made by scholars researching first-growth redwood trees, I can follow links to Web pages of other university researchers, different U.S. government agencies, state government boards, environmental groups, timber industry companies, and news media. Each offers a perspective, and may cite and rebut another agency's opinions.

Berners-Lee and Cailliau's proposal introduces the two technical faces of the Web:

The process of proceeding from node to node [Web page to Web page] is called navigation. Nodes do not need to be on the same machine: links may point across machine boundaries. Having a worldwide web implies some solutions must be found for problems such as different access protocols and different node content formats. These issues are addressed by our proposal.

The solutions they arrived at were the hypertext transfer protocol (HTTP) for the access protocol, and hypertext markup language (HTML) for the content format. HTTP codifies the way computers request, send, and receive Web data to and from each other. HTML "marks up" Web page text with emphases (e.g., colored italics or bold type), but also "marks up" tables, lists, and, most important, links to other Web pages. The two protocols work together to solve Berners-Lee and Cailliau's problems with building what is effectively a web of pages across the Internet, hence the name World Wide Web — a web of electronic connections. They also developed a do-it-yourself global address system, known as the URL (uniform resource locator), used to find different Web sites, as in www.amazon.com.

An experimental protocol was demonstrated in December 1990. Five months later, in May 1991, the HTTP protocol was put on a number of CERN computers. Shortly thereafter Stanford University's Linear Accelerator (SLAC) began to use HTTP to allow its scientists to search a database containing abstracts of physics documents. Almost at the same time, CERN made the source code for the software public — available to anyone who wanted to use it.

The Web is not just a network of communicating computers. It is a method for people to view and interact with Web pages, choosing themselves the links they want to follow. Berners-Lee and Cailliau's proposal outlines the manner in which this would happen:

> A program which provides access to the hypertext world we call a browser. When starting a hypertext browser on your workstation [your computer], you will first be presented with a hypertext page which is personal to you: your personal notes, if you like [a "home" page]. A hypertext page has pieces of text which refer to other texts. Such references are highlighted [in various colors] and can be selected with a mouse.... When you select a reference, the browser presents you with the text which is referenced: you have made the browser follow a hypertext link.

> [This explanation is what Nelson means by "transclusion." The highlighted reference "points at" something else. When I click on the highlighted reference — a word, phrase, or a picture — it becomes "necessary" for my computer to show the object which is stored somewhere on the Web, on another computer.]

Information on the Web is thus stored on thousands of computers, known as WWW servers. When a highlighted reference on a Web page is clicked, the WWW server can deliver the document to my computer at once in the form of words or pictures on my computer screen. For scientists consulting abstracts and experiment reports, the ability to move from one document to another, and to follow the subject in one memorandum through multiple follow-up memoranda, made this aspect of their research a great deal easier and much quicker. In fact, its "intuitive nature" made it so easy that inexperienced computer users could navigate the Web, giving rise to the image of "surfing." If a way could be found to "surf" easily from one highlighted reference to another — even if the documents were stored on different servers located in different countries on different continents — the HTTP protocol was an invaluable research tool. More important, it would open another, entirely new world of communication in the Information Age. The irony — if that is the right word — is that neither Cailliau nor Berners-Lee, who has been called the Johnny Appleseed of Cyberspace, made money off it. That would be left to others.

Part of the benefit is the intuitive ease of use, the immediate responsiveness of the medium, and the search capability. The other part of the benefit is the uniform format. In 1991, when CERN made the source code publicly available for the HTTP and HTML protocols, only simple text-based browsers, such as Lynx, had been developed; the Web remained an academic backwater. But when a "graphical user interface" was added to Web browsers, it had dramatic impact. In early 1993, Marc Andreessen and Eric Bina, at the National Center for Supercomputing Applications at the University of Illinois in Urbana, created a graphical browser called Mosaic for X. One year later Mosaic Communications Corporation was formed to develop a commercial browser, using the HTTP protocol. In 1994, Mosaic for X was transformed into a more sophisticated browser called initially Netscape, then Netscape Navigator.

Today, for anyone in their thirties or younger, Netscape is a household word. But I had never heard of Netscape when I was having lunch with Nalini in the courtyard of the Stanford Business School in June 1995. She told me that Netscape would become a publicly traded company in August, and that I should buy some shares. I hadn't seen a prospectus and that made me nervous, but I had a lot of confidence in Nalini, so what do you think I did?

Berners-Lee and Cailliau had foreseen the outline, but who could have recognized the importance of moving beyond the realm of just reading scientific stuff on a computer screen? As they wrote in the their original proposal:

> Nodes [and Web pages] can in principle also contain non-text information such a diagrams [like the graph of a stock's performance], pictures [satellite photographs], sound [news broadcasts], animation [video], etc. The term hypermedia is simply the expansion of the hypertext idea to these other media.

When Netscape Navigator became commercially available for use in 1995, it changed everything once again. The search for information now became instantaneous. Use of the Internet was opened up far beyond just the realm of scholars. Out of it would emerge Web sites. One of the unintended consequences would be a revolution in how we conduct business. We would call it electronic commerce — symbolized today by companies that didn't exist then, such as eBay, Priceline, and Amazon.com.

Since 1995 enterprising computer users all over the world have created thousands of Web sites and millions of Web pages (documents) for business, for politics, for education, for the arts and sciences, and for government — in short, for almost any subject imaginable. And there has been intense competition to design browsers to surf the Web. In May 1999, World Wide Web Statistics listed no less than sixty-nine different ones, and by February 2000 Yahoo! (more about that later) listed more than one hundred-thirty. Netscape is, of course, one of them. Another well-known one is Microsoft Internet Explorer; and there are others called Arena, Euroseek, Galahad, Fountain, CyberDog, Cello, MidasWWW, Minuet, Netshark, Pythia, Opera, SlipKnot, SurfIt, and Tapestry.

By mid-1997, estimated Web sites in operation numbered only about one million. By April 1999 more than 5 million existed, and more than 1.5 million Web pages were being added each day — more than one billion of them existed by January 2000. In the spring of 1998, there had been a mere 320 million Web pages on the Internet. By January 2000, there were well over 100 million Netscape browsers in use, and Netscape's home page, www.netscape.com, was being looked at ("hit") millions of times daily.

The ability to navigate the Web, to move from node to node on the Internet, made it infinitely easier to go anywhere electronically, to sites in Moscow or New York, to Singapore or Paris, or to the Web site of my colleague, Annelise Anderson, at the Hoover Institution. I only have to type in the Web site address on my Netscape browser; that's why, as an example, I have inserted addresses throughout this book. If I don't know the specific Web site address, I can use another software program called a "search engine" (or portal) to locate the subject and site I am looking for. A search engine is also just a Web site, but one with a great deal of data about other Web sites. When a search engine Web site appears on the computer screen, I type in the name or description of what I'm looking for. If, for example, I type in the name springer spaniel, the search engine will list for me, on the screen, all of the sites in its bank of Web site listings where the words appear in the form of text, photographs, or video. To find out if a Web site contains the information I need, I have to go to that site and look at it. It's just like looking up a bibliography in the back of a book, then checking each of the references to see if any of them are useful — except it's a lot faster.

Search engines are essential to the use of the Internet and the World Wide Web. Their names are not only colorful, but send a message about the power of imagination. So, for example, you can choose any one of the following search engines to help you:

www.dogpile.com ("Fetch Arfie Fetch")
www.lycos.com ("Search the Web")
www.excite.com ("twice the power of the competition")
www.yahoo.com ("Yahoo!")
www.infoseek.com ("proof of intelligent life on the Net")
www.hotbot.com ("The Wired Search Engine")
www.altavista.com ("OnSite Knowledge")
www.google.com ("The Best Search Experience")
www.northernlight.com ("Just what You've Been Asking For")

A search engine, in concept, is like a car being driven down the electronic super-highway, going from destination to destination (from node to node). When it arrives at the Web site I've typed into my computer, it stops. The Web page appears on my screen. I look and see what is there — such as the Web site of Microsoft Corporation at www.microsoft.com. When I'm finished, I return to my "car" and continue my drive — in other words, I keep on "surfing" — until I decide to stop at a new destination. One of the remarkable Silicon Valley success stories is that of a search engine called Yahoo!, at www.yahoo.com, created by two Stanford students in 1994-95. By February 1998, Yahoo!'s site, the most popular of all Web sites, registered 31.2 million users. In early April 1998, Yahoo! reported it was getting 95 million Web page views per day (one electronic page of information displayed in response to a user request), an increase of 46 percent over the 65 million views per day it reported for the fourth quarter of 1997. By January 1999 Yahoo!'s home page had no less than ninety highlighted references, which, with the click of a mouse, linked you immediately to pages for other subjects, such as music, books, or stock quotes. By the spring of 1999 Yahoo! was registering an average of 235 million Web page views per day and recorded 47 million registered users. And by the beginning of 2000 Yahoo! was getting 465 million views daily, counted almost 125 registered million users (40 million of them outside the United States), and was providing service in twelve languages. During the fourth quarter of 1999 Yahoo!'s users spent an estimated $6.7 billion in on-line transactions for shopping and auctions, and in travel and banking services. In January 2000 the company reported net revenues of over $201 billion for the fourth quarter of 1999, compared to net revenues of $91 billion for the 1998 fourth quarter, an increase of 120 percent.

The ability to browse, to search, and to surf opens up new vistas, but also brings with it a problem of major proportion. There is an enormous amount of information available. It is impossible to digest it all. Critics call it "information overload." There is little time to reflect on what it all means, as we surf from one Web site to another by reflex action. But, like everything else, the value of the Web is *what* we do with it and how we use the information we gather. Does the Internet allow me to find information in new ways? The answer clearly is yes. Just think of conducting research without having to go to the library, as was the case for much of the research for this book. This latter example alone is a change of enormous magnitude. But if you don't believe it's impressive enough, consider this completely different and disconcerting kind of example. On a recent evening I typed into the AltaVista search engine the name "Dennis Bark" because I was curious. To my utter amazement I learned that there is another Dennis Bark in this world, an assistant district commissioner for Cub Scouts in Lincolnshire, England. I don't know if this discovery has value or not. But it definitely told me something about the information gathering power of the World Wide Web. It also convinced me that a new network of relationships between human beings is being created; I thought I understood that already, but the appearance of another Dennis Bark confirmed it. But perhaps it didn't, after all. I wrote Dennis Bark a letter, with a typewriter, introducing myself, and he never replied. Several months later I typed in my name again and found a third Dennis Bark, at the University of Marburg in Germany. I told Gaku Sato about it and said, "That means there are three of me!" Gaku replied, "One's enough!"

It is true, simplistic pundits point out, that to manage and to use the vast quantities of information on the Web forces us to make choices. But so does everything else in life. Search procedures, however, are becoming more refined and sophisticated, so that an interactive relationship exists between the search engine and the person using it. Critics of the Web cry "information chaos." But to me that's like crying wolf.

The value of information is what I do with it. This is one reason why the revolution in communication technology — the technical world of virtual freedom — will continue. Another reason is that a new way has been found to use what we euphemistically describe as personal computers. By using them to create networks, we pass through the portal of the Information Age, and that changes our life once again.

5.

THE NETWORK TIDAL WAVE

The tidal wave devours the shore:
There are no islands anymore.

{Edna St. Vincent Millay, 1892-1950}

Thee are different kinds of networks, but basically they all accomplish the same thing. They allow a person hooked up to a network like the one at Stanford University, which has more than 38,000 users, to communicate with another person in, say, France. From my home in California, for example, I can exchange messages with Le Père Petit near Clermont-Ferrand, who uses the Wanadoo network. Both of our Internet service providers allow communication between these networks. Hence the word Internet.

There is, however, also communication within the same organization. We call that intra-communication. Hence the word "intranet." This is a network with a different kind of communication purpose; it connects people within the same university or business or government agency. The principle is simple. Intranets, and there are many different kinds, are designed to allow one person to communicate with another, or with many. IBM has an intranet, as does Yahoo! Banks and insurance companies have intranets. In short, as sophisticated communication tools that are easy to use, they are indispensable. Why? Because they are efficient, cheap, and exceedingly quick. They link accounting with purchasing, with shipping, with receiving, with the warehouse, and so on. They also are designed in different ways to meet different demands, to be of use to different kinds of companies, large or small. So, for example, there are local-area networks (LANs). There are also wide-area networks (WANs). There are wireless networks, and there are "home networks" being developed by Microsoft and Sony that will combine the strengths of computers with con-

64

sumer electronics — television and video, disc players, digital cameras, and digital printers.

One of the most successful Silicon Valley companies whose products make these systems work is Cisco Systems, headquartered in San Jose, California. It produces the routers, switches, and network-management software that allow different computers within a network to connect to each other. It also produces the dial-up access connections that computers use to enter the Internet — the "on-ramps" — to the information superhighway. These items also are made by other companies, such as Alcatel, Ericsson, Siemens, and Lucent — which in 2000 was the most widely held stock in America.

The elegance of networks is miraculous to me. But what I think is really extraordinary is what you can make them do. You direct your computer to dial the local telephone number of your ISP, and you're connected regardless of differences in time, place, or type of computer system. Using networks as a means of searching for, locating, and exchanging information saves money, stress, and time. It's highly efficient, and in many cases eliminates the costly, long, and stressful trip by car, train, or airplane from one place to another and back again. Moreover, instant communication via e-mail has a dynamic all its own that builds closer relationships with friends, customers, business partners, business prospects, suppliers, and employees.

That's why demand for access services is growing at an incredible rate of speed. By March 2000, AOL, the largest ISP in the United States, counted more than 22 million subscribers paying its $21.95 monthly fee. CompuServe, which is owned by AOL, accounted for another 2.5 million subscribers. AOL was serving 1.2 million users simultaneously, an increase of more than 65 percent from the previous year. Users averaged sixty-three minutes each of on-line activity daily (in the spring of 1997 it was thirty-six minutes), and were sending 110 million e-mails daily (in the spring of 1997 it was 13 million). AOL itself provided 200 million daily stock quotes.

In France, Wanadoo, while much newer in the service-provider marketplace, was growing too. In December 1998 it was charging a basic subscription price of 95 FF per month. This was exceedingly expensive. But I predicted then, in a draft of this manuscript, that prices would come down because competition would force them down. And in fact that is exactly what has happened. By June 2000 there were about 1.7 million Wanadoo subscribers, and they could access the Internet for as little as 39 FF per month for three hours' usage, or for as much as 159 FF for forty hours of use.

What this means is that telephone companies have entered the business of selling the use of real time as ISPs (such as Wanadoo), in addition to remaining in the business of charging a price for providing normal local and long-distance phone service.

They have been forced into it. No one ever anticipated that one local call that might normally last five or ten minutes would one day also be used to access the Internet via a commercial ISP and turn into a local call lasting one or two hours. There is no such thing as a "long-distance telephone call" on the Internet, if you have a modem and know how to dial the phone number of an ISP in your local calling area. Anyone connected to the Internet could surf the Net or send e-mails around world for the flat rate of one local call. The real money, therefore, was to be made by the ISP that charged for real time on-line. The telephone companies figured this out and became Internet service providers themselves. The reason their prices are dropping for access to the Internet and for consumption of real time is because they are competing for customers with other commercial Internet service providers, such as AOL.

How is real time used? Consider the following illustration.

In May 1996 the board of directors of the United States Institute of Peace (USIP) held a two-day meeting in northern Virginia. It took place at Airlie House, on Dumfries Road, often traveled long ago by a young surveyor on horseback named George Washington. In the early 1800s the road was the highway between the Potomac River and the Shenandoah Valley. Today Airlie House, a Georgian Revival mansion, is one of the most beautiful conference centers in the United States. So it was that we gathered there for our annual review of USIP's activities. There are fifteen board members, four of whom are the designated representatives of the secretary of state, the secretary of defense, the secretary of the Arms Control and Disarmament Agency, and the president of National Defense University. The others are nominated by the president and confirmed by the United States Senate. It's an interesting and sophisticated group.

The opening session on Thursday evening, led by the secretary of state's representative, Toby Trister Gaty, then director of the Bureau of Intelligence and Research, concerned threats to peace and security. On Friday morning we moved on to a presentation about the Internet. It's fair to say that enthusiasm for computers among the board members was not overwhelming. I don't know what our average age was, but I would guess somewhere between sixty and sixty-five. The presentation was being made with an overhead projector. It cast the image of a computer screen on the wall. We were looking at the home page of the institute, www.usip.org, on the World Wide Web.

By this time, Gaku had been teaching me about the Internet for six months. So as Bob Schmidt, the Information Systems Manager at USIP, began telling us about the wonders of the Web, I sat there nodding my head authoritatively; although if I had been asked to explain what the Web was, I couldn't have. He was describing why the Web was an ideal and inexpensive way to introduce the activities of the USIP to the public. But as I watched the faces of my fellow board members, they looked bored, bothered, and bewildered.

Bob was followed by Sheryl Brown. She went into more detail, and moved the arrow on the screen with her mouse. She clicked on different hyperlinks. New information immediately replaced what had just been there. "Unbelievable" was the only word that would do. The idea was for us to see and appreciate the modern world of communication, and to recognize that the USIP was on the cutting edge of new technology. It was impressive. Dr. Brown was telling us about the Information Age with credentials that were astounding. At USIP she was Director of Communications, Virtual Diplomacy, and Multilateral Information Sharing. At Georgetown University she was a professor of Greek history, teaching Thucydides' History of the Peloponnesian Wars and Xenophon's Cyropaedia and Hellenica. (I told her in February 1999 that I was going to put both worlds together in this book, and said, "Cheryl, your two lives are so fascinating because the juxtaposition is so dramatic. Neither has anything to do with the other." "Oh, but they do," she countered immediately. "Dennis, technology changes the dynamics, but the questions are still the same. What people do in their own self-interest hasn't changed a bit since Herodotus and Thucydides.")

The frustrating aspect of Dr. Brown's presentation was that it had the same effect as Bob Schmidt's. The members of the board didn't know what either one of them were talking about. We weren't stupid. We were just ignorant.

I noticed the desperate expression on the face of my fellow board member, seated next to me, as he vainly tried to follow what was being said. Max Kampelman, in his mid-seventies, finally gave up and his head began to nod, but for a different reason. He was falling asleep. He obviously didn't have a clue what it all meant. The arrow was moving so fast around the screen you couldn't follow it unless you were operating it yourself. Moreover, the computer language used to explain the tremendous possibilities of the Internet might as well have been Greek. Max couldn't understand it, and neither could any of the other board members, including me.

Max is one of the people on the board whose wisdom and judgment I greatly respect. He is a distinguished attorney and partner at Fried, Frank, Harris, Shriver & Jacobson in Washington, D.C. He is also an equally distinguished diplomat. His contributions to the conduct of American foreign policy over the past thirty years are legend. But Max couldn't understand the Internet because he didn't know how to use it. In the world in which Max grew up, it didn't exist. He didn't need it for the analysis of foreign affairs, for arms control negotiation, or for the practice of law. Students are the only group in American society being taught systematically how to use the Internet. And they are all the age of Max's grandchildren.

So the presentation made little sense to Max. It made some sense to me, thanks to Gaku, but I have to add that a less sophisticated presentation had been given in the spring of 1994 and 1995 and I fell asleep both times. I wanted Max to recognize the potential, but it wasn't being explained in terms that made sense to someone whose trusted tools of communication were telephones, typewriters, envelopes, and stamps. So, during the coffee break, I told him the following story:

> Ten years ago, Max, if you were writing a paper on the economic policy of the European Community and needed the text of the laws passed by the European Parliament during the first three months of 1987, you sent a letter to Strasbourg requesting photocopies. The letter was mailed on April 1. On April 17 a response arrived from Madame Plaisance in which she explained that another office handled such requests, and that she had forwarded your request accordingly, to a certain Monsieur de Bontemps.
>
> On April 29 a letter arrived from M. de Bontemps in which he explained that his office could indeed make photocopies available, and would be delighted to send them to you. The office only required payment in advance, in French francs, in the form of a check. On May 4 your office sent the check. Three weeks later, on May 25, the requested material arrived in the form of seven sheets of paper photocopies. Your office then thanked M. de Bontemps for his kindness, and indicated that you might be in touch with him again soon.
>
> The entire process had taken almost two months. It had also required, (1) three exchanges of correspondence, (2) $17.00 worth of French and American postage, (3) $15.00 to buy a cashier's check in French francs from the bank, (4) the fee for the photocopies, which was less than the fee for the cashier's check, and (5) the time spent by your office completing all of the above, which included a trip to the bank.
>
> [By this time Max knew something was up, but didn't know quite what.]
>
> Had the Internet been in existence (that is to say, the World Wide Web), you or your research assistant would have searched for and found in less than one minute the Web site (the home page) for the European Parliament (www.europarl.eu.int). You would then have looked (on your screen) through the table of contents, found the infor-

mation (files) you were looking for, and highlighted them with your mouse (in other words, instead of marking them with a pencil, you mark them with a little arrow on your screen).

You then would have pressed the buttons necessary to make the visual text on the screen come out of your office printing machine on paper. The whole process might have taken thirty minutes, if you dawdled.

Max got the point! And it made sense, because it was explained using real-life references that older people like us understand. Our stock-in-trade, after all — both his and mine — has been discharged throughout our entire adult life with a pen and a piece of paper — *not* with a mouse and screen. That's not our fault, that's just the way it is.

The illustration I like best, though, offers a perfect example of the convergence of computers (my laptop) with communication technology (the telephone and the fax). What's more, the result proved that all the time I had spent with Gaku had been worth every minute.

I was in my room at the Hotel du Parc, high above Lake Geneva in the late evening of April 10, 1997. I was attending the fiftieth-anniversary meeting of the Mont Pelerin Socicty (MPS). My speech was to be given the next morning on the role of Germany in Europe and on the European Union. During the Thursday morning session we got into an argument about the value of history. All afternoon and during dinner I stewed about it. At 11 P.M. I decided I had to change the first three pages for the next morning. But I had no typewriter, and if I had written it all by hand it would have been illegible. I did, however, have my laptop.

The speech was stored as an electronic document, in a file I had labeled MPS. So I plugged in the laptop, booted it up, and opened up the file. I made the revisions in the speech. So far, so good — except my speech was just words on the screen, and I couldn't very well take the laptop with me to the podium the next morning. I had to have the new version on paper. I connected my laptop to the telephone jack in the wall, dialed AT&T Direct (a very useful and inexpensive service travelers use), then the telephone number of the Stanford University computer and was connected (the bill would be sent to me at my office at Stanford). I sent an e-mail with the new text to my assistant, and asked her to print it and to fax it back to me in Switzerland. She sent an e-mail back almost immediately, and wrote, "Why don't you fax the text to yourself at the hotel, using your laptop?" Typing on the keyboard, I told my laptop to dial the fax number of the hotel (my room was on the third floor). My fax modem connected with the hotel's fax modem. When the laptop indicated that the two were connected, I was connected too. By pushing a couple of buttons, I sent my revised paper over the telephone line downstairs to the concierge as a fax, with a covering note. It said, "Please deliver this fax to Dr. Bark in room 322." Ten minutes later there was a knock at the door. The bellman handed me my revised paper and said, "Dr. Bark, ein Fax für Sie." It was now about 11:45 P.M. He had no idea who had sent the fax. Ecstatic, I went to bed.

6.

COMPUTERS AND COMMUNICATION CONVERGE

The history of the world is strewn with wonderful inventions,
but most of them were designed to solve specific problems.
The wheel to move things, engines of all kinds to supply power, and clocks and
compasses to tell time and direction.
The inventions that made possible the information revolution were of a different
sort. They changed the way we solve problems.
When Johann Gutenberg pioneered movable type printing in Europe about 1438
and when the little group at Intel designed the integrated circuit in the 1970s,
the way we record, store, access, and peruse knowledge
made a quantum leap forward and affected not only how we do our jobs,
but what we do.

{Walter Wriston, "Bits, Bytes, Power & Diplomacy," from a speech delivered to the Conference on Virtual Diplomacy on April 1, 1997, sponsored by the United States Institute of Peace, Washington, D.C.}

What I have just described is, for me at least, overwhelming. I still find it difficult to believe I was actually able to send that fax — and today, three years later, I do it from everywhere, whether it's Paris, Berlin, or Lake Tahoe. Think about the time saved or gained in the illustrations, and about being able to communicate by letter without a post office. Think about the speech in Switzerland. How could I have changed it in the hotel without the laptop, the modem, the telephone line, and then have gotten a new copy? This is one of the things that the revolution in information and communication technology is all about, and I am delighted. But I can't leave it at that, because as we change how we do things, we ourselves change as well.

Unintended Consequences

What I have described alters dramatically not only how *I* do things, but also how my assistant does things, and how millions of other people do things. It changes as well *what* I am doing. I carry my laptop with me everywhere I go on business trips. When I was using an IBM Selectric typewriter in the 1980s I had to leave it in my office when I got on the airplane. It was too heavy to carry, and I couldn't have used it anyway, because I couldn't have plugged it into an electrical outlet. But my laptop has a battery in it, and on some airplanes I can even plug into a connection at my seat. And airplanes now have telephones, so I can write and send a fax with my laptop, from my seat to anyone I wish. And I do! To Burkhard Koch in Berlin, or to Bertrand Jacquillat in Paris. It's called "wiring the skies," and it takes just a double-click.

That the world has changed so much is not surprising, but how it has changed is staggering. To me it seems like yesterday that I was submitting my Ph.D. dissertation to the department of history at the Freie Universität Berlin. When it was ready on January 8, 1970, it had taken Fräulein Zapfke five weeks to type it. I had never heard of the word "fax" or of the phrase "double-click." Today the dissertation would be written on a computer in a fraction of the time it took thirty years ago.

How we talk about this revolution is critical to understanding it, at least for those of us who went to grammar school when teachers were still diagramming sentences. That was in the early 1950s. Our vocabulary was completely different, and our world was listening to "The Lone Ranger" on the radio. My parents never talked about computers, and most of their friends didn't either. I remember very well when my father and my uncle, Thomas Swain Barclay, used to sit in rocking chairs in front of the fire in the study at our house on Escondido Road, on the Stanford campus. They talked about history, and philosophy, and politics. On Saturday nights they talked about what they called "the old alma," after Stanford had played a football game that afternoon. My father's world was a medieval one, and my uncle's was one of political science. They had secretaries who took shorthand, wrote letters on Underwood typewriters, and filed things.

I try and explain this difference in time and technology to my children, and I get bemused smiles, a shaking head, and sometimes an indulgent nod — I'm never sure if they understand my astonishment, or whether they're just being polite. I don't think they really get the point I'm trying to make. When I tell them that their language is different, I see a blank look. A perfect example is the word *database*. They use the word database all the time. But what is a database? This is a serious question, because computers use databases, and at a place like Stanford University you hear the word every day. Believe it or not it took me a while to figure it out. We used to have another word for database. We called it a *manila folder*. We'd say to Miss Babbit, "Please file the carbon copy in the Younger folder." The carbon copy was part of the Younger database; in other words, copies of all the letters we had sent to Mr. Younger, and his letters to us. That explains that word, but there are all kinds of new words, and we have to learn the meaning of all of them, if we are going to communicate with the younger generation. So, for example, there are also *relational databases*. These, as any fool would know (except those of us who were born fifty years ago), are related to the Younger file. And, of course, there are *file transfers* that are sent over the Internet. In olden times a file transfer was just a fancy name for Miss Babbit making copies of the correspondence with Cisco Systems concerning the network we are trying to set up, and mailing the copies to our attorney in San Francisco. In other words, she transferred a copy of a file from one place to another.

We used to do that with carbon copies, a large envelope, and a stamp. Then we took it to the post office. And four or five days later it would arrive at its destination unless we sent it special delivery, and that was expensive. Many of us, indeed, always will transfer our databases this way. That's not going to stop merely because *Wired* magazine has become just as well known as *Time* magazine in Silicon Valley. But in the 1970s most of us did stop making carbon copies, and started using the photocopying machine. Today, without paper, we are transferring more and more copies of our files — letters, memos, and documents (whatever they might be, e.g. wills, legal briefs, speeches, articles, and so on) — via networks. No photocopies, no ink, no paper, no envelopes, no address labels, no stamps, no glue, no sticky fingers, no post office, no skilled assistant acting as a clerk. We even have digital cameras we can attach to a computer or to a printing machine, so that we can print out a photograph without film or send it via the Internet to Aunt Monique. Sony Corporation, for example, makes such a camera, called a *Mavica*. The film is a computer disk. The post office is the computer and telephone line. And what does Sony say? — "Now, E-Mailing the Sights and Sounds of Your Life Has Never Been Easier."

In his 1993 history of the Internet, Bruce Sterling tried to define the information revolution in four categories. And while new inventions since then, like the World Wide Web and the use of the mobile telephone to send e-mail without wires, continue to redefine the meaning of the Information Age, Sterling's straightforward explanations help us understand the magnitude of the digital tidal wave that is changing marketplaces and mentalities. In 2000 the categories are no longer just four; but his explanations still provide the foundation on which computing and communication continue to converge.

His first category is electronic mail. In the conventional sense it is a message in the form of a note, or a letter, or the draft of a speech we send to someone else. But instead of sending it on paper, we send it digitally.

The real advantage of e-mail is that it's a network — for doctors to communicate with their patients, for the elderly whose mobility is limited and who often feel isolated, or for parents and grandparents to exchange news with each other and with their children and grandchildren. A perfect example is a fax I received on December 20, 1999, from an old friend, Brigitte Rühland, who lives near Münster, Germany. She wrote:

> Since I now am a computer freak, I am writing my Christmas letter on a computer. It's supposed to be faster, but that's only a rumor.... For me a lot of things are still going wrong, the whole system crashes, and the text is lost. But I'm not giving up; I want to communicate with my grandchildren later. Please send me your e-mail address.

To use e-mail all Brigitte needs is a software program in her computer. One of the best, introduced in 1989 and the one I use, is named Eudora, after the American writer Eudora Welty. It's made by Qualcomm and is used today by over 20 million people. The name, incidentally, is the idea of a young man named Steve Donner at the University of Illinois, who designed the software using the protocol called POP (post office protocol). He had read one of Welty's short stories, written in 1941, called "Why I Live at the Post Office."

First the fax revolutionized how we communicated using a telephone. Now e-mail is doing the same thing all over again. It doesn't isolate. It does the opposite, by bringing together older and younger, distant friends and far away relatives, without having to write a letter and go to the post office. I am a case in point. More than 10,000 kilometers separate California from Europe and there's a nine-hour time difference. It's not easy for me to telephone my godchildren in Germany, so they send me e-mail. I communicate with my relatives in Sweden the same way. In fact, on November 4, 1998, my brother and his wife and son, my wife and I, and our Swedish cousin met in Paris at La Bastide Odéon for lunch. My brother's family had come from New York. Our cousin had come from Ghent in Belgium. We had come from southern France. Everything had been arranged via e-mail.

Was all this just about having lunch? Well, that was certainly part of it, but another part was about "the new digital order." I asked one my of my sons, who had just returned from Cairns in North Queensland, what e-mail means. He said, "I was in no-man's land in the middle of Australia, but I wasn't isolated from you. I sent you e-mail. It's direct, it's immediate, it's one step, it's a straight shot." In spite of the skeptics, e-mail is not turning us all into rootless, laptop-toting, cell-phoning nomads and it's not going to replace real neighborhoods. On the contrary, it's expanding them! That's why CyberAtlas could report in 1999 that there were over 263 million e-mail boxes throughout the world, and that over 3.4 trillion e-mail messages had been sent in the United States in 1998.

Computers and Communication Converge

Sterling's second category is long-distance computing. Scientists, for example, can use supercomputers located a continent away. So, even though German and American physicists may be separated by the Atlantic ocean, they can work together on the same project. Indeed, initially such use was one of the goals of ARPANET, and that was one of the main subjects of the First International Conference on Computer Communications in 1972 (referred to earlier in this chapter). Long-distance computing has also created an unintended member of the workforce, the telecommuter — the preferred way of making a living for 19.6 million Americans who have traded what one observer described as "mind-numbing commutes, stress-filled workdays and office politics for the freedom to work at home." Indeed, we have one at the Hoover Institution with whom I communicate; she lives in Santa Fe, New Mexico!

Newsgroups — "the world of news, debate and argument" on USENET — is Sterling's third category. It is within these — newsgroups, chat rooms, bulletin boards — that freedom is allowed to run its full, undisciplined course. There is, as one would expect, a great deal of information-trading about computers, software programs, and networking systems, as well as about bugs, viruses, or about how to keep your computer screen clean. There are also discussions you can join on high energy physics, Elk hunting in Wyoming, gourmet cooking, or about the tragic death of Princess Diana in Paris in 1997. In fact, there is even a discussion group called "Eudora Welty." In my own case I subscribe to an IBM ThinkPad bulletin board for owners of IBM laptops (thinkpad@cs.utk.edu), where I can ask questions, get answers and trade comments with other ThinkPad users. Whenever someone "posts" a message to the board (that means to send an e-mail message to the electronic bulletin board) the e-mail is sent to my address automatically. I look at the heading of the message to see if it interests me, and either read it or discard it, as I wish.

Newsgroups, however, is also the generic phrase for another side of the Internet. You can, if you know how to search for them, join discussions about bondage, masochism, sadism, and other assorted activities. You can read, and write yourself if you wish, observations containing every conceivable vulgar word known to man, and probably a few no one has ever heard of. You can post messages to bulletin boards, send them to discussion groups, and view hard core pornography as well. The liberty to do so is the price for protecting freedom of speech. But it should be added that one does not just *turn on* dirty pictures and filthy prose, heat up the TV dinner and sit back for a little friendly self-indulgence. You have to seek it out. That's why the medium of the Internet is called interactive! And that's why it's non-intrusive. How we use the Internet is our choice, no one else's.

Sterling gives the fourth category the innocuous name of file transfers, already referred to. Whoever dreamed up this phrase could hardly have found a weaker description to describe an exceedingly powerful tool — namely, a way to attach/send/transfer a file, whatever size, that completely changes the communication equation. A file transfer, literally, is to send a file (containing one letter or the draft of this book) from my computer to another. That does not sound very important, but it affects everything. Getting stock quotes uses file transfers. Making a bid at a wine auction involves file transfers. Purchasing CDs requires file transfers. Ordering books requires file transfers. When I wanted a friend in Copenhagen to read the draft of this chapter I sent it to him as a file transfer, by "attaching" the draft to my e-mail message.

File transfers, therefore, also present a multitude of new possibilities. For example, you can scan the text of Edmund Burke's *Reflections on the French Revolution* into your computer. Then you can send the text as a file transfer to your daughter who is in her junior year at Colby College in Waterville, Maine. This could be important if her political science professor had assigned Burke as required reading, and the copy in the library were checked out. That's one kind of file transfer. Another kind, for example, is what Quorum Communications in Irving, Texas, has done. It has transferred onto its Web site the technical manuals for some of its satellite remote sensing systems. If you use the Internet to find the site — www.qcom.com — you can read the manuals and you can also tell your computer to print them out on paper. Quorum's manuals are just several of millions of books and articles that have been loaded onto Web sites for educational, commercial, and private purposes. They are all files and they can all be transferred.

We used to go to the library and check out a book. We also went to libraries to read foreign newspapers, because most of us couldn't afford to have our own, private subscription at home. We used to carry files from one office to the next. Monique would take it down the hall to Susan, or would send it via inter-office mail. Susan's boss would read the file, write a note to Monique's boss, and the file would be sent back. Very simple, but it took a lot of time.

Then modern technology gave us the photocopying machine. That made it easy and inexpensive to make copies. So we began to photocopy newspaper articles, chapters in books, and letters we had written. We sent the copies all over the place in envelopes with stamps. (How did we ever get along without that machine?) When the fax machine was invented that changed things once again. We began to fax files everywhere, whether it was one page, or many pages. I remember being at a house in the country in France in September of 1993. A friend called me from the United States and said he wanted to fax me a contract. So I gave him the fax number, and went to have dinner. When I came back fifty-seven pages were scattered on the floor and my roll of paper was gone! Today that same file can be transferred via the Internet in less than five seconds, and there will be no paper on the floor.

Will e-file transfers make the use of paper disappear? Of course not! Does it mean good-bye to data (letters and memos and reports) being carried down the hall in cardboard file folders? No, that will continue too, but old-fashioned paper transfers will be overtaken by file transfers of information via electronic networks:

> Data traffic is the dominant driver of corporate broadband networks. By 2002, around 90 percent of worldwide corporate traffic will be non-voice, compared with just 10 percent in 1992. This rate is increasing with information flow in formats such as video, data, text, graphics, and voice.

The merits of paper versus e-mail are not at issue here. Given a choice, I prefer paper, pen, and ink. But the wired world prefers e-mail, and its use is causing the biggest technical, managerial, and political challenge government record-keeping archivists have ever faced. The National Archives in Washington, D.C.,

> ... must keep 'record copies' of all documents deemed significant — under laws written when documents were created and filed on paper.

> The archivist's understandable first stab at the problem was a ruling that executive branch e-mails could be deleted if paper printouts had been made. It was properly rebuffed by the courts because so much information about an e-mail is lost when it is printed out, including when it was written and sent and who sent it.... How the government ends up storing its records for posterity also will help shape the approach of libraries and academic institutions. The stakes in this project are as enormous as its daunting complexity.

Whether we welcome it or not, we will learn how to make this new technology serve us, or we will be left in the aftermath of the tidal wave. It's an individual choice, and I've already made mine.

7.

IS THE WORLD ROUND?

Civilization ... has to do not with things
but with the invisible ties
that join one thing to another.

{Antoine de Saint-Exupéry, as quoted in
Theodor Holm Nelson's *Literary Machines*}

The information revolution is like the reddest, juiciest apple hanging from the Tree
of Knowledge. The difference between this succulent, secular snack and the forbid-
den fruit in Genesis, however, is that we are promised that one bite will lead us
back into Eden, not cast us out.
All will be within our reach, instantly. No waiting, no longing, no distance to
travel, no disappointment at dreams that don't come true.
Our computers will be genies gratefully out of the bottle, ready to grant our wishes
without a second's delay. The promise is pernicious but hard to resist. There before
us is the digital portal, with the lush garden of earthly delights just within.
The serpent flicks his tongue. No more struggling with doing.
How easy will the future be?
Click.

{Owen Edwards, *Forbes ASAP*, October 4, 1999}

I began this chapter with Hedwig Kiesler and a piano. Who would have thought the story would lead from a Viennese dinner table to the strange and fast world of nets and webs that fill this book? The idea of wireless communication, of unseen signals hopping from one anonymous frequency to another, has finally become a wired world of dramatic substance, fed by information technology.

This chapter could never have been written when Hedwig Kiesler arrived in Hollywood in the late 1930s. She wouldn't have thought about an Internet. She didn't need to. And neither did the people who watched her films. They all had their own networks. They consisted of the telephone and of Hollywood cocktail parties, that continued on moving trains going from Beverly Hills to Chicago and on to New York City, of luxury liners that sailed between Europe and the United States, of clubs and dinners and balls. They had networks, all right! And they were social, elite, and expensive. For a few it was the "old boy network." For others it was the world of the WASPs. Still others called it being socially prominent. And for some their networks were political, southern, ethnic, or racial, as in Mayor Daily's political machinery in Chicago, or in the arcane world of Huey Long in Louisiana, or in Tammany Hall in New York, or on the streets of Chinatown in San Francisco. But whatever it was, everyone had a network.

Today, we still have social, economic, political, and cultural networks. But they are no longer defined by just age, power, and money, nor are they as conventional and influential as they once were, because there's a new one! It's called the Internet. It puts both information and social, economic, and political power into the hands of individuals. It's a flat world, based on communication. This world makes me, at least, part of a network where new relationships are formed with people whom I would never have met, using the old networks. Would I have developed what I consider real friendships with Gaku or Nalini, otherwise? Highly unlikely! Nor they with me. But networks are changing all of this, with a powerful impact. Vint Cerf calls it "serendipitous communication." My own encounter with Gaku is the perfect illustration (I wonder what Gaku would say? He hasn't read this part):

> One doesn't know with whom one might be communicating when you post on a discussion group or put something up on a Web site and have someone find it then get in touch with you. It is this discovery of others with similar interests that I think is an incredibly powerful force.... New ideas, inventions ... mean that the true meaning of serendipity can emerge from this unexpected encounter with an idea or person with whom you share some interest.

The Internet is proving much more powerful than any network that has ever existed, because it is so much larger. Every scholar knows that ideas emerge from what we call brainstorming. When you're looking for a title for a book, as for example this book, you just start throwing titles out on the table, and hope there's a bottle of Jack Daniel's to help your imagination. Eventually the interaction of several minds will produce a good idea. On the Internet, brainstorming follows the same principle, but there are enormous resources to draw on, and the size of the table is the size of the Internet — that was 300 million users in April 2000. Another way to express this same concept was put to me by Vipin Gupta when I called him in early June of 1998. I asked him why networks are important. He said, "If you can have universal access to people, ideas, and products, the sky's the limit."

What Vipin really meant, without saying so, is that the convergence of computers with communication technology is producing a world of unparalleled freedom of speech, where sex, social class, and wealth are not distinguishing measures on the Internet. Today there are no racial or religious barriers to entry to electronic networks. You just have to be able to afford to buy a computer, and be intelligent enough to figure out how it works (or have the good fortune to know Gaku!). To paraphrase British statesman William E. Gladstone from 1835, the ranks, classes, and the new estate are now all flat. Indeed, I went to Gaku for help, not vice versa. When knowledge reposes in new places, and you want it, you have to go there. So I went. Would Gaku's generation have had anything I needed twenty years ago? I don't think so! The latter conclusion is a change with profound social implications — is it clear who is making the rules now, as our roles and places and responsibilities change in wired society?

Is there a digital divide? If we listen to opportunistic politicians and hand-wringing alarmists of any social persuasion, we would think so. But, in fact, there will not be computer haves and have-nots, any more than there are television haves and have-nots. The assertion that we are "separate and unequal on the Net" is heady stuff for op-ed pieces, and maybe there is some truth in it. But there is also some truth in the conclusion that we have the freedom to choose, a point put well by the chairman of the Afro-American Studies Department at Harvard University:

> The Internet is the twenty-first century's talking drum, the very kind of grassroots communication tool that has been such a powerful source of education and culture for our people since slavery. But this talking drum we have not yet learned to play.

> Unless we master the new information technology to build and deepen the forms of social connection that a tragic history has eroded, African-Americans will face a form of cybersegregation in the next century as devastating to our aspirations as Jim Crow segregation was to those of our ancestors. But this time, the fault will be our own.

Is the World Round?

Computers were expensive, and so was Internet access, at the beginning. So were horses at one time, and cars, and television sets, and mobile phones. But as production processes improve, prices drop. As more people buy, the user base broadens. As the user base broadens, prices drop further ... and so it is here. This is another way of saying that equality doesn't define the quality and price of products, competition does. Makers of television sets had everything to gain by seeing to it that as many people as possible could afford one; so it is also with computers. The Internet today is not price-discriminatory. Whether or not we use a computer is becoming a matter of choice, not of price, just as was the case with horses, cars, televisions, and mobile phones. For example, in March of 1998 the price of a PC was dropping about one percentage point a week, just another old-fashioned way of saying that companies which get their quality computers to market quickly gain manufacturing advantages. So prices continue to drop; just look at the price of computers made by Dell or Compaq (I'm not going to do it for you; go to the store and compare). The same thing happened with the television. The price of a television set, indeed, has never proved a barrier to entering the world of the soap opera. Neither will the price of a computer prove to be a barrier to entering the Internet. Political policies of control and monopolistic practices by governments may erect artificial barriers to entry, but that's not technology's fault.

During 1997, for example, the number of households in the United States with at least one personal computer rose by 11.4 percent. Lower prices for personal computers drove the market, so that by January 1998, 44.8 percent of all homes in the United States owned a PC. In September 1998, superb systems equipped for the Internet, with state-of-the art software, were selling for $900. They were three times as fast as mine bought in 1995, had eight times the memory, and almost fifteen times the storage space. The following analogy, cited in the December 1998 issue of *Wired*, makes the point: "The Model T did for cars what the $900 PC has done for computers — it made the automobile an affordable commodity." By April 1999 sophisticated personal computers were available in the United States for less than $400. And when I purchased a new IBM laptop in January 2000 I paid less than half of what I paid five years before. By March 2000 there were about 220 million PCs in use in the United States and approximately 110 million Internet users, expected to increase to almost 150 million by 2001.

Politicians, of course, argue that everyone must be equal and that translates into everyone must have a PC. And that means that politicians have a lot to gain by claiming the existence of "haves" and "have-nots" — and then, a lot more to gain by claiming that they will end it. So President Clinton made a commitment in February 2000 to bridge the "digital divide" with $2 billion in government funds (tax moneys) to develop Net access. It was a laudable goal, by any standard. But government didn't have a monopoly on serving the common interest. In February 2000 Ford Motor Company announced that each of its 350,000 employees would be offered a PC, a color printer, and Internet access for $5 per month. Delta Airlines made a similar decision at the same time for its 72,000 employees. The article about Ford Motor Company's initiative that ran in the February 5, 2000, edition of the *San Francisco Chronicle* was headlined "PC Could Be Next Standard Appliance."

Is this interconnected system of nets and webs really as important as I have convinced myself it is? What is all this, after all, except an interconnected network of computers? We went through the same thing with the invention of the electric telegraph in the late 1840s, "the Victorian Internet." What can I say, but the obvious? That's exactly what the Internet is, an interconnected network of computers! The Internet is fast, cheap, accessible, and covers the globe. Computer networks break down hierarchical worlds, destroy knowledge monopolies (that also means opinion monopolies), and unleash imagination, in powerful, creative ways. Telegraphs, telephones, and telexes couldn't do that in the same way. That is the difference. That's why so much depends on how we use what we have made. Using a fax machine, for example, was a new way to use a telephone. What new ways will we still invent to use computers? For those of us my age and older, it's time to climb aboard this computer train of communication networks. Because if we don't learn how to use a computer soon, we're not going to be part of the future. As one IBM executive wrote to me, following a discussion on an airplane flight from San Francisco to Chicago in July 1997, "Power in the future will belong to the Builders and Users of technology." And that's exactly what we see in the year 2000.

Another way to put this is to emphasize again — and it can't be said too often — no one controls the Internet. That is the beauty of a decentralized system of computers, operating independently from one another, whether they are located in Boston, Paris, Singapore, or Capetown. Governments cannot control and censor their operation, unless they shut down the entire communications system — and if they do that they isolate themselves from the global marketplace. The builders and users of computer and communication technology will prove more powerful than politicians who would like to tame technology they can't control. By no means, however, are all politicians ignorant of the potential of the revolution. Perhaps that is why Vice President Albert Gore sought to take credit for its popularity in March 1999, with his widely quoted comment that he had taken "the initiative in creating the Internet."

This new world is obviously of little value to us if we reject it. I did that, successfully, for some time. But if we aren't part of it, how do we send e-mail messages or send a fax from the computer? How do we locate newsgroups and brainstorm? How do we find information in the form of documents and print this information on paper? How do we make Web sites appear on the computer screen? How do we send and receive documents and files? How do we know they are even there? How do we search for an e-mail address if we know a friend has one, but don't know what it is? The counter question, of course, is do we want to do any of these things? I suppose the answer to that is the crux of the issue — with one little footnote. If I don't become part of this world and thus contribute my share, I will have no say in its future shape. And, if I don't like the shape I'll have nobody to blame but myself. So, I am not willing to sit back and say, "I'll stick with paper, pen, and ink," while time and technology pass me by. I had only thought in passing about these things when I met Nalini in 1995. But she knew that the computer would change my life. And I now know it will change yours, too.

While some, such as Bruce Sterling, may argue that the Internet was "originally ... a post-apocalypse command grid," that is certainly not what J.C.R. Licklider had in mind when he moved to Washington, D.C., in 1962. What we call the Net, or the Web, is a new dimension involving how we relate to each other in an elegant universe of time. We don't know all the shifts and meanings yet. We don't even know if we are asking all the right questions. But we do know, as Sterling concluded in 1993, the following:

> No one really planned it this way. Its users made the Internet that way, because they had the courage to use the network to support their own values, to bend the technology to their own purposes. To serve their own liberty. Their own convenience, their own amusement, even their own idle pleasure. When I look at the Internet — that paragon of cyberspace today — I see something astounding and delightful. It's as if some grim fallout shelter had burst open and a full-scale Mardi Gras parade had come out.

Today our round planet is still a globe, but we are playing out our electronic lives in a digital age. More unforeseen and unanticipated change is on the way. We can see some of the effects, and cannot see others. We don't know what it all means, yet. But we do know that our traditional world of networks is being transformed. That transformation is what we called, just a decade ago, at the end of the 1980s, the fax revolution. Few of us recognized that our entire civilization of communication would never be the same again, either. "The fax," one heard in 1990, "shall set you free!" How many of us recognized then that something much more powerful would soon change relationships between cultures, peoples, governments, and nations in ways we had never contemplated?

As the head of Microsoft Corporation, Bill Gates, put it in *The Road Ahead*

(Penguin Group), by late 1995 — just as John McCarthy was putting my ad on the Internet — "… there was no turning back … we had crossed the threshold."

> More users meant more content and more content meant more users. The Internet had spiraled up in popularity, achieving critical mass.…
>
> We're experiencing the early days of a revolution in communications that will be long-lived and widespread. There will be some surprises before we get to the ultimate realization of the information highway because much is still unclear. We don't understand consumer preferences yet. The role of government is a troubling open question. We can't anticipate all of the technical breakthroughs that lie ahead. But interactive networking is here to stay, and it's only just beginning.

Knowledge, electronic access to information via the wireless telephone, the satellite and the Internet have become capital assets in global competition for commercial power, financial markets, and political influence. It is no longer a tidy nexus of power, class, and money. It is a revolution in communication which changes the nature of power and the role of money. It rewrites the traditional definition of class, as we have been using it since the French Revolution. The word *class*, in all its divisive and disruptive meaning as used by labor union leaders and political activists who haven't yet got the message, is an antediluvian concept that was disappearing at the end of the twentieth century, just as it will be redefined in the twenty-first.

A fountain pen gave a feature and flourish to the art of writing by hand. IBM Corporation followed with the art of processing words by electric machine. The Internet is giving, one fragment at a time, new meaning to the art of discourse. As the organizers of the 1998 conference of the International Telecommunications Society put it, we know that, like rings on water, "the new world of communication reaches well beyond telecommunications as we know it today, promising far-reaching changes in … social, political and economic institutions, on a global scale." This new world is driven by ourselves. It is we who are finding new ways to satisfy our needs, and in many cases the needs themselves are new. This search is challenging every stable force we have traditionally drawn upon to bring order and balance to our lives. Two elements, especially, are knocking at the door of every institution we know. They are time and knowledge. How we use the first and what we do with the second will determine the future of our cultural, economic, political, and social lives. Whether we like it, accept it, or embrace it — or not.

CHAPTER TWO

THE CONNECTED

*What do they do, these microchips, these silicon
brains ... that have changed the end of the twentieth
century, just as its beginning was transformed by the
Industrial Revolution? Remember the horse and buggy
versus the motor car? Skeptics held sway in 1900, too,
just as many do today, one hundred years later.
Who won?*

{Dennis L. Bark, talking to himself in his kitchen on
Friday morning, March 27, 1998}

86

1.

LES BRANCHÉS

I, Sir, am a person of most respectable connections.

{Samuel Butler, 1835-1902}

*The links of connection make
a certain kind of law between us.*

{Ovid, 43 B.C.-A.D. 17}

In Paris my wife and I have a good friend named Hubert Jousset. Each September since 1985 we have had lunch together, normally just the three of us, though sometimes another friend, Bertrand Jacquillat, joins us. We first meet at Hubert's office, in the Rue Saint Honoré.

We used to set up these lunches by letter. Then we switched to a fax machine. Today we do it via e-mail. The routine itself hasn't changed.

On September 3, 1997, a Wednesday, we arrived at Hubert's office at 12:30. He was obviously very pleased with himself as he announced, "Today I'm taking you to a special place. We are going to *l'Hôtel des Branchés*" (the Hotel of the Connected Ones)." My wife and I didn't know what he meant, but we trust Hubert, so off we went. We walked three hundred meters to the Hôtel Costes, which used to be known as "France et Choiseul." The lobby was dark, swathed in deep reds and golds, its table lamps adorned with pleated lamp shades. Very elaborate. Socialites dressed in full-length gowns would call it Napoleon III. You couldn't help feeling you were entering an expensive, *très chic* nightclub.

Unintended Consequences

But then Hubert took us through a doorway and we emerged in a perfectly lovely courtyard, filled with sunlight and flowers and ivy. Square tables were nestled together, covered with white linen, under the shade of umbrellas. The courtyard was full. It was hard not to notice how well dressed the customers were, and that most of them were young men and women. There was also something else. Almost all of them had their own mobile telephones. The phones were either lying on the table or they were being used. As we sat down, the young man at the next table picked up his telephone as it rang. Hubert, with a wry smile, said, *"Et voila! Les Branchés!"* In English that means, "There they are! The Connected Ones!" I said, "I'll bet he asked his secretary to call him!"

This story has a point, besides just being cute. Being connected touches everything we do. Some people in this restaurant undoubtedly wanted to look like a big deal, so they had their friends call them. But others were using time in a way they never had before. Hearing private, wireless conversations at the adjoining tables annoyed me, because I wasn't there to listen to someone else's calls. On the other hand, used discreetly and appropriately, a mobile telephone introduces a brand new world, just as being connected to a computer introduces us to the wired world of the Internet and real time.

Since Nalini and Gaku "connected" me, I have been living in parallel worlds. When I read about twenty-first-century technology in a magazine called *Wired*, which Nalini introduced me to four years ago, I find it ironic in the extreme that the printed words I see date from a fifteenth-century technology called moveable type. We're all aware of the changes during that five-century period, but there were also amazing changes during just the five-year period, from 1993 to 1998, when *Wired* celebrated its fifth anniversary. Publisher Louis Rossetto wrote about them in the January 1998 issue:

> When Jane Metcalfe and I first carried our business plan around to publishers and investors in 1991, we were met with looks of incredulity and pity.
>
> Digital Revolution? Most publishers were barely aware of the Industrial Revolution.... What we were dreaming about was profound global transformation. We wanted to tell the story of the companies, the ideas, and especially the people making the Digital Revolution. Our heroes weren't politicians and generals or priests and pundits, but those creating and using technology and networks in their professional and private lives — you.

> ... [A] lot *has* changed in these five years. The Internet has mush-
> roomed from an obscure academic mail system into the fastest
> growing medium, marketplace, and community in history. Genetic
> engineering is conquering disease, and new energy technologies
> promise to save our environment. The global financial network has
> created a force for change more powerful than the nation-state.
> And digital citizens are reinvigorating democratic discourse and
> reinventing civil society.

Since 1995 I haven't stopped thinking about this digital world, not only because it is so different from the one I grew up in, but also because I like living in both. I, for example, now have a mobile telephone, a fax machine, a printer, a scanner, a PC in my office, a laptop at home, and an e-mail address. The Hoover Institution has even created a "Dennis L. Bark" Web page, and my sons gave me a digital camera for Christmas 1999. The only thing I'm missing is a Palm Pilot. My brother tells me it will change my life, to steal Nalini's phrase.

The symbols of this new world have exploded in the form of new terms and words, such as *Google, virtual reality, Ethernet, cyberspace, real time, applet, Netizens, Eudora, ASCII, cyberpunk, Jivi, hypertext markup language, RAM, don-gle, cyberstyle, Binhex, http, Netiquette, cybersoirée, digirati, surfing the Net, Veronica, cybernaut, CD-ROM, modem, Java, MIME,* and *Cyberia.* All are words and terms in daily usage in newspapers, magazines, or on radio and television in the year 2000. But all are also names which still only a minority can define properly. In some ways I wish it stopped here, but it doesn't. Acronyms, widely used on the Internet, are becoming new words themselves, and might properly be called a lin-guist's nightmare. Abbreviation, contraction, and condensation have produced an "alternative dictionary" for "Netcronyms." It's called *Tribal Voice,* with over six mil-lion users, at www.chatdictionary.com. There you can find such titillating items as GFUG (good for you, girl), YOOC (you're out of control), POS (parent over shoul-der), JK (just kidding), or TTYL (talk to you later).

Ignorance of how the Internet works — without doubt the word Internet is used incorrectly more often than any other in the English language at the present time — does not make the Internet all smoke and mirrors, as several of my colleagues at the Hoover Institution claimed at the round table in the Senior Commons in 1995. On the contrary, the revolution in communication technology is moving us relentlessly forward as it continues to transform the content of our lives, piece by piece. That's what revolutions do. Because the changes occur gradually, we don't see them as rep-resenting a revolution in how we live, with whom we live, where we work, what kind of work we do, and how long we take to do it. We don't find a headline in the morning paper announcing the arrival of the revolution, from one day to the next. And we won't. Many of us won't recognize what's happened until long after it has changed our daily lives forever.

Yet there is also reason to recall the French expression *plus ça change, plus c'est la même chose* (the more things change, the more they remain the same). And, at least in one respect, this is true. The eighteenth-century concept of the *salon* is still valid, for instance, although today it has a new name, *cybersalon*. As reporter Ann Grimes noted in a November 1998 article in *The Wall Street Journal*, only the connected need apply:

> It's more high-tech than highbrow, more business than *bons mots*, compared with the gatherings that writer Madame de Stael turned into an art form some 200 years ago....

> Round Zero [the prefunding stage of a start-up] meets monthly at a Menlo Park hotel to discuss topics like 'Is Microsoft evil?' In Berkeley, a group chews over patents and pizza at Fred and Sylvia's CyberSalon. In San Francisco, a young Internet executive hosts elaborate Thursday dinners featuring organic vegetables at his home overlooking the Golden Gate Bridge.... The trend partly reflects the development of an elite, as the [Silicon] Valley and its high-tech figures mature and depart from the computer industry's meritocratic roots....

> People here say they are so connected electronically that they feel unconnected from fellow humans. They yearn for regular face time to swap ideas, socialize and network ... 'It's a chance to talk some real issues,' says Philip N. Sanderson, a San Francisco venture capitalist.

Social life and dinner parties haven't changed. Both continue, with different vocabularies and different menus, but otherwise they're alive, well, and updated. For young and budding silicon gold rushers, dinner parties are an extension of their office life. "E-vites" substitute for written invitations, addresses are exchanged on Palm Pilots instead of with business cards, and the gourmet food is provided by www.Webvan.com. In the Valley's "suburb" of San Francisco www.OpenTable.com lists more than 400 restaurants that accept "e-reservations" and confirm them via e-mail. Valley cafes, such as Buck's in the small town of Woodside (known as "the Beverly Hills of High Tech"), and upscale restaurants in Palo Alto are places where deals get done by "e-Forty-niners" prospecting 150 years after the original Forty-niners came to California looking for gold. While only one in thirty start-ups that receive venture capital money eventually goes public, there are 250,000 millionaires in the Valley, where a house on average costs more than $450,000, more than twice the national average. The Valley's economy, if it were a nation, would rank among the world's twelfth largest. "The Net Set," according to one journalist, has replaced "the Jet Set" as it practices "Internet interruptus."

The Valley, in Santa Clara County, was named by writer Don Hoefler, whose article on the semiconductor industry for a 1971 issue of *Electronic News* was entitled "Silicon Valley USA." But if there was one person who had the foresight and the vision of what the future could hold, it was Stanford's professor of engineering, Frederick Terman. Today, for the encouragement he gave struggling businesses in Santa Clara County, and with brilliant success, he can rightly be called the Valley's grandfather. With some of his own money he supported two of his former students in 1939, working in a Palo Alto garage, who hoped to build an electronics company around their development of an audio oscillator. From the garage emerged what became the Valley's electronic corporate pioneer, the Hewlett-Packard Corporation. In turn, William Hewlett and David Packard, and many others who have come after them, maintained their connections with Stanford, both becoming major donors and trustees. The commitments they made to their company and to the university set the standard for "how one deals in the business world with your customers, with your suppliers, with your employees, and with your communities." And through it all, as one writer for the *San Jose Mercury News* put it, they never let success go to their heads. In 1995, the year before he died, David Packard, in response to a reporter's question about whether he had any regrets, responded, "If I had studied more instead of playing football … I probably would have gone a little further."

Advancements in computer technology during the 1950s and the 1960s not only affected science and engineering, they also began to leave their mark on the Valley's character, and with much greater dramatic impact during the 1970s and 1980s. In 1975 young electronic enthusiasts, such as Apple Computer founder Stephen Wozniak, attended informal meetings in Palo Alto to discuss the technology of personal computers, a name coined in 1974 in a book called *II cybernetic frontiers*, by Stewart Brand, a member of Stanford's class of 1960 and the founder in 1968 of the *Whole Earth Catalogue*. They called their group the Homebrew Computer Club; the meetings, at first held in a garage (!), became so popular that in the 1980s they had to be moved to the auditorium of Stanford's Linear Accelerator. At the same time, the rural landscape of Santa Clara County was being slowly replaced by construction cranes and industrial parks (Stanford University and the towns of Palo Alto, Sunnyvale, Mountain View, and San Jose are all located in the county). The Valley's fruit trees were transformed into trees of technology. In the late 1950s I went often with my father as he drove down the Valley's principal thoroughfare, El Camino Real, to the disappearing black walnut orchards in Mountain View and Sunnyvale to buy firewood, which he burned with some sadness in his fireplace in "The Frenchman's House" on the Stanford campus. By the 1990s the orchards had been replaced with the gleaming green-glass buildings of companies that produced much greater profits than the sale of apricots, cherries, and walnuts; in 1940 the county had 18,584 acres of apricot trees; by 1998 five hundred remained.

The technology produced by the companies of the Valley also changed life on "the farm," as Stanford University used to be known. For a professor of medieval history like my father, who read *The Iliad* in front of a fire of burning black walnut, an Oracle continued to reside in Delphi and "Yahoo!" remained a scream of excitement. But that doesn't apply today to undergraduates at Stanford who are well aware that Yahoo! Corporation was founded by two former Stanford students, and that the Valley's Oracle Corporation is one of the giants of the software industry. Almost nine out of ten of the university's undergraduates take at least one computer course, and for graduate students entering Stanford's School of Law, ownership of a laptop is mandatory. The William Gates Computer Science Building and the Paul G. Allen Center for Integrated Systems were built with gifts to the university by the two founders of Microsoft Corporation. And lectures on computer science are held in an auditorium named after Englishman Alan Turing, whose work in the 1930s resulted in the Universal Turing Machine and earned him the reputation as the father of the digital computer.

Today's Stanford students are not only the beneficiaries of Gates' and Allen's commitment to higher education and research. They and students before them are also, in a manner of speaking, both promise of the present and keepers of the heritage originally sown by Frederick Terman, William Hewlett, and David Packard. Companies such as Cisco Systems, Netscape, Silicon Graphics, Yahoo!, and Sun Microsystems are examples of scores of start-ups given birth in the Valley by Stanford students and professors. One of them who financed the founding of Netscape, former Stanford computer-science professor Jim Clark, made the largest gift in the university's history, $150 million, in November 1999, following the philanthropic example set by William Hewlett and David Packard.

The technological inventions of the Information Age exceed the imagination as we read about them in the *San Francisco Chronicle* and the *San Jose Mercury News*. The transformation from the bricks-and-mortar world to the wired world is profound. As one of my wife's friends, Suzanne Roth, puts it: "What the hell happened?" Since a knowledge gap has emerged that separates those who understand from those who do not, each views the changing world through different glasses, and therefore sees different things. Each also speaks, in noticeable ways, different languages. The vocabulary of the present and the future is spoken by those who are "on-line." The language of the past is spoken by those who are not. The word *cyberspace* separates one generation from another, both in terms of time and technology.

The heart of the Information Age is the computer network, just as the dynamo and Michael Faraday's discovery of the principle of electromagnetism were at the center of the Industrial Revolution. Indeed, we coined new English words from the changes they brought. If something was sensational, we called it *electrifying*. If we used the new electrical inventions, we were *plugged in*. Not to be outdone a century later, we call ourselves *wired* if we use the Internet, and we're *surfing the Net* if we are looking for information on the World Wide Web. If we want software from a Web site, we *download* it. If we're deluged with unwanted e-mail from people we don't know, we've been *spammed*. I still have trouble with that word, because when I was growing up Spam was a spiced-pork luncheon meat. My mother put it in sandwiches I took to Stanford Elementary school in the early 1950s.

Ironically, we also have another word, invented after electricity had made its mark but long before the Information Age arrived, that we sometimes use in connection with the Internet. George Orwell's novel *1984*, published in 1949, described a futuristic world of mind control, information tyranny, and semantic oppression with a new language, *Newspeak*. The author chronicled the destruction of history, honesty, and logic — where the Ministry of Truth decreed that *freedom is slavery*, *ignorance is strength*, and *war is peace*. Such a world was called Orwellian. Similarly, the word dynamic was coined during the Industrial Revolution, following invention of the dynamo. By Christmas 1998, vocabulary came full circle with computer hardware manufactured by Fujitsu Corporation, called DynaMO 640 SE.

2.

THE SHIFT

Times Change, and we change with them ...

— Thus the days flee away in like manner,
and in like manner follow each other, and are always new.
For that which was previously left behind,
and that takes place which never was;
and every moment of time is replaced by another.

{Ovid, 43 B.C.-A.D. 17}

I n the wired world I use time differently, because time and the Internet are always connected. Though I know we still find time in its traditional places — on the sundial, on the hands of the grandfather clock, or on my wristwatch — time is now located in my laptop too, and the clock runs continuously. From there I can use time to travel incredibly far, very fast, if I move an arrow on my computer screen to a portal on the World Wide Web and click my mouse. It's as though time is traveling, although I've always been told it doesn't.

The first chapter in *Life*, a natural history of the first four billion years of life on Earth, is called "The Everlasting Sea." The author, Richard Fortey, writes about geological time and tries to put it in perspective:

> All narratives require a scale. In novels, the scale is usually com-
> prehensible in terms of the span of a human life, a few score years,
> maybe a few generations. This scale is appropriate to us. Our nat-
> ural longevity is an instinctive yardstick, the measure both of our

mortality and the changes wrought by time. We can understand shifts in history within a few generations, empathize with our grandparents, even dimly appreciate the problems of the thirteenth century. This is all but a moment in geological time, an instant which may fall between one hammer blow and the next.

If we contemplate Internet time, and compare it with geological time, we still always arrive at a specific moment. The scale is different, but not the dimension of movement, in a continuous, inexorable, unceasing flow. Is time moving, as I write each of these words? Yes, of course it is, but I can't see it move, nor can I use a yard-stick to measure the movement. On the Internet I can't see it move, either. But I can feel it. This is something new which, for lack of a better word, I call a shift. It reminds me of the following exchange in Samuel Beckett's play *Waiting for Godot*:

> VLADIMIR: That passed the time.
> ESTRAGON: It would have passed in any case.
> VLADIMIR: Yes, but not so rapidly.

Is time moving in some new way? No, the passage of time is still, as it always has been, just a question of time. But there is something else. In a manner of speaking we have become unhinged from what we recognize as "normal" parameters of time and space. Our social, cultural, economic, and political relationships are shifting. A change in control is being caused by this shift. It's not a fourth dimension, and I can't quantify it. But a sense of order, taught and practiced for centuries, is breaking up. With that, our conventional definition of reality is changing, too. In the world of net-works and cyberspace we call it "virtual reality." That's different from the reality I grew up with, where things were either real or they weren't. I am unable to define it precisely, but on the Internet virtual reality is real, and time is real time. What was it before? Is it just post-Gaku that I am more aware that I have a limited quantity of time? Or is all this just self-indulgent, phony philosophizing on my part?

Some of my friends who believe in calling it the way they see it have told me politely, "You're barking up the wrong tree!" (They think, of course, this is an uproariously funny play on my name.) They know, as I do, that time and space still define when and where we are. "The only thing the Internet does," my wife's cousin, Peter Thieriot, points out, "is to allow us to communicate faster, and more easily, than we could with letters and stamps. But once you've done that," he says, "every-thing else is the same! Your body doesn't move any faster, nor does the use of e-mail make you any wiser." When I tell him, "I can use networks to communicate with others, regardless of time and place," he asks, "So what? What difference does that make? You're still communicating with them." My only response is, "That's virtual reality. It doesn't improve my common sense, but the reality of the world I live in is expanded." Internet pioneer Vint Cerf describes the virtual world as "embedded in the real world." So what you do has real consequences, not just make-believe consequences that disappear when you shut off your computer. Cerf puts it this way:

> You can imagine creating what looks like a bank lobby and going in and interacting with a simulacrum of a person only to discover that you've actually smoothly moved from interacting with a program to interacting with a real person on the other end of a call center that you're now talking to through the Internet.

While the virtual pictures of things we see on the computer screen are not what they look like in the *real* world, what we see is nonetheless real. But having said that, I'm not sure how to describe for Peter what is really happening. So I asked an old friend at *The Wall Street Journal*, Amity Shlaes, what I should call this book. She said, "Why don't you try *Unhinged?*"

One B.D. Thomas, a third of a century ago, thought about the relationship between time, space, and reality. I didn't meet him until he was in his early nineties, in 1996, when he was writing a small weekly for the community where he was living in Montecito, California. The publication was about what it is like to be in the ninth decade of life. His observations fascinated me, and I said so. Among other things he told me he used e-mail. That surprised me even more, because I thought few people older than I used e-mail. So we started exchanging messages. Then I mailed him a copy of my introduction to this book, and he sent me a copy of what he had said about time and reality thirty-four years earlier.

He hadn't heard of the wired world, of course, since his observations were made in November 1962, one month after the Cuban missile crisis. I was twenty years old, in my junior year at Stanford University, studying theater. I remember sitting in a seminar on the meaning of Bertolt Brecht's play *Mother Courage*, worrying about Khrushchev's threats and about President Kennedy's blockade of Cuba. The relationship between the reality of time and space had not yet crossed my mind. I had never heard of the Battelle Institute in Ohio, either — where Thomas was the director, and where the idea of the photocopy machine was born — an invention that was going to affect life everywhere in the years following, but hadn't yet.

When I first read Mr. Thomas's remarkable speech in 1996 I told him that if it appeared in *Wired* magazine, one would think it had been written today. I'm not sure whether he considered that a compliment, but I know he understood the world changing beneath him in 1962. Could he also have known that what he wrote would eventually mean something to nontechnical people like me many years later? I found it fascinating that he, as a trained chemist, was thinking about time and reality in a virtual world that didn't exist for me in 1962, but which preoccupies many of us now:

> ... [F]rom the contemplation of outer space and galaxies too remote and too gigantic for easy comprehension, we can penetrate instead into the microcosmos. Elementary particles, electrons, protons, neutrons, mesons, photons, wave mechanics, the quantization of physical concepts, mass, energy — time? Who knows? Time has resisted quantization. Why? And what of the ultimate question of the reality of these things? Are they but the weak, ponderous, ineffective and approximate devices of finite human minds seeking to comprehend the infinite and the incomprehensible? Or do they represent a reality? — the projections of a real world in which man himself is the real unreality?

If time has resisted quantization, it is at least, in the wired universe, defined in a new way. It's called real time on purpose. The Internet isn't simply a timesaving device. Real time, there, does have a meaning, just as it does for live television broadcasting. It means "right now!" Messages, news, information, all move so quickly that there isn't a gap between the event and learning about it, between sending an e-mail and receiving it, or between locating a Web page and looking at it. That speed creates a different kind of reality, just as the unstoppable movement of information on the Internet, across invisible territorial boundaries, is a different kind of sovereignty.

Members of the Internet Generation use the phrase *real time* constantly, almost as though it were a person, with a life of its own. As I thought about it, I decided a great title for this book would be *Mr. Real Time*. So I sent my introduction, along with a draft table of contents, to a good friend in Chicago. I was startled when he raised the question of whether or not the phrase was sexist. That thought had never entered my mind. He didn't like the title because, although he didn't exactly put it that way, it was offensive to females. It worried me enough that I asked Nalini if she thought it insensitive. She said "No!" Well, from my viewpoint, I didn't have time to fool around with it, so I changed the title. Here is what my respected friend wrote:

> While I abhor the spread of androgynous terms like 'chairperson,' I think you should drop 'Mr.' My girls [his daughters] are on the

computer all the time and they would resent the title.... Maybe
Nalini would too. Perhaps you could work into the title the notion
of citizen of the world or something.

The Internet is, indeed, about citizens of the world, called Netizens in computer parlance. But it is really about all of us. We can refer to it as a world of
Mr. Real Time or Mrs. Real Time. But in the whole scheme of things it doesn't
matter. What's important is how we perceive this new wired world, and how
we play our parts in it.

Anne Heenen lives in Grosse Pointe Farms, Michigan. She and I exchange e-mail,
since that means she doesn't have to go to the post office. She doesn't worry about
whether she's Mr., Mrs., or Ms. Netizen. She doesn't have time. She has a professional career as a paralegal, and a private profession as the manager of a household.
When she's cooking she becomes, as her husband has been known to observe, the
Vicomtesse of Vegetables or the Duchess of Desserts. But she has been known also
to call herself Mrs. Wrong Time when something burns on the stove. There's not a
word of truth in it. She loves cooking and she's good at it. But it amuses me because,
although she doesn't know it, she has a counterpart in San Francisco.

He calls himself Mr. Lag Time, but he's really my trusted friend Hodge. It is from
Hodge that the phrase Mr. Real Time comes. He doesn't like anything modern,
including modern food, modern art, modern music and modern life. He doesn't
know how to use a computer, and he doesn't want to learn. He locks up his television in the closet so he doesn't have to look at it unless he's watching a football game.
He thinks that mobile phones are an abomination, and considers fax machines an
insult to the civilized world. From his viewpoint, he's right. From mine, he's living on
another planet. But I've known him since we were in the seventh grade together, and
I admire him. He's one of the best-read people I've ever met, and also one of the most
intelligent. If he could ever bring himself to put pen to paper, he would be one of the
best writers I've ever read. But he contents himself with drawing me verbal pictures
as he speaks, and if I'm quick enough I write his words down. So it was one Saturday
night in June 1998. He was sitting in front of the fireplace in the kitchen. He had just
finished his first Jack Daniel's and soda — we have that in common too — when out
of the blue he announced, "I know you're writing this computer book. Big deal! The
Internet is just another crank call to civilization." So, I got my pen and said to him,
"Give me your best description of the Internet Generation."

His answer was not as cute and trite as it may sound. A lot of people my age agree
with him. Lifting lines from *Business Week*, as well as from his pals — they all frequent a bar on Potrero Hill in San Francisco called Bloom's — he advised me that
"in high school we called them nerds. Now we call them millionaires, who can't get

a date! They have a corner on the new human experience called the Internet, but they aren't part of the historical *us*. They have no conception of how things really work, and no conception of rules. They have a new outlook on everything; and they are loaded with money and power. That's great! But dealing with them is like trying to herd cats!"

Hodge was just warming up, and he was anxious to continue: "Mr. Internet, my ass! He thinks he's the measure of all things. Does he march to the tune of *noblesse oblige*? No! He thinks it's the latest Paris fashion. Look at the way he dresses. Ponytails and Levis, as though sartorial splendor is some kind of Internet protocol. He's got plenty of dough, but no taste; so he always tells you how much money he paid for the bottle of wine. Apparently the quality of wine is determined by what it costs."

Waxing eloquent, and now on his second drink, Hodge was right in stride: "He probably thinks *sophistry* is the name of the newest piece of software! He flies first class to Malaysia, checks into Raffles Hotel, and stays in the Noël Coward Suite. Money's no object. He sits at the famous Long Bar with his cell phone in his pocket, giving new meaning to the phrase Singapore Sling. It used to be known as a drink. Today it's known as *International Man*! — as international that is, as pot, porno, and apple pie. Mr. Internet? He knows all the angles, but he doesn't know dick! He's never heard of Noël Coward, either!"

Hodge is good at tongue-in-cheek. But he'd never know the "wired hotel room" of the future unless he learned how to work it. He doesn't read the in-flight magazines of today, such as United Airlines's *Hemispheres*, which tell us hotels no longer offer only "business centers." They *wire* your room instead, with a fax machine, fax lines, and telephone jacks in the wall made especially for your e-mail. If you are in Southeast Asia and don't have the right telephone adapter or power socket, your hotel concierge probably does. A March 1998 story in the *International Herald Tribune* described one hotel chain's plunge into the world of electronic amenities:

> Inter-Continental claims to be the first hotel chain to provide … help in the form of a 'cyber-relations manager,' known as CRM, to provide twenty-four-hour computer support for road warriors. A cyber-relations manager meets you at check-in and offers to help set up your computer and get connected to the hotel's phone and power systems. The managers are trained to support popular word-processing and spreadsheet programs, Web-browser and e-mail applications, and provide scanners, printers, and other hardware — free of charge.

Daniel Desbaillets, president of Asia-Pacific for Inter-Continental Hotels & Resorts, in Singapore, says: 'More than 60 percent of our guests travel with a laptop and many of them have a problem of some kind — they don't have the right dialing speed, the right software, or they need a CD-ROM. The CRM can solve the problems on the spot.'

As a writer for *The Economist* put it in a 1997 article, the older generation mourns the transformation of Raffles into "a smarter ghost of its former self — a rather tacky tourist haunt serving Singapore Slings by the sickly pitcher.... It is hard now to believe that in 1902 a tiger was shot under the billiard table." But the Internet Generation has never known it, except by reputation. While "ghosts stalk the billiard room at Raffles" for those over sixty-five, the Inter-Continental Hotel in Singapore now has a cyber-relations manager, as mentioned above, for the Internet Generation. So does the Ritz-Carlton hotel group in the United States; he's called "a twenty-four-hour technology butler." The customers they serve are, for the moment, primarily business travelers, nine out of ten of whom were using their laptops in their hotel rooms by the end of 1999. And should one of these cybernauts be flying from the Detroit Metro airport to Singapore, and has time to spare, he can read his e-mail and send his faxes from a cubicle in the airport's Laptop Lane.

* * *

HODGE'S DESCRIPTION OF THE INTERNET SOUNDED PRETTY GOOD ON SATURDAY night. But it has nothing to do with Nalini's, Gaku's and my world. For the wired world is one which Hodge has deliberately chosen to ignore. And he's not alone. But, secretly, he wants to understand it. He can see the revolution in communication technology change the way we are living. So, while he won't admit it, he's curious. That's why he has been calling me every other night since he first read the draft of this chapter, to give me the benefit of his new perspectives on Mr. Real Time, Hodge's deliberate and derogatory phrase to describe what he thinks is the artificial world of the Internet. Yuppie phrases, like "virtual reality," bother him a lot. But he also knows that this is a world he can't escape. It's a world both virtual and real — in other words, one that is *almost*, and one that *is*. Because this world is changing so fast and moving forward so quickly, Hodge's frustration is easy to understand. He's not equipped to deal with it, and he doesn't make the effort. He is part of the same century as the readers of *Wired*, but he's living in ancient times. In his heart of hearts Hodge doesn't want to be enlightened, and he certainly doesn't want to be wired, unless it's at his favorite watering hole. In fact, he would agree entirely with the response I got from Bob Queller in Detroit, whom I asked to read my introduction.

He told me to call this book *Confessions of a Born-Again Internet Geek*. Then he noted at the bottom of his letter, "the spell-check on my December 1994 computer doesn't recognize the word 'Internet.'"

And that's one of the problems. When we learn how to use one of the new technology tools — a new software program, say — something else has improved or replaced it by the time we've mastered the old tool. The other problem is that most of us who are the parents of the Internet Generation don't use language the same way those of this new generation do, and won't in our lifetimes. Consider, for example, an ad in the June 11, 1997, edition of the *Financial Times*, placed by Siemens and Newbridge. Even if you know what both companies do, the words are difficult to understand. Newbridge Networks Corporation in Canada builds switches that allow voice, video, and information (data) to travel over networks at very high speeds, and has clients in more than one hundred countries. Siemens, headquartered in Munich, develops and manufactures all kinds of advanced communication equipment, from telephones to networking systems. The advertisement is reprinted here, exactly as it appeared:

Run
with
us

Run globally reliably fast lean smart *Run* modular flexible secure *Run* multimedia *Run* robust protected ahead efficient *Run* wireless voice data video image *Run* internet intranet LAN WAN *Run* MainStreetXpress 36150 36170 36190 46020 48020 *Run* to the future *Run* without limits

R u n

Discover how MainStreetXpress, the definitive broadband architecture, can benefit you

One way to interpret the meaning of changing language and technology is to call it an accelerating evolution of human events. But if that's true, the speed is clouding our vision. It is difficult to see clearly what's happening around us, because information is everywhere in new languages and shapes. We're being deluged with it in the form of e-mail, and we're being drowned in it on the World Wide Web. As a result many find it difficult to concentrate or to focus. What should we try and learn next? It may well be, as a foreign policy analyst in Washington, D.C., speculates, that one of the most important commodities on the Internet will be *attention*. Who, in the Information Age, will get whose attention, for how long, and toward what end? In Internet time, according to Intel Corporation in March 2000, the attention span of a customer is just eight seconds — a problem, Intel estimates, that costs e-commerce retailers $58 million in uncompleted orders each month.

This changing way of looking at the effects of real-time delivery of information presents big problems for those of us who have never thought in terms of real time. Our children and their children are part of this world, but we're not. So for those of us who live now, who have been brought up to use words as tools as I was, wired-world vocabulary is confusion writ large. Many of the words and phrases of the Internet world, as well as the way they are used — and I am not referring to silly abbreviations like GFUG and inane words like cyberpunk — don't make sense to any of us who appreciate the craftsmanship and beauty of great literature. *Virtual reality* is one example. *Cyberspace* is a second. *Real time* is another. Look at the government keepers of the French language! They view the Internet as the end of culture. They're having fits dealing with the vocabulary as they struggle to preserve the purity of the language of diplomats. Indeed, French frustration has produced such comical observations as that from the minister of justice, Jacques Toubon, that the English-dominated Internet is "a new form of colonialism."

In some ways I sympathize with the concern. In 1999 English was the language used on more than 78 percent of Web pages, and French just 1.2 percent. But Parisian civil servants at the Ministry of Economics, busy translating Internet vocabulary into French, were overdoing it. Thus, the word start-up is now *jeune-pousse* (literally "young bud"). As Carol Liscia, marketing director at French Internet service provider Liberty Surf Groupe SA told the *International Herald Tribune*, "What's worthwhile is translating Web sites into French because it increases the audience of the Internet.... But how will international investors understand us if we use words like 'jeune-pousse'? It's absurd." If she doesn't already know it, Madame Liscia would surely laugh on learning that the origin of France Telecom's Internet access provider Wanadoo, is the American phrase "I want to do" — but I doubt that the *Academie Française* would be amused.

The French are not alone. Iceland encountered a similar linguistic threat in 1998, since Microsoft's Windows was unavailable in Icelandic. But in an April 2000 interview with the *International Herald Tribune*, the country's Prime Minister, David Oddsson, also recognized that "we are very small and isolated, so to be prosperous we must be connected to the world." By April 2000 almost 70 percent of the population was connected to the Internet.

And what would Shakespeare and Charles Dickens do with words like Netizen and digirati? Probably neither Englishman would find beauty in the words, but would they insist on writing with a pen in the year 2000? I wrote this book as a Netizen using the tools of the wired world. As the manuscript progressed from one draft to the next, the corrections on each were simply typed into my laptop. The only piece of paper in the whole process is the end result. Whatever we call it, electronic ink or electronic paper, *time* gains new meaning. Is that "value added"? For me, it is!

I did, in fact, use two computers as I wrote this book. My laptop served as my typewriter, sitting in front of me on the desk. I could move paragraphs around, go from chapter to chapter in seconds, and print a copy of one chapter at the same time I was working on another. In the old days I would have had to cut and paste. It would have taken forever. To my right was my office computer. Each day, I connected it to the World Wide Web as soon as I arrived at my office. If I needed to add more information, I used a search engine to find it for me.

The World Wide Web saved me enormous quantities of time. Otherwise I would have been obligated to go to the library, on foot. I did use both resources, and I went to each electronically. Side by side, old libraries still have real books in them, and new ones are building collections of digital books. The idea isn't new. It originated in the 1930s with a Belgian, Paul Otlet, who sought to put all human knowledge on three-by-five-inch library cards in a special library he called a Mundaneum.

Digital books are not only here, they're here to stay. Rare first editions of books such as Lewis Carroll's *Alice's Adventures in Wonderland* with original drawings by Sir John Tenniel are being put into digital form (for a CD-ROM), and great libraries such as the New York Public Library and the Huntington Library in San Marino, California, are granting exclusive digital rights to a company called Octavo. The paper never turns brown or crumbles, because there isn't any paper. And at The Fiction Network (www.fictionnetwork.net), which made its debut on the Web in November 1997, we find the best of literature from both the nineteenth and twentieth centuries.

Does all this mean that libraries and librarians are passé? Well, search engines are very quick, but they don't have minds. Librarians, on the other hand, have been organizing information for more than 2,000 years. That task will become more important, not less so, as more and more information is produced and preserved, decade by decade. The tools and the names will change, but for all practical purposes a database with 750,000 entries is the same thing as a library with 750,000 books. Except there are no bindings and no shelves. We will use the virtual library differently, because we will travel to hundreds of libraries, both public and private, via the World Wide Web, without getting in our car. The process of gathering information is the same. I'm not sure whether the Internet is threatening the printed word, but it is changing how we see it.

The force and power of communication in the wired world was once the force and the power of the words of Samuel Adams and Alexander Hamilton, written with quill pens. While their quills have been replaced with paperless words, the importance of what they thought and wrote hasn't diminished one whit. One of the best-known manufacturers of fountain pens in the United States, A.T. Cross, has concluded there may be a place for real ink in the wired world as well. It's producing a pen to write words on a notepad, which can be read on a computer screen, then printed out on paper. With IBM, Cross is developing the CrossPad, with the goal of translating handwriting into computer text.

The wired world is not a mindless, empty one, filled with gadgets and gimmicks, and populated by cybergeeks. Some, however, claim the contrary. As writer Theodore Roszak observed in a March 1999 article in *The New York Times*:

> Information is worthless if it is not informed by ideas, values and judgment — or worse than worthless if one recognizes why the Web exists at all. The Web is the product of a predatory entrepreneurial sensibility. Like a spider's trap, it exists to ensnare attention with high-tech effects and eye-popping tricks. Those who weave the Web are seeking desperately to transform the medium into the new television, the new movies. Their objective is to lure millions to their sites so they can make lots of money.

The latter is just unadulterated nonsense. There is, however, no question that computers, the Internet, the language used to describe the wired world, and the electronic ways we enter this world via e-mail and the Web are intimidating — at least to many people my age and older. A computer on every desk, for example, won't make us a nation of thinkers, but neither will blind adherence to a goose quill and an inkwell. The Internet and its webs of communication open our imagination and increase our options, not vice versa. For the elderly, however, just the concept of electronic connections can be overwhelming; how can we send messages without paper? Luddites don't like the concept either (how do they feel about the photocopier?). German Nobel laureate in literature Günter Grass thinks that computers and the Internet exert a bad influence on writing: "I write all manuscripts still and first of all by hand, with pen and paper, and then there's my old Olivetti for the second version and the third and the fourth and so on." But this is more a matter of style and preference than of substance. I am writing this book with my laptop, but I am correcting the drafts with pen and ink.

Twenty years from now information that I can find on the Internet is going to be more valuable to me than it is now. When my generation is in its late seventies, and my age may limit my ability to travel, I will still be connected to my grandchildren, to libraries, to art galleries on-line, to digital art dictionaries and encyclopedias, to museums, to concerts, and to the news. I'll be able to visit the Metropolitan Museum of Art from my living room, and in Paris I can already go to the French national digital library and look at photographs taken by Eugene Atget. The physical isolation of old age won't be as frustrating. And, if I can still see and use my fingers, if I can still think clearly and use my head, the Web won't limit the horizons of my world. It will broaden them. And culture? The Internet isn't the end of it. It's the expansion of it.

* * *

AFTER I FINISHED THIS CHAPTER HODGE READ IT. I ASKED HIM WHETHER HE FELT any more comfortable about the world of the Internet. Instead of answering "yes" or "no," he told me a story about what happened to him on March 27, 1999. It was late on a Friday afternoon. Hodge wanted to know if A.B. Frost, a popular magazine illustrator from the late nineteenth century, made mono-types. So he went to the San Francisco Library. When he got there the librari-an told him that if he typed the illustrator's name into the computer, it would print out a list of books about A.B. Frost. So Hodge tried to type in the name and to press the right buttons to get the list. He couldn't work the computer, and he was too embarrassed to ask the young man next to him what to do. He went back to the librarian and asked if there wasn't a real card catalogue he could use. The librarian told him he needed special permission, and she could-n't give it to him. Instead, she came over to the computer, typed in the infor-mation and printed out the list.

"I was just stunned!" Hodge said when he finished this story. "All I wanted to do was look it up in the card catalogue. But you needed special permission. I couldn't believe it! Web sites and uniform resource locators are replacing the Dewey Decimal System. Moreover, it's crazy! Every five-year-old out there can look up *The Little Engine that Could*, and I couldn't. You can't even use the library today without a computer. You can't escape it! 'Sorry pal,' she said, 'you have to use the computer.' And I suppose, Dennis, to add insult to injury, there's probably an A.B. Frost Web site."

Well, of course, you know what we did. With Hodge watching I used a search engine to see if there was one. We found 140 of them.

There is a postscript about Hodge, which in some ways I would rather skip, because selfishly I would prefer to leave his image unchanged; but I owe it to him. It is now, as I write this, February 2000, and I am making revisions on this chapter with my new IBM laptop 600 E. Hodge is coming to dinner. We're going to play dominos and drink Jack Daniel's. When he leaves, he will take my old IBM laptop 755 CE with him. Hodge has finally decided he wants to be a wired man after all! He told my eldest son on New Year's Eve 1999 — undoubtedly after midnight — that he wanted to learn how to use the computer.

It is now April. For the past eight weeks my son's been teaching him, and I have been getting reports on his progress. But the phone call I received on April 10 was completely unexpected. "Dennis," Hodge said, "you'll never believe what just happened. I was reading my e-mail and there was a message from 'China' Pete. He wrote that since we hadn't been in contact for twenty-five years, he had no idea where I lived, but that he'd found my e-mail address on the Web. He wants to know if I would fly to Las Vegas on April 29 to attend the twenty-fifth reunion of the graduates of Death Valley High School, where I taught the children of Indian talc miners in the 1970s." This time it was my turn to be dumbfounded, and I could only think of one thing to say: "There's a message here somewhere, Hodge, and I believe it's more than just about e-mail."

3.

PRIVACY FOR THE PUBLIC GOOD

*They that can give up essential liberty to obtain
a little temporary safety deserve neither liberty nor safety.*

{Benjamin Franklin, 1706-1790}

"The wired world," Gaku said, "is like Swiss cheese. There are a lot of holes in it." That made me wonder, at first, how we protect copyright on the Internet. How would I protect my words written here if someone scanned this book onto a computer and made it available on a Web site, thereby depriving me of royalties? And what about the copyright for songs and music available on the Web? That made me think about property rights as well as privacy. As I thought about both, I knew I didn't really understand how to deal with these problems. And I was sure I didn't know what questions to ask. I became even more confused when Gaku introduced me to encryption and showed me how to send e-mail messages in code, so nobody could read them except the person I was sending them to. Gaku even said it was probably next to impossible for *anybody* to crack really sophisticated codes. Should this be true, I wondered, would it give the word privacy a brand-new meaning? Encrypting communication on the Internet would affect a multitude of worlds, in which operate scholars, bankers, political extremists, stockbrokers, business men and women, students, law enforcement agencies, journalists, tax collectors, government leaders, teachers, spies, bureaucrats, criminals, politicians, terrorists, intelligence services, and diplomats.

My curiosity coincided with a conference about "intellectual capital" at the Hoover Institution in June 1997, the first of its kind we ever held. I was looking forward to going. I even volunteered to comment during the session dealing with

The Connected

"International Issues." I was anxious, to put it mildly, to hear what would be said about copyright, and I did know something about foreign policy. But the subject of encryption was also on the agenda, and I didn't really know why. I had never thought very much about secret codes — certainly not as a means to protect intellectual property. The way I looked at it, if someone stole my words, used them without my permission and violated my copyright, I would call the Hoover Institution's lawyer. It hadn't occurred to me that digital technology has made it easy to pirate songs, and to copy or alter all sorts of information, from art to computer software. As *The Economist* put it in a 1996 article headlined "The Property of the Mind," "all copyrighted works can now be digitized, and once on the Net, copying is effortless, costless, widespread, and immediate." Nor had it occurred to me that music and movies would be major targets, as software with names like Gnutella and Napster would be used to acquire and exchange copyrighted works without the payment of royalties to the owners.

Encryption was a word which, as a scholar of the classical tradition, I found suspicious. It applied to the clandestine world of spies and intelligence. The words *code* and *cipher* made me feel a little more comfortable, but not much. All three words were really distinctions without differences, as far as I was concerned. I understood that the world of secrecy was a necessary government responsibility. Namely, it existed to keep information confidential that could be used to protect my country's borders and, more to the point, to protect my country's citizens, which included me. But the real world of that responsibility was not part of mine. I wasn't very interested in learning about it, either, until I discovered during the conference that the U.S. government classified encryption as a *munition*. I also learned that some of my scholarly friends were using encryption to protect not only their manuscripts, as they sent these to colleagues around the country electronically, but also that American and foreign companies were using encryption to protect the confidentiality of proprietary information sent over the Internet. Encryption could be used to protect personal privacy, commercial property, and public security. The right to privacy in a democracy, I thought, is for the public good.

If I was ever out of my element, it was at this conference. It was attended by experts from, among other places, Microsoft Corporation and the Securities and Exchange Commission. On the foreign policy panel I was sitting next to a man named Donald Alford Weadon Jr. While we were waiting for the moderator to introduce the speakers, Mr. Weadon and I started talking. Well, what I knew about encryption you could put in a thimble, and what he knew would fill several volumes. I explained to him that I was trying to write this book. He said, "It surprises me that you are interested in this. I will help you, if you need help."

I needed help. I called him on June 27, 1997, and we've been exchanging e-mail ever since. I recognize now, as a result of Don's tutelage, that the issue of encryption and control in the wired world is of major importance to all of us who believe in the integrity of free and open communication. The security of proprietary information (like a financial statement), as well as the protection of copyright and intellectual property, is closely related to how encryption is used, and by whom. If the Internet is like Swiss cheese, then I wanted to know how to keep my communication private. The idea of being able to write my messages in code seemed brilliantly simple, and the phrase "encrypting Swiss cheese" had a nice ring to it. Therefore, if any of the following makes sense, Gaku and Don Weadon get a large part of the credit.

It hadn't dawned on me until Gaku had mentioned it that with the interactive medium of the Internet, access, control, and privacy are two-way streets. So I asked Don to tell me about the relationship of encryption to "Swiss cheese." As it turns out, electronic tunnels can wind their way through our e-mail messages and into our computers. Tunnels don't exist in my typewriter, but they do in the Web. I have to respond to their existence, even if I don't know where they are. Are there holes leading into my files? Can anyone who knows how to get inside read what I have written?

The answer is, it is possible for other people to read our e-mail, and it is possible to break into computer systems. There are holes in them. This is why system managers at Stanford, for example, devote so much effort to protecting access to the university's computers. That's why elaborate electronic programs called "firewalls" exist to protect privacy at such diverse places as banks, research labs, defense ministries, and the Internal Revenue Service. The goal is to keep people out who don't belong there. We guard our files from prying eyes in different ways. We can exercise control with passwords. We keep them secret. The only people who know my password are my wife and my assistant. (Although when Gaku read this, he pointed out that he knows it too!)

We can protect the privacy of our e-mail messages by encrypting them, and I protect my personal financial statement, stored on my computer, the same way. We protect ourselves with both passwords and encryption when we use e-commerce and have to divulge our credit card numbers, for instance, when buying books at www.amazon.com. But this conclusion raises another question about our privacy. How is control actually exercised over the use of information, passwords, and encryption on the Internet? Are there people gathering information about our private lives, or about our shopping preferences, without us knowing about it? Does the United States government read our e-mail messages? Do system managers have the right to check which Web sites we are looking at? Do they have the right to censor which sites we may visit? Do computer hackers really snoop into our computers?

In his book *The Cuckoo's Egg*, Cliff Stoll writes vividly about the nightmare created by a hacker in Germany who began breaking into the computer system at the University of California at Berkeley in 1986. Stoll discovered a group whose members, sometimes working in tandem and sometimes individually, were breaking into computers in North America, at high-energy physics labs, and at the offices of the National Aeronautical and Space Administration. They also found their way into the computers of defense contractors, military installations, and intelligence agencies. It took an entire year, but with the help of his girlfriend's creative mind, Stoll finally trapped his hacker. After a cyberspace mystery that rivals any novel by Tom Clancy, the hacker was arrested in June 1987 in Hannover, Germany. The arrest itself was an adventure, but so is the story of how the hackers did their breaking and entering using a cuckoo's egg. To find out what that is, you need to read Stoll's book.

The hacker's real name was Markus Hess, but he broke into computers using pseudonyms like Hunter, Jaeger, and Sventek. He was twenty-five years old. On March 2, 1989, Hess and four others were charged by the German government with espionage, and three of them were later brought to trial in a little town called Celle, in Westphalia, famous for its centuries-old *Fachwerkhaeuser* (Tudor-style house). After being released on probation Hess began working for a company in Hannover, writing software. Another, known as Hagbard, had been paid by the KGB (the Soviet intelligence service) for the information he had stolen. But, to quote Stoll, he had "avoided prosecution for espionage" by cooperating with German police. Stoll continues:

> Hagbard was last seen alive on May 23, 1989. In an isolated forest outside of Hannover, police found his charred bones next to a melted can of gasoline. A borrowed car was parked nearby, keys still in the ignition.
>
> No suicide note was found.

During that year of 1986-87 Stoll made a discovery he had not anticipated concerning the irreplaceable, classical values of trust and integrity. He didn't call them that, but when he wrote his story in 1989 that's what he was describing:

> I learned what our networks are. I had thought of them as a complicated technical device, a tangle of wires and circuits. But they're much more than that — a fragile community of people, bonded together by trust and cooperation. If that trust is broken, the com-

munity will vanish forever.... I saw the hacker not as a chess master, teaching us all valuable lessons by exploiting the weak points in our defenses, but as a vandal, sowing distrust and paranoia.

... Hacking may mean that computer networks will have to have elaborate locks and checkpoints. Legitimate users will find it harder to communicate freely, sharing less information with each other. To use the network, we all might have to identify ourselves and state our purpose ...

To have the networks as our playground, we have to preserve our sense of trust; to do that, we have to take it seriously when people break that trust.

As I was reading *The Cuckoo's Egg* I began to wonder how computer security really worked. I had seen very different reports in the newspapers, and I really didn't know where to begin. A computer-system manager at Stanford explained it to me. System managers, by definition, watch over the operation of Stanford's computing system twenty-four hours a day, seven days a week. System managers are the overseers. In their world preserving trust is vital, because they have the freedom and expertise to abuse it. They are, in a manner of speaking, the trustees of the system. If the system breaks down they fix it. If it needs to be improved — *upgraded* is the proper computer word — they upgrade it.

If thieves or vandals — originally known as "crackers" and now called hackers — break into the system, system managers are supposed to detect it, stop it, and catch the culprit. Unfortunately, in the virtual world as in the real world, thieves and vandals abound. Thus, just as we are concerned about protecting our homes from robbers, protecting the security of our computers must be a concern for everyone who uses the Internet. And unauthorized use occurs, although not nearly as often as breaking into real houses or stealing real cars. For example, a break-in at Stanford occurred on October 11, 1998, and was discovered on October 26. The hackers, who had logged onto Stanford's system from Sweden and Canada, stole 5,000 passwords. Stanford system managers spent more than 200 hours plugging the "hole" and notifying the victims.

Not a great deal of damage was done at Stanford, but the message, although simple, is a powerful one. The unscrupulous and the dishonest, as well as avowed enemies of freedom, are on the Internet just as they are on city streets. They have no compunction about wreaking havoc or committing crimes. This sad aspect of the human condition doesn't mean we should stop using our computers, but it does demand vigilance. There are people who will try, on occasion with success, to sabotage Internet service networks by so overloading them with requests that they collapse. This happened to Yahoo!, Amazon.com, E*Trade, eBay and CNN.com in February 2000. Among the world's biggest commercial Web sites, they became overloaded with thousands of phony information requests, until the systems, finally overwhelmed, shut down for several hours. Did this attack mean, as one software engineer asked in a February 2000 article in the *International Herald Tribune*, "the end of Internet innocence?... Is the house of cards about to crumble? Can we move to an Internet-based economy while the potential exists for a group of hackers to bring it to its knees at any time?"

The answer, of course, is that we will continue to move forward. But the attacks won't stop, either, and there will be more serious ones. They could take the forms of electronic eavesdropping, of electronic espionage, and of computer viruses. If a virus-infected program were sent to the Internet address of a bank and somehow got into the computer system, it could do serious damage, as in erasing account balances or mortgage statements. This is why computer-system managers are employed by major banks to protect their systems. Virus attacks also could be launched by terrorists for subversion and blackmail. Their weapon could be as simple as a threat to insert a virus into the computer records of the Social Security Administration or the Department of Commerce, or into library systems, public utility companies, or stock exchanges.

There is a message here about the Information Age. If we are leading our private and professional lives in a new, digital society, we need the legal means to deal with computer crime and punishment. There is a need for better Internet security, and it is being addressed by both business and government. The financial cost, of course, is significant. For the fiscal year 2001 President Clinton's proposed budget contained a $2 billion package to finance computer security efforts. In private industry the FBI estimates that computer crime costs $10 billion annually, and the annual cost to U.S. companies for firewalls and other anti-hacker measures is already at $4 billion. Information is private property and guarding property is both costly and part of life; how that protection is carried out by business and government agencies is vital to preserving the freedom of all of us. A balance must be struck. Law enforcement agencies must have the electronic means to pursue computer criminals, and the private citizen must able to communicate privately on the Internet, free from the prying electronic eyes of government. In the long term, it is private industry that must design Internet software and establish hardware standards that thwart attackers, and it is the critically important role of system managers to protect the integrity of our networks.

The rate at which information technologies are changing provides more than enough grist for speculation about threats to personal freedom. To what extent intelligence gathering technologies and law enforcement measures may represent an invasion of privacy is a legitimate question. It is true that I don't know, for example, what information is being gathered about me (if any), by whom, to what extent, or what happens to it. Moreover, the debate about Internet privacy and Orwellian futures is a legitimate one that should and will continue. But I do not consider legitimate government intelligence activities to be a threat to my individual liberty.

Not only governments, however, are gathering information. Knowledge about our shopping preferences, for example, can be collected as well, via the use of little files called *cookies*. They are located on Web servers such as Netscape, and can write information to the hard disks on our computers. Cookies can track every move we make on a Web site, including what hypertext references we click on, what articles we read, what information we request, and record all of it. The owner of the server can then sell this information about our interests to someone one else without our knowing about it. But there is nothing new about that either; this practice has been going on for years. That's how mail-order houses get our names and addresses; they buy such lists from someone else. For e-commerce, however, information gathered by cookies can be of enormous value. Since normal information can be saved and used again in legitimate business transactions, cookies make it unnecessary for Amazon.com, for example, to request the same address and billing information each time we go shopping on the Internet.

Nonetheless, the use of cookies, if I am not told how personal information about me will be used, is a violation of my right to privacy. So whose responsibility is it to draw the line? It's a dual one. It's in the interest of the information technology industry, on the one hand, to act responsibly; otherwise pressure mounts for government agencies to regulate. On the other hand, it's also in the interest of Internet users to shoulder the same responsibility, and object when the privacy line is crossed.

There is a great deal we can do to preserve our privacy on the Internet. Public debate is one avenue. Another alternative is to learn how to protect, electronically, what we write and how we sign it. This applies not only to our private interests, but also to how we conduct business: digital signatures are not only the key to privacy, but are also the key to widespread use of electronic commerce. This means using encryption.

4.

ENCRYPTING THE SWISS CHEESE

*As the digital revolution takes hold, laws that were written
for another era will become increasingly difficult to enforce. Americans can
choose either to jettison these laws and take advantage of new technologies
and the opportunities they create, or keep the laws and pay the price in economic
inefficiency, technological backwardness and government intrusiveness.*

{Richard W. Rahn, "Financial Privacy in Peril," *The Wall Street Journal*, June 1, 1999}

I s encrypting the Swiss cheese really important? What's the likelihood of someone reading my e-mail? And even if someone does, so what? As far as just e-mail is concerned, encrypting each message probably isn't worth it. I don't spend a lot of time worrying about whether someone is going to open my snail mail or read my postcards. Moreover, there are simply not a lot of people out there interested in what I have to say, any more than there are a lot of postal employees waiting in the shadows to open my letters. And if someone does read my e-mail and doesn't like what I've written, that's his or her problem, not mine. In the whole scheme of things, protecting the confidentiality of my financial statement stored on my computer isn't a major concern either, unless my computer is stolen. And if it is, no one can read the documents stored on my laptop, unless they have my password that has to be typed on the screen each time I boot up my computer.

But as far as business is concerned — whether it's buying books at Amazon.com or having my bank send me my monthly statement via the Internet — confidentiality is of great importance. Just one question that we hear over and over again makes the point. Hodge, for one, has asked it several times: "What makes it impossible for someone to steal my Visa card number when I enter it on Amazon's Web site?" He then answers his own question: "It's just too dangerous to put my credit card number on the Internet. Anybody can get it."

Is it really dangerous? More dangerous than giving the number to an unknown person over the telephone? Many of us do that all the time, and we never give it a second thought. But we do worry about security on the Internet. The reason is fairly simple. The Internet is still new. Many of us don't understand how it works. There's a lot of mystery about it, and newspaper articles about hackers tell us horror stories about risks, not success stories about safety.

So, is it really true? Can any Tom, Dick, or Harry get our credit card number? The answer is no. It stands to reason that companies doing business on the Internet want to make sure that stealing credit card numbers is extremely difficult. That's why Amazon, for example, uses what is called a *secure server*. In other words, when I type in my credit card number, the Amazon Web site encrypts it to prevent anyone from reading it. A hacker may steal it, but if he can't decrypt it, he can't use it. That's a lot safer than losing my wallet.

How all this works is fascinating, as is the history of how we have protected the privacy of our correspondence. Using digital encryption is no different from using sealing wax; it's just more refined. In the nineteenth century and well before, we closed our letters with hot wax and pressed our seal into it. So if the letter arrived with the seal broken, the conclusion was obvious. No one uses sealing wax anymore, except romantic eccentrics (including me from time to time). Instead, we can send a letter three different ways, and most of us believe all three ways are safe. We put a letter in an envelope, lick the flap, and mail it. Or we send a fax. Or we send an e-mail. If we had time, we could write our letters in secret code. We would make it up, perhaps using numbers and letters. We would give the key — that is to say, a copy of our code — to Aunt Monique, and only she could decipher the letter. But few of us do it, because it takes so much time.

In 1997, when Gaku and I started talking about electronic security, I just wanted to know how it worked. Both he and Don Weadon said it was easy to use encryption. So what do I do if I want to send a confidential message to a friend, to my bank, to my stockbroker, or to my lawyer? I scramble it up electronically, in a hopelessly complicated way, like alphabetical hash. But unlike hash, it is scrambled in a mathematically specific way, using a mathematical "key." The only way it can be read is if the recipient has a cryptographic key to unscramble my message. This means, in turn, I actually have to hand over the key in advance, or send it in the mail if I am willing to take that risk. How do I give my key to Gaku, or to the bank, if I can't do so in person?

The answer is via *public key cryptography*. The idea is simple. I have two keys, a public key and a private key (in other words, a public code and a private code). A message encrypted with my public key can be decrypted with my private key. When I send Gaku my public key via e-mail, he stores it in his computer. I keep my private key secret. When he writes me a letter, he encrypts his message to me using my public key. When I receive his message, encrypted with my public key, I use my private key to decrypt it. That's safe since I am the only person who has my private key. This allows Gaku and me to communicate without anybody eavesdropping, and in a code that presumably no one can break. Obviously, the more complicated the key, the more difficult it is for someone to crack it. So we can send each other letters no one can read, except Gaku and me.

To demonstrate the process, Gaku and I downloaded the so-called "military grade" cryptography software "Pretty Good Privacy" (www.pgp.com), made by a company in San Mateo, California. I didn't believe what I was seeing when Gaku showed me what an encrypted message looked like, and it took a while to learn how to use the software. But I finally sent my first encrypted message to Gaku on June 5, 1997, with my digital signature. Here is (1) what the encrypted message looked like, and (2) what my digital signature looked like (for this message only, since, by definition, my signature can never be the same twice. It is a shorthand and scrambled version of my message, and thus always unique.):

_ _____BEGIN PGP MESSAGE_____
Version: 2.6.2

hIwDLeOaAdnQfLkBA/sHPeXB+sFVvr/fBZAwYbVXlCUPfOigmfSPpPOe+Y0PK
PDCEYlqAVoVl4lx6hDoUE7Xcc8IOlUG79GXyj1GWHHvV4pwGAFn0Yn20Xb
/oURxjLl9FQOIrWOEy8qYOeKeEJvE9NvSIwC2GAzkpU8d6tsvsBi8r6Ubd4GdD
jrqe1WY7qYAAAIYeYPdZ4FxBGW8/5gU1dykQmOXB73nMyGysZw9OoDxN
70BAJgNbYhy3Rh78TidEwBC3fumEa19WUMq7GCjl2NX4ddURD7PfKRo5mp
ZylRTWMEAWdC3XTWcQTC/Jubcc1hajaAsfhIw+MvaI6R6pXqIwV0pgjf3rPw
3hgwcjV//tfVe6p1Siq7kJyXlfeJeX00z+IFeKi2DrReCbtB7n9j9EbVn8zoWdNzRBa
9Db3+WsTiohWaYx/L48inQiqiBhcOoX9TFaFWlXimpMZUG7F9HED44mzYvE
Rtu5L2TQMwmZCWCNx2XKyF+p29NG0uyNULE1UpOT/486eddBPL/h8pkC/
TryUt/VIx7gd4N61opksr54R113eEicaNTdaOUeyqe288AwrKgcfOZJBBX4K26E
CGTpi1kbBFvEQ/VJ32NWzOlX3+0Qfvknna4ejT2T08V9dO/TuAhIxEy/ECUv5q
u06yXdrj7Z+AbAov8ofOUsDDl86ynC/uctEDesoc/1L/3oENOB6gqWVRUJ0hQiE
erDX4ME81IF+vP8bD4LCvNWUzlDKEpwn70ci7c/+dJsMHqpl5HqttpoGgKx4a
PaUbqb9EzhsACtLlY/Ss+H1Qn8PKaww2snryXxmsYVJMAeuNxZe1g4e4ZGhh
mn0xssQrL2ZdMNfrvd9d6sGHE3cbQXnQ5XSd4AqfoAkOu23peEp2WkOBz0
DIdu34==24M3

_ _____END PGP MESSAGE_____
_____BEGIN PGP SIGNATURE_____
Version: 2.6.2

iQCVAwUBM5d7ndCvoGnjAEn9AQFmeQQAqOWMhjj9lYBlvAl+KPGt4pQ4K
dZRhgZNnLZvJFhgAfdPmB7HHzGeINE5QrGvNb19+WHq1phIzFvAxpRN7db
5l8POubPlRdJDLsho3Ms6lg18C8GLVMP8jPcxh9kheURPC1zzRZjJLFVcy7mWh
W2orJAPQHThsO9stzWyVQgnmtw==cji5
_____END PGP SIGNATURE_____

And here is the message I sent, as written before I encrypted it:

To The Prof!

Gaku: This message will go into Chapter II. I am encrypting the message and am digitally signing it. I am using 1,024-bit PGP. What the reader will see is my message, encrypted with your public key, and my signature, signed digitally. Please confirm when you have read it. Be creative, and say something intelligent. Our readers will appreciate it!

The Student!

This system is so simple that anyone can send a protected message using the recipient's public key. The irony is I can't decrypt my own message, even though I wrote it in the first place, because I don't have Gaku's private key. That, indeed, is what the private key is for. Gaku's response to my message arrived on June 30. Decrypted, this is the text:

Dr. B.,

In ancient times, for example, the early 1980s, there were certain guarantees built into mail communications. The sealed envelope, the postmark, and the signature are all more than formal elements of a letter; along with federal laws against tampering with the mail, that are part of that guarantee.

Given the fact that forging e-mail is easy to do, PGP or other forms of digital signatures and encryption should be considered just a normal part of day-to-day e-mailing, much as signing and sealing a message are part of sending a letter.

Signed, sealed, and delivered,
Gaku

If the privacy of communication on the Internet is to survive, being able to encrypt a message and/or digitally sign it is vital. The security and therefore the success of electronic business and commerce depend on it. Indeed, the security factor is so important that we should stop using the word "cryptography" and eliminate the aura of mystery. An easy way to do so would be to rename it "privacy protocol." In 1997 Gaku and I both thought that digital signatures should become part and parcel of every business transaction on the Internet. In January 2000 digital signatures still weren't widely used. But by June, President Clinton had signed legislation to allow the use of electronic signatures as an alternative to hand-signed documents. It would mean that all kinds of financial transactions could be carried out on the Internet.

As Gaku said, "The encrypted part is easy. The creative part is hard." How we use encryption, in other words, is the challenge. Some see it as a way to protect free speech, others as a way to protect electronic commerce. And government agencies, such as the FBI, view strong encryption as a way for terrorists and criminals to destabilize democracies. So, when it became possible in the mid-1990s to send encrypted e-mail messages and documents on the Internet, the battle between privacy and government control was a foregone conclusion. But this is getting ahead of the encryption story itself, which is far stranger than fiction.

It began unfolding in earnest in 1990, when a nondescript man in his mid-thirties sat down at a table in his house in Colorado. He wanted to write a code no one could break. It was ironic, because the end of the Cold War suggested that spies and secret codes were out of business, and had been replaced with the freedom of the fax revolution. Moreover, in America in 1990 no one opened our mail. There was a law against it and we were confident that postal employees and Internal Revenue Service agents didn't violate it. If there was a reason in 1990 why private citizens needed an unbreakable code, I wasn't thinking about it. But that's not surprising, because I was still using snail mail. I didn't know that communication technology made it possible to read someone else's electronic letters. Neither was I aware that the same technology could also make it easier to protect e-mail from prying eyes — but *only* if e-mail were encrypted. (Recall that in 1990 I hadn't ever heard of e-mail.) E-commerce and the Web didn't exist either, so no one was yet thinking about how to protect my credit card number from hackers.

The story, as significant as Hedy Lamarr's, is about Phil Zimmerman, whom *The Wall Street Journal* described in an April 1994 story as "a paunchy, bearded" computer consultant. In 1990, when he was thirty-six years old and worried about the nuclear arms race, Zimmerman had already been arrested twice for anti-nuclear activism. He became "an electronic-freedom fighter." At that time various agencies of the United States government were lobbying for legislation

> ... that would ban certain forms of encryption, and force computer makers to build into their machines hardware that would allow law-enforcement agencies to decipher any code that was used. The proposal outraged confidentiality-minded corporations and computer users alike.

It also outraged Phil Zimmerman. So he

> ... took it upon himself to thwart the government's purpose by working on what came to be PGP.... 'I did it to inoculate the body politic' from the danger of government prying.... [He] stopped consulting and holed up in the computer-filled workroom in the back of a bungalow in Boulder, Colorado.... He says he spent six months of twelve-hour days writing the program, drained his family's savings and missed five months of mortgage payments. He finished the program in June 1991, and named it Pretty Good Privacy — in deference to Ralph's Pretty Good Grocery in humorist Garrison Keillor's *Prairie Home Companion* radio show.
>
> When ... [Zimmerman] was through, he gave the encryption program to friends. One of them, whom he won't identify, placed it on the Internet sometime around June or July 1991.... Once there, any computer user in the world with access to the Internet could download it. Almost immediately, many did.

As Zimmerman put it in *The Wall Street Journal* story, "I wanted to make cryptography available to the average person before the government tried to make it impossible to do so." What followed was an adventure involving the FBI, the top secret National Security Agency (NSA), the Departments of State and Defense, the Department of Commerce, and the White House. For

Zimmerman, however, it was an ironic and dreadful story that didn't end until January 1996.

PGP is called strong encryption. It has a key length of up to 4,096 bits and has proven unbreakable so far. When it became available on the Internet — free to anyone who downloaded it — government law enforcement agencies and national security experts recognized immediately the significance of unbreakable digital codes. Encryption, depending on who uses it and for what, is a double-edged sword. Encryption is obviously valuable for legitimate security purposes, whether it's for e-commerce or for classified information communicated among government agencies. But it can also be used as a weapon by dictatorships and terrorists, and drug lords can use it to conceal the illegal transfer of wealth.

Whether encryption is electronic or done by hand, its diverse uses prompted the United States government to define encryption in 1934 as a "munition" in a document known as ITAR (International Traffic in Arms Regulations). Licensing authority for its exportation abroad — to Europe, for example — has been governed by the Arms Export Control Act, and is overseen by the Department of State and the Department of Commerce. Since strong encryption was considered to be a munition, the U.S. government restricted the exportation of any commercial encryption product in excess of forty bits. There was, however, one exception. Encryption of fifty-six bits could be exported if a key recovery system had been devised in advance and deposited with a designated holder of the U.S. government. There were two reasons for the distinction. Encryption of forty bits could be broken easily, and stronger fifty-six-bit encryption was, for all practical purposes, unavailable to the public. So its exportation never became a major issue.

But the export laws never anticipated creation of the Internet as a means of communicating throughout the world. Thus, when Zimmerman's strong, "military-grade" encryption of 1,024 bits was first put on the Internet, its availability made the export control law moot. Export licenses were no longer needed because PGP was free on the Internet. Moreover, because it couldn't be cracked, it meant that government agencies — in Asia, Europe, or the United States — could no longer read strongly encrypted information. Its strength, indeed, gave the word privacy real meaning. As the Deputy Director for the National Security Agency put it in testimony before the U.S. Congress in March 1997,

> If all the personal computers in the world — 260 million computers — were put to work on a single PGP-encrypted message, it would still take an estimated 12 million times the age of the universe, on average, to break a single message.

Encrypting the Swiss Cheese

To put the significance of unbreakable encryption in perspective, the following examples (from the April 1998 article in *The Wall Street Journal*) illustrate the risks and advantages. The advantages first:

[1] ... During the battle between Boris Yeltsin and the Russian Parliament last October [1993], with Russian freedom hanging in the balance ... Zimmerman received an electronic-mail message from Latvia. 'If dictatorship takes over Russia,' it read, 'your PGP is widespread from the Baltic to the Far East now and will help democratic people if necessary. Thanks.'

[2] ... For human-rights advocates, the consequences of compromised sources can be devastating. Daniel Salcedo, who works for the Human Rights Project of the American Association for the Advancement of Science in Washington, teaches activists in El Salvador and Guatemala to use PGP. 'In this business, lots of people have been killed.'

[3] ... Craig McKie, a sociology professor at Carleton University in Ottawa, encrypts chapters of a new book with PGP as he sends them to his publisher, fearing that otherwise 'a gazillion copies would go flying off into the night.' Lance Cottrell, an astronomer at the University of California at San Diego, says he uses PGP to share unpublished observations with collaborators to keep others from claim-jumping a discovery.

[4] ... PGP also helps make the otherwise leaky Internet safe for commerce. Members of the Electronic Frontier Foundation ... can pay dues by sending PGP-encrypted credit-card numbers over computer networks. S. Soloway Inc., a Palo Alto, California, accounting firm, scrambles backup tapes with PGP, so that clients needn't worry about lost confidentiality if the tapes are lost or stolen. Kenneth Bass, a Washington lawyer, communicates with some clients and other attorneys in PGP code.

[5] ... Alan Dawson, a writer living in Thailand, says rebels opposing the regime in neighboring Burma are using PGP to encrypt information sent among rebel groups. Before use of PGP became widespread, Mr. Dawson wrote Mr. Zimmerman, 'captured docu-

ments have resulted directly in arrests, including whole families, and their torture and death.'

There's also a dark side, far from romantic, illustrated by the following examples:

[1] ... In Sacramento, California, police lament that last year [1993] PGP encryption blocked them from reading the computer diary of a convicted pedophile and finding critical links in a suspected child-pornography ring.

[2] ... investigators say PGP and other encryption systems aid crime. William Spernow, a computer-crime specialist with Search Group, a federally funded police-training firm in Sacramento, California, predicts criminals will routinely encrypt information within two years [by 1996]. 'This could signal the end of computer forensics before it even gets off the ground,' he says.... Mr. Spernow studied one case where a criminal conducted a fraud by keeping a double set of books — the real set encrypted in PGP.

So, when PGP suddenly became available on the Internet in 1991, the horse was out of the barn: "There's no way anybody can stop the technology,'" according to Leonard Mikus, the president of an encryption software company in Phoenix, Arizona, called ViaCrypt. Stephen Walker, a former cryptographer with the National Security Agency and president of Trusted Information Systems in Maryland, hammered the point home when he told *The Wall Street Journal* that the availability of worldwide encryption programs makes export controls "a farce.... We have to recognize what's out there."

The response of the United States government, on the other hand, was very different and perhaps predictable. In April 1993, *The New York Times* reported, the White House proposed creation of "a new system of encoding electronic communications that is intended to preserve the government's ability to eavesdrop for law enforcement and national security reasons while increasing privacy for business and individuals."

Two separate keys would be made for every single communication system using encryption and would be deposited (escrowed) with two separate government agencies. If law enforcement services felt there was reason to suspect criminal activity the escrowed keys could be made available, but only with a court order. Therewith, according to the proposal, the honest public's right to privacy would be protected — as long, of course, as the escrow system wasn't misused. The means to escrow an encryption key would be called the Clipper Chip, a microprocessor developed by Intergraph Corporation, of Huntsville, Alabama, and manufactured by military contractor Mykotronx, in Torrance, California, and VLSI Technology Inc., in Silicon Valley. The chip would be built into all government and eventually into all private telecommunications equipment: telephones, fax machines, computers, and all wireless communications equipment. As noted in the *Times*, the White House proposal reflected an effort

> ... to resolve a long-standing dilemma of the Information Age: how to preserve the legitimate right for businesses and citizens to use codes to protect all sorts of digital communications — be it a doctor's cellular phone call to a patient or a company's electronic transfer of a million dollars to an overseas client — without letting criminals and terrorists conspire beyond the reach of the law.

The *Times* also offered this summary:

> While the administration currently has no plan to try imposing the technology on private industry, officials hope it will become a standard. Any communications or computer company doing business with the federal government, from AT&T to IBM, would presumably have to incorporate the technology into their products.

The White House called the announcement the Voluntary Escrowed Encryption Initiative. But there was nothing voluntary about it. The proposal was designed to force private companies to comply. The intention, according to one unnamed government official quoted in the *Times* article, reflected the view that "there is a trade-off between individual privacy and society's safety from crime.... Our society needs to decide where to draw the line." This conclusion ignited the inevitable dispute.

Critics of the Clinton administration asserted that the proposal amounted to nothing less than total government control over the privacy of communication. All a government agency would need is a justification and a court order to use the escrowed keys to violate privacy. At issue were two basic constitutional rights: (1) the right of free speech (the First Amendment), and (2) the right to protection against unwarranted search (the Fourth Amendment). In other words, the proposal launched a debate over where to draw the line and who should draw it.

Stephen Bryen, a former Pentagon official and president of Secured

Communications Technologies, Inc., in Silver Spring, Maryland, told *The New York Times* in April 1993, "I think the Government is creating a monster." A firestorm followed, but went largely unnoticed in the press. Throughout the remainder of 1993 the response "was overwhelmingly negative," according to a report by a special panel of the Association for Computing Machinery. It took the form of written commentary and oral testimony before the National Institute of Standards and Technology (NIST), held at the Computer Systems Security and Privacy Advisory Board. Less than two months after the proposal was made, experts were called to present testimony. One of them was Whitfield Diffie, who held the title of Distinguished Engineer at Sun Microsystems in Sunnyvale, California. But Diffie was much more than that. With Martin Hellman from Stanford University, Diffie had developed in 1975 what became known as public key cryptography, described by a colleague at Sun as "the most revolutionary concept in this discipline since the Renaissance." In 1993, Diffie said:

> … The standard would call for the use of a tamper-resistant chip, called Clipper, and embody a 'back door' that will allow the government to decrypt the traffic for law enforcement and national security purposes.

> … The effect is very much like that of the little keyhole in the back of the combination locks used on the lockers of school children. The children open the locks with the combinations, which is supposed to keep the other children out, but the teachers can always look in the lockers by using the key.

What concerned some critics of the escrow system was that the world of communication technology was changing in fundamental ways, and that the White House proposal was nothing less than the imposition of government control over an element of the Information Age. Other critics went further and concluded that the old adage still applied: The road to hell is paved with good intentions. Only one rhetorical question was necessary to make the point: what could have happened if Nazi Germany had been a computerized society and the Gestapo had a Clipper Chip?

The issues were simple and fundamental: free speech and control in a wired world, or the need to prevent crime versus the rights of the honest citizen. In June 1997, *Wired* magazine framed the case this way:

When Thomas Paine published *Common Sense* in 1776 — arguing

Encrypting the Swiss Cheese

that the American cause was not merely a revolt against unfair taxation, but a demand for independence — he had no idea that more than 200 years later, the struggle for freedom would be waged between privacy advocates and the national-security establishment. This time, the dispute is not over taxation without representation, but communication without government intervention.

The concerns were ignored. On February 4, 1994, the Department of Commerce announced adoption of the Escrowed Encryption Standard (EES) "as a voluntary Federal Information Processing Standard (FIPS)," according to the Association for Computing Machinery report. The "voluntary" EES had George Orwell's *1984* written all over it. It prompted encryption specialist Bruce Schneier to draw the following conclusion in his 1996 book *Applied Cryptography* (John Wiley & Sons):

> Some dangerously Orwellian assumptions are at work here: that the government has the right to listen to private communications, and that there is something wrong with a private citizen trying to keep a secret from the government. Law enforcement has always been able to conduct court-authorized surveillance if possible, but this is the first time that the people have been forced to take active measures to *make themselves available* for surveillance. These initiatives are not simply government proposals in some obscure area; they are preemptive and unilateral attempts to usurp powers that previously belonged to the people.
>
> Clipper and Digital Telephony do not protect privacy; they force individuals to unconditionally trust that the government will respect their privacy. The same law enforcement authorities who illegally tapped Martin Luther King Jr.'s phones can easily tap a phone protected with Clipper.

The latter debate was only one of two government-inspired events. Focus on the second was brought to bear on April 28, 1994, in a *Wall Street Journal* article headlined "Cipher Probe." Guess whom it concerned? Philip Zimmerman! At this point he was "fast becoming a folk hero on the information highway." The article, and subsequent ones, reported that a federal grand jury in San Jose, California, had been convened to determine if Zimmerman had a role in placing PGP on the Internet, and had, therefore, violated the law concerning exportation of strong encryption without a license. If the investigation produced indictment and conviction, it carried with it imprisonment of up to five years and a fine of up to $1 million. It was a serious matter. In an April 1995 *Washington Post* article, William P. Keane, a U.S. Attorney, explained the issue with a question:

> What — if any — policing is to be done on the Net? Are we going
> to throw up our hands and say, 'There's no accountability. It's too
> big to enforce.'?

As far as encryption was concerned, the question was beside the point. By early 1995 PGP encryption had already been available on the Internet for four years, and "400 encryption products [were] readily available overseas — including 164 that use encryption methods that the U.S. government has declared illegal to export." But the law was on the books, and the investigation of Zimmerman continued while he drew up a list of attorneys prepared to take on the case pro bono. The issue was not one of the left or right. It was about the privacy of private information. Zimmerman told the *Washington Post*:

> Privacy is as apple-pie as the Constitution. Perhaps you think your
> e-mail is legitimate enough that encryption is unwarranted. If you
> really are a law-abiding citizen with nothing to hide, then why don't
> you always send your paper mail on postcards?

As the investigation continued, so did support for Zimmerman. Lance J. Hoffman, an expert on encryption issues, concluded in the *Post* story that a prosecution "'would be the Dreyfus trial of this century' — a landmark case for the culture of cyberspace. 'It will put on trial a culture and a set of mores and rules ... that is in conflict with the established, written-down rules and laws.'" If indictment and conviction followed, concluded Jerry Berman, the head of the Center for Democracy and Technology in Washington, D.C., "'it will rightly make Phil Zimmerman a martyr.... The Clipper Chip polarized the discussion of the balance between privacy and security ... and 'Zimmerman will square that — without accomplishing anything for the government.'"

The counterargument, which must have confirmed the views on government respect for privacy held by Zimmerman and his friends, was put the following way in the April 1995 *Washington Post* story by a "source familiar with the case" from the government's point of view:

> ... Zimmerman [is] 'muddleheaded and naive' for thinking that he
> could escape prosecution for software that appeared on the

Internet: 'He's playing at this stuff, and when it has real consequences, he wants to deny it. How far do you think you'd get arguing you didn't cause the export of nuclear technology if you sold it
in an international airport departure lounge?'"

The irony in this conclusion was that this kind of thinking was already
debris floating in the technological wake of the Internet. Nonetheless, an old-
boy mentality was still ruling in some echelons of the U.S. government. To
argue that it was necessary to prevent exportation of strong encryption in order
to protect the national security of the United States was absurd. It wasn't possible to prevent the spread of strong encryption by using customs controls to
guard the territorial borders of the United States. For whatever reason, in
January 1996 the U.S. Attorney's office told Zimmerman that he wouldn't be
prosecuted.

In the meantime, three things had become crystal clear. First, the Internet is
not a medium that can be controlled effectively by the U.S. government, or by
any other. The consequences of the convergence of the computer with information technology really does represent a shift — however it may be defined
— that requires new ways of thinking about the world in which we all live.
Second, the outcry against the Clinton administration's proposal of the Clipper
Chip not only sent the government back to the drawing board on the issue of
encryption export, it also forced the White House to rethink its position on the
significance of the revolution in communication as a whole. Third,
Zimmerman was awarded the Pioneer Award by the Electronic Frontier
Foundation in March 1995, the same award that Hedy Lamarr would receive
two years later. The postscript was written in March 1996. Zimmerman founded his own company, Pretty Good Privacy, to sell "digital-privacy products for
private communications and the secure storage of data for businesses and individuals." Today well over one million people are using PGP.

The concept of the Clipper Chip, and the redefined Key Escrow proposal of
1995, had been already passed over by time and technology the day they were
proposed. The only people who would be hurt by the Clipper Chip scheme
were the honest. Clever criminals would remain unaffected; encryption was
available on the Internet. Moreover, what would prevent criminals in the
United States from importing strong encryption? And how would the government enforce such an import prohibition, if one existed? PGP does not make
the world more dangerous. Criminals and terrorists do. PGP does, however,
protect my privacy, and I like that idea very much. As Nalini put it when we
had lunch in June 1997, "If government officials want to control the use of

encryption, they should go use the Navajo language." (Navajo Code Talkers, 400 of them, were a major asset during World War II. The Japanese were never able to decipher the language, and it was kept a classified secret until 1968.)

Following the decision to drop the investigation against Zimmerman, the White House did not give up its effort to establish some sort of escrow key system, phrased as key recovery, even though non-U.S. encryption software companies were producing encryption software far stronger than fifty-six bits and selling it on the open market. Indeed, the use of encryption was continuing to spread rapidly; by the end of 1997 there existed more than 650 encryption products in twenty-nine countries outside the United States.

The year 1998 did not see the end of the debate. But the issues were all out on the table, thanks to people with courage and common sense, like Phil Zimmerman, Bruce Schneier, and Whitfield Diffie. What was ultimately at stake was discussed by the head of the Central Intelligence Agency, George Tenet, and by the chief executive officer of IBM Corporation, Louis Gerstner Jr., before an audience of 800 CEOs and security experts at the Sam Nunn NationsBank Policy Forum at the Georgia Institute of Technology in April 1998. Tenet admonished "U.S. industry ... to get off its butt" to resolve the stalemate with government over the use of software to scramble, or encrypt, computer data," and concluded that "we are staking our future on a resource we have not yet learned how to protect." In an April 1997 report in *USA Today*, Gerstner drew a different picture, one of

> 'a future threat to our national economy' if government is successful in forcing industry to turn over encryption keys. 'It is simply impossible to overstate how much is at stake' in securing the future of the Internet.... He compared its potential with that of 'the printing press, radio, the lightbulb or manned flight.'

When all is said and done, security *and* privacy in the Information Age were at the heart of the matter. But the debate had taken place in a kind of twilight zone occupied by government law enforcement officials and intelligence gathering experts on the one hand, and by sophisticated computer users and encryption producers on the other. The two sides were both talking about security, but their respective definitions of security could hardly have been more different. Does less freedom mean more security? Or is it the other way around?

As explained in a *San Francisco Chronicle* article, the issue was resolved in January 2000, when the White House announced new rules that would permit U.S. companies "to export any encryption product available on the retail market to businesses and individuals in almost every country in the world," subject to a one-time review. Complicated licensing procedures did remain in place, but the wired world had achieved a victory. In the words of the general counsel of the Electronic Privacy Information Center in Washington, D.C., "encryption software shouldn't be treated any differently from word processing or spreadsheet software."

As a private matter my "Swiss cheese" is safe because my e-mail is encrypted, and so are all my shopping orders placed on the Internet. So is e-mail communication with my bank and my stockbroker. This safety and ease of communication are the result of products of the Information Age. They are not going to disappear, but will, on the contrary, become more sophisticated. Why aren't they welcomed by governments? A June 1999 story in *The Wall Street Journal* put it this way:

> ... Technologies are coming together in ways that will allow people to move money and financial assets instantaneously to almost any point on the globe without the knowledge of any government.

> Many in government wish to squelch these developments, either because they fear the loss of their own roles as economic gate-keepers, or because they genuinely believe that the new technologies will make life easier for drug dealers, money launderers and other assorted criminals. To be sure, these technologies do make a criminal's life easier — as do the telephone and automobile. Yet it is also true that the digital age has given law enforcement many more tools to observe and detect criminal activity. Law-enforcement officials must learn to adapt new technologies to their purposes, rather than outlaw them in the futile hope that they will simply go away.

Today, all users of the Internet owe a major debt of thanks to people like Zimmerman. He had the courage of his conviction, that freedom of speech is more important than government claims it should be restricted in the interests of law enforcement. In fact, some persuasively argued, in connection with the debate that followed creation of PGP, that law enforcement in a democracy is the consequence of a free society, not vice versa. Why should law-abiding citizens be denied the means to protect their right of free speech? It was a rhetorical question. The issue was one of freedom versus control. Who had the right to watch, monitor, and control the activities of whom?

Virtual freedom of speech is an issue in the interactive world, where the nature of communication is being transformed. Old institutional approaches no longer apply.

The problem isn't encryption. It's how we deal, in a free society, with the electronic means of communication in the Information Age.

Most of us over fifty grew up in a world where control was exercised by those who had more authority than we did; namely, our parents and our government. We were used to it, we accepted it, and as we grew older we were often part of this hierarchy, even if we nonetheless didn't always enjoy the consequences. But today the Internet gives both young and old a means to communicate that weakens and challenges hierarchical authority. The result is that we are all in the middle of a new conflict. It's about the effects of unlimited freedom of speech in a wired world, where, for many, electronic sovereignty is a reality.

Part II

VIRTUAL CERTAINTIES

The sovereignty of man lieth hid in knowledge;
wherein many things are reserved that kings with their treasure cannot buy,
nor with their force command.

{Sir Francis Bacon, 1561-1626}

CHAPTER THREE

Marketplaces and the Information Age

*... Every month, 4 quadrillion transistors are pro-
duced, more than half a million for every human on the
planet. Intel's space-suited workers etch more than seven
million, in lines one four-hundredth the thickness of a
human hair, on each of its thumbnail-size Pentium II
chips, which sell for about $500 and can make 588 mil-
lion calculations a second.*

{*Time*, December 29, 1997}

1.

WEB SITES AND WINE?

*"It wasn't the wine," murmured Mr. Snodgrass, in a broken voice,
"it was the salmon."*

{Charles Dickens, 1812-1870}

Toulouse-Lautrec's Moulin Rouge was the cover for the October 15, 1998, edition of the *Wine Spectator*, the most prestigious bimonthly magazine about wine published in the United States. The issue was devoted to "A Wine Lover's Guide to Paris," so, as you would expect, the magazine was full of articles about Parisian restaurants and French wines, small hotels and fashionable shops. There was also a great deal of advertising. But something surprising struck me when I opened the issue, just by chance, to page 222. There was a full-page advertisement for an Internet brokerage firm, DATEK, with a Web site address of www.datek.com. The ad read:

> I found this on the Internet ...
> Now I make trades instead of phone calls.
> At only $9.99 per trade, I get free news, research and unlimited real-time quotes.
> Making my own investment decisions has never been easier.
> Datek updates my account instantly and provides me with what I need to manage my own portfolio ... **and my broker wonders why I don't call anymore.**

I thought to myself, "This is odd, but maybe it's a sign of the times. Obviously, there must be some connection between people who like wine and use the Internet. I wonder how many other companies are advertising in the *Wine Spectator* with Web site addresses?" So I started to count. The results amazed me. Between fifty-five and sixty companies had placed ads that included their Web sites. Among them, in addition to the *Wine Spectator* itself, were Joseph Drouhin of Beaune, but also Rémy Martin, Bulgari, the Inter-Continental in Paris, the Principality of Monaco, and companies throughout the United States, including wineries. Equally interesting were the famous companies advertising with just telephone numbers. You will certainly recognize some of the names: Hermès, Louis Vuitton, Chanel, Cartier, Bang & Olufsen, Rolex, Cellini, and Van Cleef & Arpels. Why didn't they list Web sites, too?

There is a message here. It's about business, about the Internet, about who's got money to spend, and about how it's being spent. It's about bricks-and-mortar enterprises like PlumpJack, the wine shop on Fillmore Street in San Francisco that introduced its own clicks-and-mortar Web site in November 1999, www.PlumpJack.com. The site now caters to customers across the country who can connect on-line to its restaurants, PlumpJack Café and Balboa Café, to the PlumpJack Squaw Valley Inn, to the PlumpJack Winery in Napa Valley, or to the wine shop itself.

2.

PARALLELS AND PRODUCTIVITY

Companies doing business on the Internet generated
$300 billion in revenue and created more than
1.2 million jobs [in 1998]

{*San Francisco Chronicle*, June 10, 1999}

Industries built on telecommunications and computers accounted
for nearly one third of U.S. economic growth in 1999.

{U.S. Department of Commerce, May 2000}

In the year 2000 U.S. companies were expected to create
1.6 million new high-tech jobs.

{*San Francisco Chronicle*, April 10, 2000}

People everywhere are talking about money, markets, and information. A "massive reallocation of wealth" is taking place in Europe. Money is moving from investment in banks and bonds to stock markets and venture capital. This change is not a European phenomenon. Look at Asia, despite its economic problems, and look at America. In the United States we see the same thing reflected in the enormous market values of companies traded on the New York Stock Exchange and on the NASDAQ, in the unprecedented growth and competition in the marketplace, and in the technological revolution fueled by companies such as Amazon, Oracle, Microsoft, Yahoo!, Rambus, Lucent, AOL, Qualcomm, Intel,

Cisco, and Sun Microsystems. Few people had ever heard of any of them in 1989. In fact, half of them didn't even exist. By November 1998 they had a combined stock-market value of almost $900 billion and estimated annual revenues of $130 billion. Six months later, in May 1999, their combined value was $1.225 trillion. By April 2000 that value had increased to $2.340 trillion and annual revenues had reached $169 billion. Then, however, the stock market went in the tank, but did that mean the technological revolution was a fraud?

Corporations in Asia, Europe, the Middle East, and the United States are becoming global forces; to wit, the purchase of Random House (American) by Bertelsmann AG (German) in April 1998, or the merger of Daimler Benz (German) and Chrysler Corporation (American) one month later. European companies are being bought, sold, and merged as well. One example is the merger of the chemical conglomerates Hoechst (German) with Rhône-Poulenc (French). Another illustration is the purchase in May 1998 of Rolls-Royce Motor Cars Ltd. by Volkswagen. Equally noteworthy was the purchase, in the same month, of the 231-year-old British auction house, Christie's, by Frenchman François Pinault, followed later in the year by TOTAL's (French) announced purchase of Petrofina (Belgian) for an estimated $11 billion. And the year 2000 began with the announcement that AOL would merge with Time Warner, a deal worth $156 billion.

What is economic power in 2000, and what is driving the marketplace? Is it the power of governments to regulate? Is it wealthy investment banks? Is it e-commerce and e-business? Is it access to competitive, international markets of trade and finance? Is it the breakdown of traditional government telephone monopolies? Is it pressure on public institutions to let private business operate more and more services once provided by governments? However economic power is defined today, it is part and parcel of commerce conducted in an electronic marketplace on the Internet. Information technology markets, and markets of all kinds in Asia, Europe, and in the United States, are growing and expanding by leaps and bounds. It is no longer banks that are driving marketplaces. It is markets, where venture capital firms are investing pooled funds, and where new start-up companies are raising money by selling their stock directly to the public via initial public offerings.

Does this mean that tried and tested economic statistical measures are becoming poor yardsticks of economic performance? Or, if they are still valid (which they are), are there new ones that are valid too? Is the increasing strength of global markets, electronic commerce, and information services making the old steel and wheat measures obsolete? Is it true that, as the nature of markets changes, the way we measure and understand them also changes? And does that in turn affect everything else: unemployment, labor markets, salaries, interest rates, inflation, housing prices, and so on?

138

Not all the answers are in yet. But it is clear that traditional marketplaces for capital equipment, chemicals, insurance, defense, energy, health care, industrial commodities, transportation, finance, and banking, have a new competitor. It's called the marketplace for information technology — where what is being valued, measured, traded, bought, and sold are computers, software programs, wireless telephones, palm-sized organizers, scanners, Internet access, bandwidth, Web sites, switches and routers, microprocessors, operating systems, and networks. What these digital things do, and how they are used, are adding value to the operation of businesses internally, to the conduct of businesses with each other, and to the relationship of businesses with their customers. It's a new economy that is changing the meaning of banking and investing, and the face of financial analysis as marketplaces become connected electronically, everywhere.

There are many examples, but one I like especially concerns a friend of mine in Frankfurt. In 1990, as the closed societies of communism were collapsing, he had a simple and brilliant idea. Greater political freedom in Europe, he believed, would be translated into increased economic growth on the Continent. As the size of the European marketplace expanded, he reasoned, so would the value of major publicly owned corporations listed on Europe's principal stock exchanges. In turn this would mean that the value of comparative financial analysis of stock portfolios held by large banks — for example, in Amsterdam, Frankfurt, Munich, Rome, Vienna, Paris, and London — would increase too, if such information could be gathered and analyzed each month. So he founded a company to do just that, called Financial Asset Associates. He made agreements with two dozen banks to prepare a confidential comparative financial analysis of their respective portfolios on a monthly basis.

He had cornered a market on proprietary financial information, provided his clients a new and powerful analytical tool, and was building a valuable company. In December 1999 he decided to sell it, and found a buyer. But in February 2000 the deal fell apart. Why? Because although the Internet hadn't existed in 1990, it did ten years later. Statistical information on the performance of European stock markets and publicly traded companies was available everywhere on the Internet. Anyone could get it, analyze it, and distribute it. It was true that traditional yardsticks to measure the financial value of bricks-and-mortar companies were still valid. But these companies were operating in parallel with new clicks-and-mortar companies whose productivity, market values, and economic performance had to be measured and analyzed in new ways as well.

He understood that information technology was changing the nature of marketplaces and the nature of business. But he couldn't explain why, because he didn't understand electronic networks — how they worked, and what can be done with them. He did know there was a continuing need for financial analysis, and he recognized that the way markets were measured and analyzed was changing. But he didn't know what companies like Cisco Systems, Intel, Oracle, Qualcomm, or Sun Microsystems made, how their products were used, and why their products added value. When the impending sale of his company collapsed, he drew the consequence. Today he is developing new yardsticks and measures for producing new analytical tools to use with the old, to analyze the world of e-commerce and e-business. The point here is that time and technology are bypassing traditional ways of measuring growth, productivity, and value. My friend sees it, and so do his associates. They recognize today that they must learn what networks do, and that they must develop their ability to use the Internet more effectively so that they can analyze the electronic commerce and business markets of tomorrow.

In Europe e-commerce will drive growth geometrically. The common currency of the Euro has eliminated exchange-rate risk and, therefore, greatly expands the size and scope of markets. Thomas Kamm, writing in *The Wall Street Journal* in December 1999, summed it up:

> 'People who thought they were hot shots with 20 percent of their domestic market are nothing in Europe' [said the chairman of the French insurance company Axa SA].... 'Everyone is asking himself: Oh la la, will I survive in this environment?' ... Companies that could raise money only for bids [to buy other companies] in their domestic markets or couldn't pay for foreign targets in shares because they were denominated in a foreign currency now can tap into a much bigger pool of money that has fueled a booming corporate bond market [in Euros].

The buying power of the European Union at the beginning of 2000 was measured with a gross domestic product of $8.345 trillion, compared to $8.230 trillion for the United States. Competitive advantages are everywhere, unless, that is, European politicians succumb to an old statist temptation and seek to regulate the Internet. If, for example, European governments tax commerce on the Internet, and seek to control its electronic operation with "back door" encryption, Europe will remain a second string player in the global marketplace of the twenty-first century. That's why, as early as 1998, the former chief executive officer of Bull Computer in Paris, Francis Lorentz, encouraged the Europeans to hurry the development and use of information technologies. Otherwise in his view, they were "liable to see their foreign competitors — especially American businesses — reshape the market to their own advantage."

Europeans have lagged behind for three reasons. Computer hardware and software are still much more costly in Europe than in the United States (a fax machine costs two to four times more in France, for example). The cost of fixed-line telephone calls, although it is dropping, remains exorbitantly expensive in Europe in comparison to the U.S. Finally, European political leaders have suspected, rightly, that the Information Age is changing the role of government power and the relationship between government and citizen. Some European politicians, who believe in free markets, welcome this. Others, who believe in the power of the state, do not. So Europe as a whole has been slow to embrace the concept and practice of competing in the global, electronic marketplaces that information technologies make possible.

The trans-Atlantic technology gap, however, is narrowing fast. Closure is being driven by both competition with the United States in the use of information technology, and by the recognition that e-commerce and e-business will drive the global marketplace in the twenty-first century. European businesses understand that they must compete successfully or remain in second place. In March 2000 approximately 85 million Europeans were on-line, compared with about 110 million in the U.S. Internet users, according to Ireland-based Internet Surveys, included about 16 million Germans (20 percent of the population), almost 16 million in the United Kingdom (27 percent of the population), and 9 million in France (15 percent of the population). But perhaps a measure of even greater significance is where international Internet traffic originating in Europe in 1999 was sent. In 1998 more than half of it went to the U.S. In 1999 66 percent of it stayed in Europe; the London-New York Internet traffic route was the busiest, and traffic in the next six hubs, led by Frankfurt and Amsterdam, all began and ended in European cities.

A milestone on Europe's way to greater competitiveness was the breakup, beginning in 1997-1998, of Europe's state-owned telephone monopolies, and privatization of other industries as well. In 1998 stock in France Telecom was being sold on the Paris Bourse. That constituted a revolution in itself, which perhaps is what had prompted France's then minister of economics, Dominique Strauss-Kahn, to conclude in frustration in late 1997 that France "is a capitalist country without capital or capitalists." By March 2000 European leaders were no longer just recognizing the handwriting on the wall, they were writing it themselves. European Union leaders, meeting in Lisbon, set as a formal goal the creation of a strong and dynamic knowledge-based economy that would surpass the United States in the Internet age. To this end they committed themselves to further deregulation of their economies, to reducing the cost of Internet access, to encouraging business start-ups, to passing legislation supporting e-commerce, and to wiring their school systems. Prime Minister Jospin of France did argue that each country should proceed at its own pace on matters such as privatization of state-owned industries, an issue which he said had no place in a European summit meeting on the new economy. But his argument was undoubtedly made for domestic political reasons, because private initiative and risk, contrary to his remark, have everything to do with the success of the new economy.

Is it the Information Age that is driving these changes? Is there a connection among free markets, economic competition, and the revolution in information and telecommunication technologies? The answer to both questions is yes. But some people still choose to ignore it. They are the political collectivists, whose theories and practices were thoroughly discredited by the bankruptcy of communist economies in 1989. Their views did not disappear with the collapse of dictatorship in Central Europe and the Soviet Union. They continue to assert that free marketeers know no moderation, as though government regulators do. They collectively opine that ours is "an age whose technology ensures that competition brings changes ever more rapidly," as though speed defines the quality of change. Not surprisingly, according to Angus Sibley in the *International Herald Tribune* of May 1998, they assert that free markets constitute

> ... a recipe for rapid, persistent, accelerating, ubiquitous change. No one should be surprised if the accompanying pains are acute and pervasive; if societies thus afflicted become disoriented, rootless, anarchic, violent; if ugly political movements seize the resulting opportunities.

> History suggests that upheavals are followed by contrasting phases of oppressive order. After the French Revolution came the Bourbon reaction. The Bolshevik cataclysm gave way to Soviet ossification. Franquismo followed the Spanish civil war. Victorian laissez-faire bred the obstructive trade unions and inflated welfare states that libertarians loathe.

> For those who desire civilized order, this historical sequence offers but partial comfort. For reckless economic revolutionaries, it threatens nemesis. Who shall say they have not deserved it?

Is it really that simple? Just irresponsible free marketeers? Competition run amok? Can the positive significance of new technologies be so easily ignored? For the ideologues, more is at stake than just the assertion that competition corrupts. They believe that freedom of the marketplace is evil. Competition, in their view, isn't fair. It produces winners and losers. By definition, therefore, free markets are not in the public interest, even though free markets produce better products at lower prices for more people than any other economic approach.

Indeed, in 1998 none other than George Soros, who made a $2 billion fortune on currency speculation in 1992 by selling the British pound short and earning himself the title "The Man Who Broke the Bank of England," published his views on free markets. In a *Wall Street Journal* review of Soros's book, *The Crisis of Global Capitalism*, Charles Wolf Jr. concluded that Soros placed

> '... market fundamentalism' on a par with communism for the supposed gap between its 'grand intentions' and 'disappointing outcomes.' And the 'imperialistic tendencies' of capitalism make it 'little different from Alexander the Great or Attila the Hun.'

But the looking glass has two sides. Those who were locked up in corrupt political states in Central Europe and the Soviet Union until the end of the 1980s knew that free markets and technological change could produce things of value, things called choices. Information, and the means to exchange it, brought freedom to choose. Free markets of ideas, information, and goods did not mark the end of "change." It marked the beginning of it. Free markets did not bring the affliction of poverty and violence. They brought the birth of economic liberty. In post-1989 Europe free markets unite, they do not divide. They bring people together, they do not keep people apart. They challenge, they do not isolate. They foster innovation and initiative. They do not stifle and choke. They breed competition, not coercive bureaucracies. They champion open societies, not closed ones.

There are interesting parallels between the Industrial Revolution and the Information Age, between the introduction of electricity in the nineteenth century and creation of the Internet a century later. Both produced entrepreneurs and visionaries. A century ago one of them wrote about the future in a novel which wasn't published in French until 1994, and in English in 1996. We are all familiar with Jules Verne's imagination in his famous story *Twenty Thousand Leagues Under the Sea* (1870). But few of us, until recently, were aware of the vision of an electronic age that Verne described in *Paris in the Twentieth Century*: he portrayed a society in the grip of business and technology, where elaborate public transit and the glare of electric illumination created twenty-four-hour-a-day commerce. He foretold what can only be described today as faxes, calculators, and computers. And he predicted traffic jams.

There are also parallels between the two ages concerning measures of productivity, and growth, and change. Electricity, just like the Internet, was far from an instant success. There was doubt, uncertainty, ridicule, and competition. Like the Internet, the idea of actually doing something constructive with electricity spread slowly, and its use was not immediately productive. And in a scenario reminiscent of the competing microprocessor systems of Intel and Motorola, or between Apple's versus IBM's operating systems, the Industrial Age saw a contest between direct current (DC) and alternating current (AC). But also like the Internet, electricity captured the imagination of the intrepid, and its use eventually spread throughout the world. And, as information technology is doing in the twenty-first century, change, growth, and productivity were inexorably propelled forward by electricity.

Whoever thought, in 1880, that one day the entire city of Paris would no longer be lit by lamplight? Many of my generation and older may not yet believe that one day we will consider the operation of electronic networks to be as natural as turning on the light. But the efficiencies of networks make their users more productive. In other words, computers, like electricity, make it a lot easier to do an enormous number of different things, more quickly. There is, however, debate about this, just as there was debate about the value of electricity or the motor car. After all, how could anyone improve on the horse and buggy? Today, if you own a stock in an outdated technology, like buggy-making, stockbrokers call it a *buggy-whip* stock. It's not difficult to figure out what that means!

In the late 1980s Stanford University economist Paul David began writing about "the dynamo analogy." His interest was prompted by the debate among economists concerning MIT professor Robert Solow's conclusion, "We see the computers everywhere but in the productivity statistics." David's point was simple: "In 1900, contemporary observers well might have remarked that the electric dynamos were to be seen 'everywhere but in the productivity statistics.'"

David argued, in a 1991 Center for Economic Policy Research paper, that there was, "on the one hand, the buoyant conviction that we are embarked on a pre-determined course of diffusion, leading swiftly and inexorably toward the successful transformation of the entire range of productive activities," but that, "on the other hand, there is the depressing suspicion that something has gone terribly awry, fostered by the disappointment of premature expectations about the information revolution's impact upon the conventional productivity indicators and our material standard of living." His conclusion was elementary. There is always a significant lag time between introduction of a new invention and its long-term effects; to coin a phrase, *these things take time.* David cites statistics illustrating the relationship:

> In 1899 in the United States, electric lighting was being used in a mere 3 percent of all residences.... [T]he horsepower capacity of all ... electric motors installed in manufacturing establishments in the country represented less than 5 percent of factory mechanical

drive. It would take another two decades ... for these aggregate measures of the extent of electrification to attain the 50 percent diffusion level....

Although the pace of the computer's diffusion in the business and public sectors of the industrialized societies during the past two decades [the 1970s and '80s] has been faster than that recorded for the dynamo during its comparable early phase of adoption, it has been estimated that only 10 percent of the world's fifty million business enterprises today [1990] are using computers, and only 2 percent of the world's business information has been digitized.

What David could not include were statistics made public by the U.S. Department of Commerce in April 1998. In the United States radio gained fifty million listeners in thirty-eight years. Television had fifty million viewers after thirteen years. The Internet had more than fifty million users in just four years.

Speaking to the same theme in July 1997, John H. Moore, president of Grove City College in Pennsylvania, addressed the changes in business structure and organization made possible by the use of electricity:

[Faraday] once gave a demonstration of the phenomenon [electromagnetism] to the British chancellor of the exchequer. Having seen the experiment, the esteemed official said it was very interesting, but asked Faraday what it was good for. Faraday replied that he didn't know, but he was sure that one day the chancellor would tax it.... It's no wonder that Faraday could not tell the chancellor what it was good for. Nobody knew, and nobody could possibly have predicted the almost infinite range of uses to which electricity has been put.

Moore continued that "to exploit Faraday's discovery and the invention of the dynamo that resulted from it has required more than a century of research, invention, creation, development, investment, construction, and organization." What the next hundred years led to, Moore declares, was the large, centralized corporation as the model of industrial organization:

This form of organization was a natural result of the development of mass production that followed the inventions of the Industrial Revolution. The success of the machine in production led to the conception of the firm as itself a machine; the efficiency of a machine became a metaphor for the efficiency of the company. If the company is like a machine, then all parts should be controlled centrally. So the corporation became a centralized hierarchical organization.

Today, the centralized and hierarchical corporation still thrives, but, like the kerosene lamp in the nineteenth century and the knowledge monopoly in the twentieth, it is living on borrowed time. Corporations like General Electric, Alcoa, and J.P. Morgan are not going to become industrial and financial relics. But how they do business, where they do business, and with whom they do business, is undergoing dramatic transformation. Take GE, whose chairman Jack Welch issued in January 1999 the battle cry "Storm the Internet." He told his executives, as reported by Matt Murray in *The Wall Street Journal* in June 1999, that every GE business should establish a Web site by the end of the year:

> [By mid 1999] GE's twelve units … [were] in the midst of a frenzied effort to accommodate the technology that Mr. Welch calls the greatest change in business in his lifetime. GE is already using the Web to sell plastics and monitor medical equipment, to market refrigerators and lease cars. To make employees more Web-savvy, GE is making its internal newsletters and some memos from Mr. Welch available only on-line … and is figuring e-commerce performance into managers' compensation.

Welch's decision had an unintended consequence. Many of the company's top 1,000 managers, in their late thirties to nearly sixty years of age, didn't know much about the Internet, nor how to adjust to the "new world." It used to be that corporate elders tutored the up-and-comers. But Welch proposed that the veterans themselves become students of 1,000 computer-savvy e-business mentors, many of whom were brand-new to GE, working with them three to four hours a week on the Web. "It was this mentor-mentee interaction," wrote Welch in February 2000, "that helped overcome the only real hurdle some of us had — fear of the unknown." He applied the experiment to himself as well, and at age sixty-three discovered that he could "go to all kinds of sites, and … go to chat rooms and see what people are saying about GE.… E-business knowledge is generally inversely proportional to both age and the height in the organization." The results were so profound that Welch sent a letter about them to share owners, customers and employees on February 11, 2000:

[T]he contribution of e-Business to GE ... is changing this company to its core.... [D]igitizing a company does more than just create unlimited business opportunities; it puts a small-company soul into that big-company body and gives it the transparency, excitement and buzz of a start-up.... E-business is the final nail in the coffin for bureaucracy at GE.

The speed that is the essence of 'e' has accelerated the metabolism of the company, with people laughing out loud at presentations of business plans for 'the third quarter of next year' and other tortoise-like projections of action. Time in GE today is measured in days and weeks.

The accelerating pace of our success in this initiative is leading to a lot of spontaneous celebrating — something big companies, including GE, have always had trouble doing as well as small companies. It generates more fun across a business than anything we've ever seen. The informality, joy of work and endless celebration that comes with 'e'-life is something on which we are thriving.

E-business was made for GE, and the 'E' in GE now has a whole new meaning. We get it — we all get it.

Welch's experience at GE wouldn't have surprised Nalini or Gaku in 1995. Today it doesn't surprise me either, and it elates GE's active and retired employees who, in February 2000, had $24 billion of GE stock in their savings plans; the total return on a share of GE stock in 1999 was 54 percent. What is really remarkable, however, is that no chief executive officer of any traditional bricks-and-mortar American company would have dared write a letter like Welch's ten years ago, and if he had tried he probably would have been fired. But today the vertical corporate world of the past is disappearing and GE's experience is the reason why. Predictions like the following, made in January 1999, may sound far-fetched, but they are an accurate reflection of what Welch calls "the greatest change in business" in his lifetime:

[W]e can write off the bricks and mortar of every downtown financial district in the world because little of it will survive competition with the cyberworld.... [V]irtual commerce has already rendered obsolete the skyscrapers, stock exchanges, bank lobbies, record stores, luncheonettes, newsstands, book stores, commuter trains, and much else that we can see from our office windows....

Commercial real estate won't be the only casualty as virtual commerce burgeons.

Since the World Wide Web gives companies the ability to sell directly to customers, America's sales force will be decimated.

Although this is inevitable, neither the companies nor their employees are eager to acknowledge it, for both have too big a stake in the status quo. Nevertheless, nearly every retailer and manufacturer in America has opened a Web site in the last two years, tactfully encouraging customers to drop in from time to time.

Information technology companies, for the most part, are not hierarchical and centralized. Networks break down organizational constraints on decision-making and corporate rigidity — in the sense that the corporation is the benevolent master and mother of all things. Software companies, networking companies, e-commerce companies, and corporations like GE are replacing the gray-flanneled system of the "organization man" with a flexibility of structure inconceivable in the middle of the twentieth century. In the 1950s, the corporation, the organization, and the labor union were the structures that provided security, and assured loyal workers and members that everything was OK. By the late 1990s the situation was reversed. The transformation is simply remarkable to behold, and difficult for older generations to grasp.

Computer and telecommunications industries have developed electronic networks that connect their employees one with another in company offices around the globe, whether they number two or fifty. The "connectedness" is the power, the force, and the value of the Internet. That is why more and more businesses, large and small, are using electronic networks. Interconnectivity is a new dimension of man's organization, making possible relationships we never had before. If we destroy the connection, we've got nothing: the Internet's value is proportional to the number of people using it.

The idea of the Internet start-up company in Silicon Valley owed much of its initial success to engineers and programmers who were designing computer networks and the software to make them work. Some of these young entrepreneurs came from large companies where they had found it enormously frustrating to present their electronic concepts to corporate committees who sparingly committed research funds to the development of an idea. Some stayed and tried to change the centralized and vertical corporate structures from within. Others decided to "start up" something new.

At the beginning of the 1990s men and women in their twenties and thirties were starting software companies with good ideas, lots of energy, and with money from venture capital firms. By the end of the decade the venture-capital landscape had become a gold rush of financing. In 1999 venture-capital infusion amounted to something between $36 and $48 billion, depending on the estimates used — in any case, larger than the three previous years combined. According to Stuart Alsop, a partner at New Enterprise Associates on Sand Hill Road in Menlo Park, California (which is considered the world capital for venture capitalists), "It is like standing under a waterfall trying to take a drink.... At any one time, I have 150 to 200 company business plans sitting on my desk." Indeed, during 1999 one third of the total venture capital investment in the United States was raised in northern California. And the pace continued during the first quarter of the year 2000 with a record $22.7 billion invested in start-ups.

If young computer whizzes weren't reinventing the concept of work in the 1990s, they were designing an approach to work that placed greater value on creativity, experimentation, innovation, and imagination than on arriving at the office "properly" dressed in Brooks Brothers suits. They did not take large salaries at first because there wasn't always enough money. They did not embrace the trappings of traditional corporations, such as plush offices, executive suites, and private bathrooms, because they couldn't afford them. They were prepared to take risks. They gave themselves stock and stock options in their small ventures, and with skill, hard work, and luck, they gambled they would succeed. Their perks were not country club memberships, but free parking and beds to nap on.

Many of them failed, but for those who succeeded, success exceeded their wildest dreams. As the potential value of their electronic inventions attracted the attention of larger corporations in the communications industry — such as Intel, Microsoft, or Cisco Systems — they sold their little enterprises or transformed them into public companies. Either way, the decade of the 1990s saw many from this young generation suddenly discover they owned stock that had become extremely valuable.

A typical example is the success story of a small company called Lightspeed International, which had developed software to enable voice transmission over data networks. In December 1997, according to a *New York Times* business story, the company's chief executive officer, Lev Volftsun, visited Cisco Systems to discuss licensing of two products. But Michelangelo Volpi, thirty-one years old and vice president for Cisco's business development,

... had something else in mind. He wanted to buy Lightspeed.... Within three hours both sides had agreed to terms.... The shares Mr. Volftsun and his colleagues received in return for selling their company, worth $194 million when they completed their deal, are now [November 1998] valued at more than $320 million.

Another example, although much more dramatic, illustrates the same principle. Anyone who uses the Internet today has heard of Netscape. As I have already mentioned, the idea came from Marc Andreessen, but financing came from Jim Clark, who had previously started Silicon Graphics. When he decided to finance creation of the Internet's first commercial browser, Clark enlisted Andreessen's help and, in Andreessen's words, "bet his own money on a motley crew of college students."

The company was founded in the spring of 1994 as Mosaic Communications Corporation, and in January 1995 James Barksdale, with highly successful careers at McCaw Cellular Telephone and Federal Express, was brought in to provide, at age fifty-one, some "adult supervision." Netscape had its first initial public offering in August 1995, and was listed on the American over-the-counter stock exchange NAS-DAQ. Its opening price was $14 per share; ten million shares were sold. The company's initial product — the one for which it is so well known — was described in Netscape's 1995 annual report as "an easy-to-use, intuitive tool for navigating on-line information — one that was truly dynamic, built on open standards, with the ability to operate with any computing platform or database." One year after Netscape became a publicly traded corporation it had revenues of $346 million.

The company had a great product and an unusual name. It also had a creative strategy which worked well, until it became involved in head-to-head competition with the Internet browser sold by Microsoft as part of its Windows operating system. Kara Swisher described it in *The Wall Street Journal:*

> Netscape's tactic of giving the initial browser away for free, and then charging for it later, resulted in stunning growth. Within six months, millions of copies of the browser were downloaded by Internet users, many of them new to the medium. For that feat alone, Netscape will always remain an icon of the digital age. It is to the Internet what Apple Computer Inc. is to the personal computer — a start-up that through innovation turned a hobby into a major global industry.

In November 1998 America Online (AOL) announced it would acquire Netscape for approximately $4.2 billion, in an alliance with Sun Microsystems. Barksdale, Netscape's chief executive officer, would leave the company with 5.1 million shares, valued at almost $210 million, and would become a member of AOL's board of directors. *The Wall Street Journal* reported that Andreessen, a struggling college student a few years previously and just twenty-seven years old in November 1998, would own AOL stock worth more than $92 million and would become AOL's chief of technology (he resigned one year later). And the return on Jim Clark's investment? His holding of 14.4 million Netscape shares would have a value of $592 million.

There were other consequences as well, of a more long-term nature. The Generation X designers and creators of hardware and software products like Andreessen's Netscape

> ... did not fit the patterns of the past. They saw their careers as their affair. They wanted freedom to operate independently and were ready to change jobs to achieve more autonomy.

> Even the concept of a career was a contradiction as it suggested a series of steps controlled by the powerful. This lot intended to control their careers themselves. If they had an idea of a career it was as a portfolio of activities that might or might not reflect an institutional framework.

Generation X, young adults born between 1965 and 1975, has come of age. The Xers represent America's second-largest generation (about 41 million between the ages of eighteen and twenty-eight and about 16 percent of the population), after Baby Boomers (about 78 million and 30 percent of the population). At the borderline between the two generations is a group that has advanced faster, become enormously successful, and has more disposable income than my or my grandparents' generation.

A stunning case in point is the success of two former Stanford students who developed a search engine called Yahoo!. It began as an idea of David Filo and Jerry Yang, both Ph.D. candidates in the School of Electrical Engineering at Stanford University. In April 1994 they began making daily entries of their personal life on the university's computer system, and soon discovered that their lists were "too long and unwieldy." So later in the year they made a decision, which was recorded on-line in "Yahoo! History" in 1997:

> [T]hey converted Yahoo! into a customized database designed to serve the needs of the thousands of users that began to use the service through the closely bound Internet community. They developed customized software to help them efficiently locate, identify,

and edit material stored on the Internet. The name Yahoo! is supposed to stand for 'Yet Another Hierarchical Officious Oracle' but Filo and Yang insist they selected the name because they considered themselves yahoos.

Once their software was made available on the Internet, computer users were able to download it at no cost. Filo and Yang received, as a consequence, a great deal of feedback on its strengths and weaknesses. They gathered enough market research — that is, they were able to count the number of people who accessed their Web site — to make an educated guess about their chances to succeed. They were then able to raise enough venture capital to form a company in March 1995. In April 1996, Yahoo! went public in an initial public offering (IPO), and is listed today on the NASDAQ along with companies like Microsoft, Cisco Systems and Intel. Yahoo! has, since then, become the most popular search engine used on the Internet. At the beginning of April 2000 its market capitalization was more than $84 billion and its revenues for 1999 were almost $229 million. The value of David Filo's stock had already exceeded $1 billion by July of 1998.

In the heart of Silicon Valley, perceptive managers at the National Aeronautics and Space Administration recognized that young entrepreneurs did not fit past patterns. So NASA inaugurated the concept of the *incubator* in 1992 to encourage risk taking. The idea was straightforward, as explained in official Web sites: "provide opportunities for start-up companies utilizing NASA technologies to grow and become robust high tech businesses [and] information resources that can be searched and consulted for research and technology, patents, technical expertise, and R&D facilities as well as for technology partnering, licensing and commercialization opportunities."

As knowledge spread about the advantages of an incubator environment, the commercial advantages of technologies developed in university research laboratories became evident as well. Academic institutions across the United States, such as Harvard, were quick to take credit for burgeoning relationships between higher education and the rest of the economy. The logical consequence was creation of business incubators and research parks closely associated with different parts of the academic enterprise. Stunningly simple and successful, commercial and academic incubators are sprouting like mushrooms everywhere in 2000. That includes the one launched by entrepreneur Burkhard Koch, chairman of IQ International Incubator in Berlin, as well as the oldest center of learning in Europe, the University of Bologna in Italy, today "on the verge of an e-renaissance."

In one sense, however, NASA arrived relatively late on the scene.

Computer company executives such as William Hewlett and David Packard had long before recognized the advantages of easy and informal communication. Their company offices didn't look like those at Chase Manhattan or Alcoa Corporation. They operated HP on the basis of wide-open access. They got their morning coffee at the same coffee urn where other employees got it. It seems Generation X's approach to the world of work wasn't new after all. Hewlett and Packard invented the practice of management-by-walking-around in the 1950s. What was new in the 1990s was that an entire generation was creating, competing, communicating, collaborating, producing, and managing by walking around on electronic networks.

Parallels between the use of electricity and the use of information technology tell us that the future will be defined by how we transform our offices, businesses, and corporations into modern communication networks. Men and women in all kinds of business settings tell us that networking saves time and money, and increases efficiency and quality — even if it's just an e-mail network between two or three people. Whether we call our machines network computers, laptop computers, or personal computers, what we are talking about is connecting computers to form a network. How does it work? Writing for the *San Francisco Chronicle* in June 1998, Jonathan Marshall explained:

> A computer network lets employees swap files with the push of a button instead of walking from room to room with floppy disks. It lets them share a high-speed printer instead of wasting desk space and money putting printers by every workstation. And it permits everyone in the office to share Internet access without the expense of multiple dial-up lines and accounts.
>
> Networks also let offices centralize files on one hard disk, so safety backups become easy and routine rather than onerous and infrequent.

Networks on the World Wide Web also represent "libraries at your fingertips," as John Gapper illustrated in a January 1999 *Financial Times* story:

> For many managers and white-collar workers, the world did not change much when the first personal computer arrived on their desk.... It was impossible to discover some things before without going to a dusty library....

A salesman can now use his laptop to carry out a rapid search for news on a company he is about to visit. A corporate financier can read on-line equity research about a target company. A health service manager may not only brief herself on a drugs company but also examine the clinical research on its latest drugs.

Examples of network efficiency abound. A famous one is a decision made by IBM. When Louis Gerstner became head of the company in April 1993, he apparently wasn't well familiar with communication technology. He was an outsider who had come to IBM from RJR Nabisco, a food conglomerate where he had been the chief executive officer. Whether he understood the meaning of real-time communication via a network is a moot point, because he did recognize that IBM could use the Internet as a vehicle for global business. That provided the motivation to create a network that could be used within IBM, and which also could be sold for use by other companies.

IBM went looking for a small company that had designed such a communication program, found one in 1995, and bought the company for a reported $3.5 billion. The program was called Lotus Notes. The enormous value Lotus Notes brought to networking was its function as an electronic platform that allowed people to work with each other on the same report, on the same analysis, or on the same project, irrespective of where they were — in a hotel room in Singapore or Warsaw, at a meeting in Copenhagen or Istanbul, in an airport in Capetown or Madrid, or in IBM's offices in New York. Lotus Notes was, in the parlance of information technology, very powerful corporate groupware which provided a document sharing platform. From Lotus Notes, IBM further developed the idea of groupware as in the following remarkable example reported by Kevin Mooney in April 1997 in *USA Today*:

> A group of computer programmers at Tsinghua University in Beijing is writing software using Java technology. They work for IBM. At the end of each day, they send their work over the Internet to an IBM facility in Seattle.

> There, programmers build on it and use the Internet to zap it 5,222 miles to the Institute of Computer Science in Belarus and Software House Group in Latvia. From there, the work is sent east to India's Tata Group, which passes the software back to Tsinghua by morning in Beijing, back to Seattle and so on in a great global relay that never ceases until the project is done.

'We call it Java Around the Clock,' says John Patrick, vice president of Internet technology for IBM. 'It's like we've created a forty-eight-hour day through the Internet.'

Critics of IBM's purchase in 1995 asserted that too much money had been paid for Lotus Notes. But by the summer of 1998, 3.4 million licenses had been sold, in comparison to 3.2 million for the software program of the company's major competitor, Microsoft. Lotus Notes gave the word collaboration new meaning in the Information Age. That's why IBM's advertising slogan really does convey a simple, but powerful message: "Solutions for a Small Planet."

For Hermès, the French luxury goods company, Lotus Notes offered an ideal solution for an old problem. Every day the company received requests for specific scarves, but not all designs were always available in all its stores. In the past, the inquiries were passed on by telephone or fax to the headquarters in Paris. Expensive and time-consuming long-distance phone calls were then made to shops around the world, to find the requested design. The introduction of Lotus Notes made possible automatic processing of the orders, so that they were communicated to all Hermès shops via the internal network. Elisabeth Burgess, my French administrative assistant, gave me this example and entitled it "Lotus Notes, or how to replace the Hermès scarf you just lost (a present from your mother-in-law and she wants you to wear it next Sunday)." For Hermès, she added, the Lotus Notes network really did create a small planet.

Another networking illustration comes from Great Britain. Llandough Hospital in West Cardiff was looking for an easy way to give administrators and doctors information about three very different departments in the hospital: pathology, radiology and patient administration. To use computer language, the data needed to be integrated. The hospital chose a network called Casablanca that provided what is called a single point of reference for all three departments. The goal was to improve patient service, provide better data access for doctors and nurses, maintain patient confidentiality, and free up more beds by quickly identifying patients ready for discharge from the hospital.

In ancient times, to use Gaku Sato's phrase, doctors had to call up the laboratory staff and talk with them, or call back later. Nurses and doctors wrote a lot of notes by hand. The pathologists either had to call in their results, fax them, or walk down the hall. The administrative staff couldn't coordinate the patient's release with the attending physician, if he could not be found. With Casablanca, information is found by accessing the system with a standard Web browser and filling in a request form. Data stored this way is consistent across all three disciplines.

Drawing, once again, on the parallel with the introduction of electricity, there are still those who argue that computers have not yet delivered a big payoff in productivity. Stephen Roach, chief economist at Morgan Stanley Dean Witter, concluded in November 1998 that, "The productivity gains of the Information Age are just a myth." In January 2000 he refined his view, but not much: "I don't think we've cracked the code yet.... I really believe that a year from now we'll be talking about slower productivity." The conclusion was especially ironic, since Morgan Stanley managed the initial public offering of Netscape. Whether we agree with Roach depends on how we define "big payoff." But rather than split semantic hairs, it is more useful to ask what has happened to the use of money, markets, and information since Ronald Reagan was elected president of the United States in 1980. What have computers done for the economy twenty years later? According to Scott Thurm in a January 2000 *Wall Street Journal* story:

> [They have caused] productivity of American workers to accelerate for the first time in a generation. Productivity, the key to a society's living standards, is defined as the hourly output of an average worker. Since 1996, productivity has grown an average of 2.6 percent a year. That is up sharply from the 1.4 percent average annual increase from 1974 to 1995. The recent uptick may not seem like much, but it would be enormously important over time: At 1.4 percent a year, living standards double in 50 years. At 2.6 percent a year they double in twenty-seven years.

More wealth has been created in the industrialized world during the last two decades than during any period in human history. Together Europe and the United States produced almost half of the world's gross domestic product in 1997 and accounted for almost 40 percent of the world's trade. In 1999 the combined exports of the European Union and the United States exceeded $1.8 trillion. Increased prosperity was found in the sheer magnitude of the industrial and capital base in Europe and the United States. The movement toward deregulation and privatization around the globe is an equally persuasive bellwether. The concurrent growth of stock markets throughout Asia, across Europe, and in the United States is another sign. Just look at the effect of the privatization of former state telephone monopolies in the European Union and how it is affecting prices. Efficiency has improved, costs have gone down, and 30 percent of the French population now uses mobile phones. The percentages for users in Scandinavia are even higher.

Any way we count it, the central role is being played by computers and information technology. How can we measure their productivity? With price/earnings ratios in the stock market? Well, that's one legitimate way, but it certainly isn't the only way. The traditional definitions no longer apply across the board. How do we measure the degree of productivity when two scientists who otherwise couldn't work together can discuss a physics problem on the World Wide Web? Or take Vipin Gupta. In the spring of 1998 he published an article on satellite imaging in a scholarly journal with a circulation of 2,000. He wanted comments from readers, but didn't expect many because the circulation was so small. Since he was curious, he created a Web site and posted the article there, as well. Four months later, his site had received more than 50,000 visits, and they were still coming.

What is the proper definition of productivity today? Is it how much we produce? What about time? How is the productivity of its use measured? Human beings began communicating with each other in the last decade of the twentieth century in ways never available before, and that human interaction, exchange, and communication are producing new ideas, new energy, and new products. Increased productivity is there. But we're still struggling with the question of how we measure it, in ways we all understand. Erik Brynjolfsson, an associate professor at the Sloan School of Management at MIT, frames the difficulty this way:

> [T]he economic value of speed, quality improvements, customer service and new products are often not captured by ... statistics.
>
> These are the competitive advantages of information technology.... We need a broader definition of output in this new economy which goes beyond the industrial-era concept of widgets coming off the assembly line.

According to the U.S. Commerce department's report in 1998 on the emerging digital economy, information technology is controlling inflation and transforming the invisible Internet into an electronic marketplace. As a result, according to Bruce Ingersoll writing for *The Wall Street Journal* in April 1998, "the high-technology industries of computers and telecommunications accounted for more than one-quarter of the U.S. economy's growth in the past five years." In mid-1999 Cisco Systems' executive vice president, Donald Listwin, said that productivity gains had only begun, and predicted that American companies would become true electronic businesses, and that productivity would see a ten-fold increase. He calculated that Cisco Systems saves $500 million per year in operating costs by using networked systems, and that estimated revenue per employee in 1998 was $700,000, in comparison to $250,000 for the average Internet company, and to $160,000 for the automotive industry.

If these examples are not signs of productivity, what are they? Electronic networks allow free markets to work faster and more efficiently, at lower cost and with greater productivity than any other method we have devised thus far. As far as salaries, stock options, and stock values are concerned, a new, young, and wealthy class of free market, information technology entrepreneur has been created. And for consumers today, more people throughout the world benefit from greater choice, better quality, and competitive prices, than at any time in the twentieth century. Karl Marx argued that free markets don't work this way. Lenin believed communism would do what free markets couldn't. Both of them had at least one thing in common: they were wrong.

3.

E-Business + E-Commerce = B2C

In 1999, worldwide B2B [business-to-business] e-commerce reached $145 billion, and the North America region accounted for 63 percent of the market with revenue reaching $91 billion. In 2004, worldwide B2B e-commerce is projected to surpass $7.29 trillion; the North America region will account for 39 percent of the market with revenue of more than $2.84 trillion.

The strongest regional growth in the B2B market can be found in Europe. B2B revenue in Europe in 1999 totaled $31.8 billion. In 2004, the European B2B market will be more than $2.34 trillion.

{Gartner Interactive, February 2000}

Christmastime on the rue Royale in Paris — it was December 4, 1999. I was looking at a figure of Santa Claus perched above the window of Christofle. Red-and-green ribboned packages were poking out of his sack. E-commerce, thank goodness, wasn't crossing his mind; but it was mine. I wondered what would happen to that merry figure whose spirit touched me so closely as I regarded him from the sidewalk. Would the inexorable steps leading us to electronic holiday cheer make his magic vanish, as buying on-line replaced my childhood world of Lionel trains going round and round in Macy's store window in San Francisco?

Or was I being too sentimental for my own good? I don't think so. The image on that Paris evening is very much alive in my mind. I can't get it out of my head, as I read the statistical figures of the revolution in on-line buying during the last Christmas of the twentieth century. The results also tell me that the old-fashioned shopping landscape is going to change drastically. I'm not at all sure I like it, and neither was columnist Ellen Goodman when she went e-shopping for Christmas presents for the first time in 1998:

> It is 3:30 P.M. and I have gone shopping. Actually, I have not 'gone' anywhere. I am sitting at my desk.... While waiting for a call back from a source in California, I send a calendar to a niece in France. Click. While on hold for an editor in Washington, I buy a sweater for a son-in-law in Manhattan. Click. While waiting for a ride home, an amaryllis wings its way back to Boston. Click. Click.
>
> ... According to the myriad articles, cover stories and TV features about the wonders of shopless shopping, I have been 'giddily' buying Christmas presents while the poor troglodytes circle the mall for a parking place and try to wrestle down a surly salesclerk.
>
> Why is it that I do not feel giddy? I feel efficient. I feel relieved. I feel rather as if the holidays were another errand that I ran. Which is decidedly unmerry.
>
> I hate to sound like a retro e-crank in an era when Martha Stewart is selling snowflake kits on-line. But after my first e-mas, it seems there is a downside to any marketplace that comes without either a market or a place.
>
> For openers, it feeds into the mass delusion that it is possible, with just a bit more organization and a few more megabytes, to lead a real life without ever leaving the office.... Consider the testimony of the shopping-dot-com crowd. Most of us brag about the time we save. But many also boast that they no longer have to deal with those hassles known as ... people!

My sympathies lie with Ellen Goodman, but logic tells me there's no going back, either. E-commerce may be anonymous buying and selling, but it's really just another developing use of the Internet. Between Thanksgiving and Christmas in 1999, an estimated twenty-seven million Americans shopped on-line, generating sales of between $5 billion and $9 billion, depending on which estimate you choose. On-line orders increased by more than 400 percent over 1998. The biggest winners were Amazon.com with 5.69 million visitors (an increase of 81 percent over 1998) and the auction site eBay.com, with 4.07 million (an increase of 76 percent). While on-line sales paled into insignificance in comparison to the $750 billion spent by real-world holiday shoppers, the conclusion was clear: in 1999 "dot-com" had entered the consumer lexicon.

Yes, there were glitches and Web site crashes, and not all the gifts arrived in time for Christmas. But most did, and credit card numbers weren't stolen. If there was a key to success, it was that "e-tailers" (retailers) like Amazon had learned how to manage their warehouse inventories efficiently, as they filled orders and packed and shipped them, using their internal computer networks. There was also another key: more and more Americans were using the Internet. The growth in Christmas sales in just two years spoke for itself.

On-line spending during the 1997 Christmas season was a little over $1 billion, and predictions for the Christmas shopping season in 1998 were more than double that. As it turned out, the dollar value of on-line purchases up to December 25, 1998, more than tripled over the previous year.

The message had already been made clear shortly before Christmas 1998, and it wasn't limited to holiday buying. The tremendous growth of e-commerce, according to the Boston Consulting Group, represented a quick convergence of the virtual and real worlds. The group concluded that retailers who have both on-line and bricks-and-mortar distribution outlets perform best. During 1998 more than eighteen million people in the United States purchased goods and services on the Web; that number was predicted to be fifty million by the end of 2000. The conclusion, according to James McQuivery, an analyst at Forrester Research Inc. in Cambridge, Massachusetts, was that e-commerce was soaring, and he estimated that forty million U.S. households would be shopping on the Internet by the year 2003, spending more than $100 billion, accounting for 6 percent of consumer retail spending. In the same year, in McQuivery's view, worldwide sales from e-commerce would go as high as $3.2 trillion.

As in any dynamic and growing market, however, such figures change rapidly. So, by March 1999, sales from e-commerce in the U.S. were predicted to be $133 billion in 2000, and to reach $202 billion in 2001, according to estimates made by Zona Research of Redwood City, California. While e-commerce figures for Europe were not nearly as high, the potential for growth was similar. In 1998, e-commerce amounted to $1.2 billion, while the retail sales industry generated $1.9 trillion in spending. For the year 2000 e-commerce sales were predicted to reach $7.4 billion, and to exceed $53 billion by 2003.

It needs to be kept in mind that firms like Forrester Research, Jupiter, Zona Research, the Gartner Group, and eMarketer are in business to sell their product — namely statistical information about the Internet. On the one hand, they are likely to be optimistic in their estimates, since optimism increases the value of their product to firms doing business on-line. On the other hand, credibility is one of their most important assets. Thus, while the estimates jump around a great deal from month to month, they nonetheless reflect what is a new economy. Indeed, the Gartner Group, so reported a major German newspaper in March 1999, predicted that by 2001, without adopting e-commerce, up to 70 percent of businesses could lose their ability to compete effectively. Nor is it surprising that the U.S. Department of Commerce considered the numbers important enough to announce that it will now publish separately statistics showing the impact of Internet commerce on retail activity instead of ganging estimated on-line sales with catalog sales in its overall numbers. And here both business and government agreed on one thing: that e-commerce goes beyond buying books or downloading software. It is about all aspects of business-to-business transactions, government services, financial services, advertising, and more.

Whether we refer to it as e-business or e-commerce, it is changing both markets and their places, and that also means the curricula of business schools. In 1998 IBM created an Institute for Advanced Commerce to encourage academic research into the phenomenon. The next year it concluded an agreement with a French business school in Grenoble to develop jointly a master's degree in e-commerce, and was discussing development of similar programs at French universities in Lille, Nice, Rennes, Toulouse, and Lyon. E-commerce management was also being taught at France's famous INSEAD business school in Fontainebleau, and at the London Business School. Similar courses were being introduced at universities in the United States such as MIT and Harvard, which announced in February 1999 that it was researching Silicon Valley businesses for material to teach in classes about Internet start-up companies. Indeed, at Harvard 11 percent of its business school's 1998 graduates went to Internet companies, overtaking for the first time those going into investment banking. Stanford University's School of Business followed suit in the autumn of 1999, with a $25 million fund-raising drive to develop a new Center for the Study of Electronic Commerce. The e-commerce programs at Stanford and MIT have been given five-year life spans, on the assumption that e-commerce will soon be so integrated into the general curriculum it won't need to be ghettoized.

At the end of December 1998, pessimists lamented that Internet sales for the year amounted to less than 1 percent of total domestic sales in the United States, and they complained also that during the next five years Web spending would increase to "just" 6 percent of retail sales. But, of course, the significance of statistics depends on how they are interpreted. So if we have no confidence in the potential of e-commerce, it would be wise to sell our stock in AOL, Amazon, and Yahoo!. But if we believe Bill Gates, CEO of Microsoft Corporation, "we are just at the beginning of the Information Age."

If the statistics we read on-line and in the newspapers are even close to being cor-

E-Business + E-Commerce = B2C

rect, e-commerce is on the threshold of an explosion. If nothing will be left unaffected, what is the potential? It is clearly seen in what the successful companies produce. Microsoft makes the operating system used on 85 to 90 percent of computers around the globe. That's why the company had one of the two largest stock market capitalizations in the world in March 2000, before the stock market went into its "dot-com" decline. Cisco Systems has the largest capitalization. When the company announced a 53 percent increase in sales, to a staggering $4.35 billion for the second quarter (it ended January 31, 2000), and a two-for-one stock split as well, its stock price went where you would expect, namely, up. In fact Cisco overtook Microsoft as the world's most valuable company on March 24, 2000, with a market capitalization of $579 billion, ahead of Microsoft by one billion dollars.

What Cisco Systems makes and how it sells its products address head-on the question of potential. It is the leading producer of the routing and switching hardware that allows the Internet to connect. Almost half of the company's revenue comes from sales to large corporate networks, and new growth is coming from smaller businesses adding internal networks and Internet connections and from telecommunications service providers that are competing to offer combined voice and data lines. "Potential" is also addressed by how Cisco sells what it produces. The company explained it like this in its 1998 annual report:

> Internet Commerce is one of the most visible business solutions of the Internet Economy. Early in 1997, customers first began placing orders on the Cisco Web site and checking order status. Since then, Cisco has created a comprehensive suite of tools to enable its customers to configure, price, route, and submit orders electronically over its Web site. With network commerce sales of more than $5 billion last year, Cisco has quickly emerged as a leading electronic merchant.

> ... Freed from urgent inquiries and routine orders, Cisco's sales organization can now focus on building stronger customer relationships and providing better service. Productivity for account executives and sales engineers has increased approximately 15 percent as a direct result of Internet Commerce. It is anticipated that orders received over the Web will constitute more than 80 percent of revenue by the end of fiscal year 1999.

[Author's Note: By May 1999, 76 percent of Cisco's orders were Internet-based, and 81 percent of customer support was transacted over the Internet.]

Cisco's example gives the phrase "new economy" real meaning, and so does the continuing history of Intel's way of doing business. In 1996 most orders with Intel were placed via telephone or fax, but the following year, with no example to follow, Intel took a new path and began shifting its business to the Web. The company learned a number of things, including that it needed more powerful network connections and that many of its departments were using incompatible electronic-data-interchange software. It also lacked a security system for its worldwide Internet sales, and then discovered, to its shock, that the U.S. government prohibited the exportation of sophisticated encryption technology. Without networks that worked together and that were safe, there was no future in e-commerce. So Intel changed. By the end of 1998, 20 percent of its $26.3 billion sales volume came from the Web. By the end of 1999 half of Intel's revenue came from e-commerce.

It doesn't take a great deal of imagination, following these illustrations, to recognize that the revolution in communication technology transforms the way business provides value to customers.

The "value-added" bombshell arrived in January 2000. In the biggest deal in the history of American business the largest Internet access provider, AOL, and the world's largest media company, Time Warner, agreed to a merger worth $156 billion. In acquiring Time Warner, AOL had found what it was missing — access to high-speed cable lines — and a partner was found to help Time Warner deal with the negative consequences of all its movie, magazine, and TV business being turned upside down by the Internet. The merger created what Thomas W. Weber, Martin Peers, and Nick Wingfield called in *The Wall Street Journal*:

> … a new world in which recorded music is piped over the Internet rather than sold on CDs, television game shows let you play along, too, phone calls are beamed over cable-television lines, and marketing blitzes span the worlds of print, television and the Web….
> [The new company's] formidable assets will include twenty-two million AOL subscribers, 130 million readers of Time Warner publications, thirty million subscribers to the HBO cable channel, and a news colossus, CNN, that claims a global reach of more than 1 billion.

It was a huge instance of dismantling the wall between old and new media. Equally interesting, a company founded just fifteen years before, in 1985, and referred to as late as 1996 as "the Internet on training wheels" had used its financial power to buy what had been a giant, before the arrival of the Internet. It was the successful courtship of the old guard by the on-line generation.

What had happened? The communicative force of the Internet and the economic potential of e-commerce were self-evident. Some people called it "the death of old media." Others said the deal would remake "the advertising, marketing and media landscapes." Still others saw in the merger "'the beginning of a huge change in the paradigm of how media are consumed, planned and bought.'" Any way it was taken, it meant that AOL Time Warner would now have a presence on the Web equivalent in potency to Microsoft's platform on the desktop.

And when the dust settles, wrote Michael J. Wolf in *The Wall Street Journal,* the merger would be "far from the last salvo in the broadband war." Everything would be affected, in Wolf's view:

> There are broadcast networks, publishing empires, Internet portals, Internet service providers, cable systems operators, cellular companies, satellite owners, regional Bell operating companies, and music labels all up for grabs. The battle won't be contained; this conflict will also involve auto companies, banks, retailers, brokerage firms, consumer products markets, and sports leagues.... [T]he clear winner will be consumers....

One question asked in the aftermath was, which consumers? Just those in the United States? Or in Europe also, where politicians with their heads in the sand love to regulate business? The immediate conclusion was pessimistic: in Europe, the Internet fragments along national boundaries. This is due to two facts: (1) telephone companies in Europe are the biggest Internet service providers in each country, but almost none of them provide their fixed-line services across national borders, and (2) consumers, therefore, don't get the advantages of competition and economies of scale (although in 2000 the convergence of mobile communication with Internet access is beginning to change all this).

The pessimists, however, received their comeuppance at the beginning of February when an even larger merger in the ongoing telecommunication revolution occurred. In a deal worth an estimated $181 billion, the world's fourth highest valued company (at that time) was created with the takeover of Germany's Mannesmann AG by Britain's Vodafone AirTouch PLC — a fusion, so editorialized *The Wall Street Journal*, "likely to shake Europe's old telecom monopolies to their fossilized cores.... [I]n the future no corporate executive in Europe is going to be able to reject the new shareholder-first model that Mr. Esser [Mannesmann's CEO] put ahead of the old system in which politicians picked economic winners and called it a social consensus." And what would this merger mean? Greater efficiency and lower prices. Combined, the company was the largest wireless telephone provider in Europe. As a part of the deal Vodafone sold U.K. mobile-phone operator Orange to France Telecom in May for almost $38 billion, thereby creating Europe's second-largest wireless company.

There is more to electronic economic opportunities than just mergers, however. There are other, broader Internet consequences as well, for businesses large and small, both wired and wireless. Wells Fargo Bank's on-line customer base grew from 20,000 in 1994 to more than 650,000 in 1998, for instance: "While far outnumbered by ... ten million regular banking customers, on-line customers are less expensive to service, do more business, and stay with the bank longer."

The world of banking is just beginning to see the extent of change. Some agencies of the U.S. government have already stopped issuing salary checks, and make direct electronic deposits instead. Treasury bills are already a virtual security; they don't exist in paper form. Smart cards will act as ID cards, debit and deposit cards, and as credit cards. Mortgage banking will take place online. In short, full financial services will be offered on the Internet. And it all has to do with information, as described by the executive vice president of Merita-Nordbanken in Helsinki, the world's largest on-line bank with 1.2 million customers, in a 1999 *International Herald Tribune* interview:

> If you think about the Internet ... you could say it is primarily a very useful way to get information. But when you talk about transactions, banking is the killer application. Because banking is information ... Money is not a physical thing ... It is the numbers on a statement. When you transfer financial payments, you are only shifting information.

The communication revolution is affecting the marketplaces of trade, publishing, advertising, merchandising, rare book dealers, cosmetics, train tickets, flowers, shipping, clothing, insurance, auctions, education, candy, postal services, groceries, stocks and bonds, fine chocolates, marketing, finance, manufacturing, and pharmaceuticals. In short, anything can be bought or sold over the Internet. Bookstores will sell digital books as well as printed books. Postal service "snail mail" will use electronic stamps. Music stores will play CDs on Web sites without a phonograph. In short, the Web gives retailers an entirely new way to sell their products. We call it e-commerce; but basically it's a twenty-four-hour shopping service, seven days a week, with no permanent address. You can't find its office on Park Avenue, New York City, or on the Champs Elysées in Paris. And it makes no difference where you live, what time zone you live in, or what time you buy or sell. Virtual stores never close.

What are some examples of available goods and services on the Web? Making hotel, airline, train, and cruise reservations is one — on-line sales for the global travel industry are predicted to hit $23 billion by 2003. But the entire gamut runs from downloading computer software to starting on-line magazine subscriptions to ordering flowers for Valentine's Day to a wedding registry at Williams-Sonoma to buying and selling old etchings and engravings to ordering Vienna's famous Sacher Torte. You can order specialty foods and wines and purchase recipes from New York City's famous market Dean & DeLuca. A scholar in California can order a book from Basil Blackwell in Oxford, England, via e-mail, or subscribe to the English horticultural magazine *Hortus*, at www.hortus.co.uk. (I found it by accident on the Web in March of 1998 and, electronically, ordered a subscription for my wife's birthday.)

And what about the delivery of all these goods? E-commerce is a boon for firms like Federal Express, DHL, or UPS. Packages have to be delivered, and it's big business. In 1998 UPS moved more than three billion parcels and documents in more than 200 countries, and shipped 55 percent of goods purchased on the Internet. Once Federal Express had the lion's share of the market in the overnight delivery of documents — photographs, letters, contracts, financial statements. Today it is collaborating with UPS. Both companies are integrating their services with e-commerce Web sites, such as book and music stores, so that with just the click of a mouse you can instruct www.amazon.com how to ship your books as you complete your order. What this meant in real numbers was announced by FDX Corporation (the parent company of Federal Express) in March 1999. For the quarter ending on February 28, net income reached $78 million, in comparison to $18 million one year earlier. Indeed, FedEx now uses networking systems to track and coordinate package shipments. And UPS was not to be left out of the financial boom experienced by Silicon Valley start-ups either. In November 1999 its first public stock offering was the largest in American history.

It's hard to miss the handwriting on the wall. But the next example makes the message indelible. The world's largest catalog retailer of outdoor specialty goods is L.L. Bean, headquartered in Freeport, Maine. Reading into the future, the company opened its own Web site, www.llbean.com, in 1997. "We are," Bean spokeswoman Catharine Hartnett points out, "reaching new customers who have never purchased from us before who have discovered us on the Internet." And you can go to sites for a myriad of other once traditional retailers, such as Lands' End, The Gap, J. Crew, Eddie Bauer, or Macy's. By mid-2000 you couldn't yet find company Web sites for Baccarat crystal or Burberry's famous coats, but you could order silver sterling candelabra or Limoges china from the sites of Christofle (founded in 1830) and Tiffany (founded in 1837). And, I suspect, by the time this book is published Hermès will have a Web site too.

An antique buyer in Chicago using the World Wide Web can make a bid at an auction held in Vienna's venerable Dorotheum (founded in 1707), www.dorotheum.com, or buy at the famous Louvre des Antiquaires in Paris, at www.louvre-antiquaires.com. Then there is www.priceline.com, known as a "demand collection system," where customers name the price they want to pay for a home mortgage, for example, or for a hotel room, or an airline ticket. During one week in mid-March 2000 more than 30,000 people bought airlines tickets alone. And there is www.ebay.com which was founded in 1995. The company proved so successful that by the end of 1999 it was able to purchase San Francisco's oldest auction house, Butterfield & Butterfield, founded in 1865. Traditional auctions are expensive to hold and reach a limited audience, but by April 2000 eBay was offering 400,000 new items each day in more than 2,900 auction categories.

Estimates in the spring of 1999 projected that on-line auctions will grow to $19 billion annually by 2003, an increase from $1.4 billion for 1998. If these numbers have any significance it was confirmed in early 1999 by the announcement of one of the world's most venerable auction houses, Sotheby's Holdings, founded in 1744. The firm planned to invest $25 million in creating a Web site that would auction, as one of its first on-line offerings, baseball memorabilia; look for it at www.sotheby.com.

What about books? In the United States, when we hear the name Amazon we no longer think of a river. The company — at www.amazon.com — "opened its doors" in July 1995. By September 1998, it had more than 4.5 million customers, an increase of 377 percent from 940,000 on the same date in 1997 — and more than seventeen million by the beginning of 2000 (6.2 million in 1998). The founder and CEO, Jeff Bezos, thirty-six years old in 2000, observes, "We are changing the way people buy books," and he's right. But the company's offerings are not limited to books; it also sells music, videos, toys, software, electronic equipment, and tools, and is in the auction marketplace in partnership with Sotheby's.

Amazon, which Bezos originally wanted to call Abracadabra, is headquartered in Seattle, Washington — in an Art Deco building across the street from a pawn shop, the local needle exchange, and a wig store. It is a publicly traded company of over 5,000 employees, seven distribution centers in seven different states, with customers in all fifty states of the USA and in more than 160 countries. Its founder had become so well known by December 1999 that he was named *Time* magazine's "Person of the Year." Net sales for 1999 were $1.64 billion ($610 million in 1998). But the company had a net loss of $390 million ($74 million in 1998), while its book division became profitable in the fourth quarter of 1999. It was these latter issues — loss and profit — that raised two key questions. How much longer could Amazon continue to lose money before it achieved a large enough customer base to generate sustained profit? And what would be the necessary critical mass — twenty-five million, thirty-five million, forty-five million customers — with 66 percent of its sales going to repeat customers? By summer of 2000, the answers are still not known, but suffice it to say that in 1999 Amazon raised $1.25 billion in the United States alone from the sale of convertible bond issues, and in 2000 planned to raise 600 million Euros in convertible notes to expand its operations in Europe.

Why do I buy books on-line? Because I don't have to drive to the bookstore, I save time, and I normally get a discount from 2 to 30 percent. Don't get me wrong; I love bookstores and I like people, too. But sometimes it's a lot more convenient to buy on the Web from my study at home or from my office. The effect of all this on the book trade is that the classic "bookstore on main street" that I grew up with is already disappearing.

Attempts by traditional retailers to control the effects of e-commerce have been futile. The Saint Louis Galleria in Richmond Heights, Missouri, in a letter to its 170 shops just before the Christmas shopping season in late November 1999, barred all of them from promoting e-commerce. But businesses like The Sharper Image, Eddie Bauer and FAO Schwarz ignored the policy. From the Galleria's viewpoint, e-commerce bit into the mall's profits, since normally a shopping mall gets a percentage of sales from its tenants. For the shops themselves, however, e-commerce brought customers into the stores since Internet shoppers at, for example, Eddie Bauer's Web site — www.eddiebauer.com — are permitted to make merchandise exchanges at the store itself. The Galleria's policy was compared by one New Jersey retailing consultant to the Luddite practice early in the Industrial Revolution of jamming machines with wooden shoes to shut them down. If shopping malls don't all fall victim to e-commerce, certainly the middlemen in all kinds of businesses will. Economists call it disintermediation.

"Cybershopping" will continue to change, and competition will make it more convenient and more profitable for the shopper. The chairman of a New York investment firm, Fred Alger Management, describes the effects of e-commerce this way:

I am often asked: How many of these Internet companies will survive? What we should ask is: How many small retailers, distributors, service providers, travel agents, insurance companies and conventional brokerage firms are going to find themselves Amazoned ... over the next five years? As Internet companies replace other goods and service providers, the result will be tremendous savings to consumers.

And if there is a consequence, it is this:

If buyers become hooked on cyberspace bargaining, the implications for the retail economy could be as wide-reaching as the introduction of fixed pricing enabled by standardized production a century ago.

The latter conclusion was also on Bill Gates's mind when he attended a conference in Paris in September 1998: "There is a need to reach out here in Europe to the companies and to the professionals and get the message out about what's possible." By the spring of 2000, 80 million of 300 million Internet users worldwide were in Europe. On-line retail grew by 200 percent during 1999 on the Continent. While only 18 to 20 percent of European homes had Internet access, and only 10 percent had bought goods and services on-line, the statistics were changing weekly. In France the number of Internet subscribers doubled during 1999, and reached more than nine million by spring 2000 in a population numbering 60-plus million, up from 540,000 in January 1998.

The president of France, who didn't know what a mouse was on Bastille Day of 1997, had learned in the meantime when he visited an incubator in the rue du Faubourg du Temple in Paris in early March 2000. It was called Republic Alley, where seventeen Internet firms worked in glass-enclosed rooms in a nineteenth century building that catered to a machine-tool assembly line during the Industrial Revolution. Internet excitement in Paris was also seen in the crowds of more than 1,500 coming to the monthly "First Tuesday," a cocktail and seminar party started in September 1999; there, young entrepreneurs mingle, look for contacts, and seek partners, and if they're lucky meet the investor who may offer the "big break." In the early spring of 2000 the crowd astounded French woman Flore Vasseur, the founder of a strategic marketing firm in New York called TrendSpotting. "A year ago," she said, "who could have imagined this craze here?"

I wasn't sure "craze" was the right word so, unannounced, I visited Republic Alley myself in June. It was about 6 P.M. on a Wednesday afternoon and at first I couldn't find the incubator, since the building houses not only Internet startups but

170

also a textile workshop, a restaurant, a nightclub, a dance studio, and a movie theater.

The first people I found were Anne-Laurence Portes and Samuel Katan, who were part of a group of ten between the ages of twenty-one and twenty-eight. Their company, called Chewing Com (www.chewing-com.com), designs interactive, animated Web sites using a flash technology called Shockwave. I told them I had heard about Republic Alley and wanted to see it for myself, since I was writing a book about the Internet. The only way I can properly describe them is to say that their enthusiasm was absolutely delightful, and profitable. "We're making money," they told me, "not just spending it." They added with big smiles that they had won first prize for their designs in an international competition of 250 projects held in Vienna at the end of 1999.

As I left them I met another young man, just thirty years old, named Laurent Edel, who, it turned out, was the founder of Republic Alley. He wanted to know why I was there, and after I explained he told me Republic Alley was receiving between thirty and forty business plans a week, and that he and his two cofounders were opening new incubators in other cities in France. This was much more than just a craze, and it gave real meaning to French economist Alain Minc's conclusion that, "Ten years ago, only one out of 200 graduates of elite universities ... wanted to be an entrepreneur. Today, it's more than half. That's a major generational shift."

4.

THE MESSAGE AND THE MARKET

The Internet spans more than 200 countries,
and has more than 151 million users.
{December 1998}

The Internet has 163 million users.
{May 1999}

The Internet has 300 million users.
{March 2000}

By 2003, only one-third
of an estimated 500 million Web users will be U.S.-based, and by 2004,
the majority of users will be people who are not yet using the Internet today.

{International Herald Tribune, May 17, 1999}

What are all these percentages and statistics? Just figures of degree? Is what Steve Case of AOL calls "the Internet century" just self-indulgent hype? Some point out that e-commerce is right for some transactions, but not for everything; to wit, people who buy pants from Levi Strauss first may want to try them on. And others conclude, logically, that the Internet as yet is not in the same league with developments such as moveable type, electricity, the automobile, the railroad, and the airplane. It will have to aspire to being more than just a device for e-mail and advertising; it will have to be economically viable. That is, e-commerce will have to move beyond today's relatively small Internet sales and deeply discounted prices.

172

E-commerce, for the moment, may be puny. But retail selling and buying is only the tip of the iceberg. What's underneath is where value is being added in business-to-business. We read a lot about the potential for the Internet to change the way people work and live, but just buying books and music on-line isn't going to do it. That's why the nebulous phrase "Internet economy" should be broken down into three parts: Internet commerce (now clearly evident in on-line buying and selling), Internet information technology structure (for example, electronic networks and wireless connections using mobile phones), and Internet business structure (for example, what's taking place at GE, Cisco Systems, IBM, and Intel).

We read and hear about the first part everywhere. But it is the second and third parts that are beginning to dwarf the first in importance — as management, inventory and customer networks, and linkages among payroll, marketing, demand, sales, logistics, and supply-chain functions, all operating effectively in real time, save millions of dollars in costs for the producer, the distributor, and the consumer. The electronics of the Internet via cable, satellite, and broadband communication — voice, data, and video, using television, telephone, and hand-held devices such as mobile phones, pagers and palm-sized organizers — will become the means to operate and conduct businesses that make a profit.

The formula for the future is E-Business + E-Commerce = Business-to-Commerce. The whole is B2C. It is e-business that is making use of interactive networks and multimedia services, both wired and mobile, within and among companies, and with suppliers, shippers, and sellers. This is why so much money is being spent on Internet infrastructure and services. For example, in mid-1999 IBM designed a $500 million marketing campaign focused on e-business (the global technology-services market, of which IBM had a little more than 8 percent, was $361 billion). Examples abound, although they don't receive the kind of publicity that Amazon.com does when its stock goes up or down, and the following provide just a flavor.

IBM helps manage on-line broker Charles Schwab's Web systems, and provides services "24/7" (twenty-four hours a day, seven days a week). Wal-Mart Stores Inc. uses an on-line system developed by NCR Corp. called Retail Link that gives suppliers access to sales, inventory, and shipping data. Wal-Mart's "data warehouse" receives detailed information on each item sold in each store. During peak periods more than 8.4 million updates occur every minute. That means more than 7,000 suppliers can access the warehouse and get real-time information on what is selling in each of more than 2,800 locations. ExxonMobil Corp. uses the Internet to provide used-oil analysis information to ship managers; they, in turn, can make their fleet maintenance programs more cost-effective and efficient. Lufthansa has created a travel portal on the Web where flyers (even non-Lufthansa customers) can make reservations with about

Marketplaces and the Information Age

700 airlines, book rooms from a list of several thousand hotels, or bid on surplus tickets in a monthly auction. Still another example is the replacement of paper tickets with e-tickets in the airline industry, where the processing cost has dropped from $8 to $1.

The message on the horizon is that "the time for talking about the Internet economy is over." This conclusion was drawn by Andy Grove, Intel's president, speaking to a German audience in the autumn of 1999:

> In some period of time, let's say five years, there won't be any Internet companies. There will be companies that use the Internet; all companies that will operate will use the Internet in their business operations, or they will be marginalized out of operations.

Whatever I have learned about the revolution in information technology leads me to the inescapable conclusion that Andy Grove is right. But for me and, I think, for many of my friends in the United States, Internet marketplaces and communication still mean, for the moment, e-commerce. This doesn't apply to most of my friends in Europe, because few of them are buying books and music on-line. They listen to my description of the Internet but ignore the possibilities. In Paris, for example, my friend Bertrand asked me in November 1999 if I would develop a collection of CDs for him of the music of George Gershwin, Cole Porter, and Jerome Kern. I told him he could do it himself on the Internet, but he said he preferred to... and mumbled something I couldn't understand. Since his good friend Marina Eloy let me use her apartment in Paris in December, January, and March, I returned the favor by building a collection using Amazon.com. As I write this, in April 2000, I have brought him three dozen CDs — a respectable beginning — and I did so without ever leaving my study.

Like a snowball going downhill, e-commerce is gathering momentum fast. Revenue generated by the Internet in the United States in 1995 amounted to approximately $5 billion. By the end of 1998 it had increased to $301 billion, and according to officials in Washington, D.C., technology companies had accounted for a third of the nation's annual economic growth.

That performance in 1998 was recorded when the Internet was not yet popular in Europe. The Europeans were not "opting out of the Information Age," as some have implied. Nor were they twentieth-century Luddites concerned with rejecting American technological imperialism. But they did have a formidable set of problems to deal with, and some of these still exist. The value-added tax (VAT) added 20.6 percent to the price of a computer in France and 16 percent in Germany. There was an estimated 25 percent less disposable income for the average European after taxes, because of the enormous costs of the continent's welfare states.

And, the Europeans used their computers differently. Sharon Reier summed it up in a March 1998 *International Herald Tribune* article:

> [T]he typical German consumer uses his home computer as much as 90 percent of the time for games, whereas his American counterpart uses his to find stock quotes, communicate with friends and business connections through e-mail and to search the Internet.

Americans used their laptops and networks to communicate; Europeans didn't. While almost 100 percent of all computers sold to Americans had modems (the device that uses a telephone line to connect you to another computer), less than 50 percent in Europe had them. While more and more Europeans had an e-mail address printed on their business cards, they didn't read their e-mail on a regular basis. In fact, by the end of 1999 I was so frustrated with Bertrand that I stopped sending him e-mail because I never knew when he was going to read it. I had no choice but to call him on the telephone or to send him a fax. But Marina was connected. On February 16, 2000, I sent her an e-mail, and wrote, "I hope this reaches you before you leave; but, if not, it will still be there when you return — one of the beauties of e-mail!" And she answered the next day: "I got your mail before our departure. It is so convenient this e-mail. I am becoming an addict. When I ask people in Paris their e-mail address (people my age), they look at me as if I was totally spaced out. Although the country is changing a lot in this field, they better get going before the train has left!"

Marina is right on both counts; namely, that her friends had better get moving, and that a lot has changed. The deregulation of Europe's major telephone monopolies on January 1, 1998, fourteen years after AT&T was broken up by court order in the United States, rewrote the rules. Usage has risen and the cost of telephone calls has dropped. This process began in Germany in March 1998, when price reductions of 30 percent were announced by the country's second-largest telecom operator, Mannesmann Arcor. New products and services followed. For example, business clients now may subscribe to "universal number" service which automatically locates a customer on his cell phone, at home, or at the office.

With competition in the field for the first time, new companies also began forming partnerships with each other across Europe. In Germany, American Express Corporation formed a partnership with O.tel.o communications GmbH to allow it to offer calling-card services to all American Express cardholders. By 2005 O.tel.o. planned to have $3.83 billion invested in building its network. Another telephone company which began to compete with Deutsche Telekom AG in 1998 was Viag Interkom.GmbH, in which British Telecommunications PLC had a 45 percent stake and Telenor AS of Norway owned 10 percent.

Until December 31, 1997, Deutsche Telekom had ruled the German Internet-access market with T-On-line. But when privatization opened up competition in 1998, the initial beneficiary was AOL, which understood the operation of free markets much better that those managers running T-On-line's former monopoly. AOL could offer better Web-page design and more efficient browsing than T-On-line was capable of producing.

T-On-line, however, quickly adjusted. In early 1998 AOL had about 500,000 European subscribers compared to two million for T-On-line. By March 2000 AOL had over one million, but T-On-line had grown to 4.2 million. It wasn't surprising that AOL's growth in Europe did not match its growth in the United States (in April 2000 AOL had twenty-two million subscribers). Deregulation of Europe's telephone monopolies unleashed European entrepreneurial initiative, imagination, and creativity. Because Europeans understood their markets Internet access charges were lowered substantially during 1998; in some cases in the spring of 2000, there were none at all.

Sparked by privatization of the continent's national telephone monopolies, growth was fueled by growing recognition in business circles — not in political circles — that e-business + e-commerce would increase the intensity of communications, generate new revenues, produce new computer hardware and software, and result in new services.

In 1999 France's Cegetel planned on investing $800 million, with the expectation of eventually capturing $8 billion in French business, 40 percent of the cellular phone market, 20 percent of the long-distance market, and 10 percent of the local residential market. In early 2000 another step was taken as Deutsche Telekom's T-On-line expanded outside Germany, when it announced plans to buy a French Internet access service, Club Internet (with about 320,000 subscribers). Owned by the French company Lagardère SCA, Deutsche Telekom would acquire 99.9 percent of the service while Lagardère would take a 6.5 percent ownership in T-On-line.

In early March 2000 the French communication group Bouygues approved a capital investment of 1.5 million Euros to finance further Internet and telecommunication development. And in the same month France Telecom announced plans to purchase a 28.5 percent stake, for 3.74 billion Euros, in Germany's Mobil-Com AG, which has 1.9 million mobile phone customers (8 percent of the market) and 603,000 fixed-line subscribers (9 percent of the market). France Telecom, which had thirty-three million fixed-line subscribers and more than ten million mobile customers in France at the beginning of 2000, would thus become a major player.

The course of the communication revolution in France is a fascinating study in contradiction, because the policies of its statist institutions stand in such contrast to the entrepreneurial creativity of the French themselves. In 1997 three events took place which would have been inconceivable just a few years earlier. The first occurred in August when France's new socialist prime minister, Lionel Jospin, announced the government's decision to wire the country with a commitment of more than one billion French francs. He warned that France's technology gap might have negative repercussions on competitiveness and employment if not remedied. The second was the privatization of France Telecom, which meant the death of the French government's telephone monopoly. By 2000 privatization had only been partially completed, but the decision to denationalize the company was a complete reversal of policy (the French government still owns 62 percent of the stock). The third, and a direct consequence of the second, was new and stiff competition in France's telecommunications industry.

To have concluded in 1990 that shares of France Telecom would be publicly traded on the French stock exchange eight years later would have been unthinkable. But in 1997 the slogan of the first corporate TV advertising campaign in the company's history was, "We are going to make you like the year 2000." The company, once privately managed, was in a good position to make good on that claim. Indeed, in March 2000, if you had invested 10,000 FF in France Telecom stock when it first was publicly traded, your stock was worth about 65,000 FF. Moreover, the market value of France Telecom, in March, was about twice as much as the entire value of the French stock market in 1980.

True Gallic meaning, however, was given the word "irony" by what the market had done to the value of France Telecom stock held by the French government. In 1997 a major political crisis had developed when then prime minister Alain Juppé, announced a tax increase of 150 billion francs. So President Jacques Chirac called a special election, and Jospin won. Despite the fact that French Socialists opposed privatization as a matter of principle, the denationalization of France Telecom went forward as planned and the new government became the largest shareholder. Thus, political pundits were ecstatic on March 2, 2000, when the price of France Telecom stock increased by 25.5 percent in one day on the Paris Bourse after the company announced it would eventually list its Internet business as a separate company. The increase in value of the stock held by the socialist government alone was 200 billion francs, bringing the value of the total holding to more than 800 billion. Elisabeth Burgess, my French administrative assistant, put a note on my desk which read "Internet au secours de l'État?" ("The Internet to the rescue of the state?").

France still has a long way to go; what is important is not the distance but whether the country is moving forward or backward. It has been hamstrung by its stubborn resistance to transform the Minitel telephone information system into an Internet system — in the 1980s, a marvel of French technology and a pre-Internet relic today. The reason for obstinacy was classically simple. Minitel, owned by the French government via France Telecom, was never equipped with e-mail capability, possibly because that would have placed it in direct competition with another state monopoly, the post office. The frustration felt by the French, who wanted access to the Internet via Minitel, was widespread and was well expressed by the following posting to a French newsgroup, www.libe.fr, in September 1999. The comment was in response to the question, "Is a law necessary to unstick the Internet in France?"

> The Minitel is the most expensive and profitable device in France. No wonder a lot of companies and on-line merchants would rather make a lot of money on Minitel rather than go on the Internet.… The Internet is free! (Or almost.) This is the reason why the Internet is not successful in France.…

Refusal to modernize Minitel was a significant error in judgment, since more than half of the French population used Minitel in the 1990s (France Telecom charged for its use). That penchant for short-term gain coupled with failure to develop modern technology cost France dearly. But by the end of 1998 France Telecom announced it would be working in collaboration with IBM Corporation to develop a network to allow its thirty-five million Minitel customers access to the Internet in 2000. How a new system would fare in competition with other companies was less important than the obvious conclusion: free market competition was working. Indeed, to make the point that low cost would be a major consideration, French Internet users staged a one-day strike in mid-December 1998 protesting France Telecom's telephone rates. In February 1999 the company announced a 12 percent reduction in long distance rates and a 10 percent cut in the cost of international calls, and combined it with the promise of a further reduction of 9 percent by the end of the year 2000.

The future of the Internet and usage of the computer in Europe is wide open, representing the largest growth opportunity since the post-World War II reconstruction of Europe. The education of Europeans in computer usage will move inexorably forward, and quickly. Computer sales in Europe rose by 21 percent during 1998 compared with 1997. Indeed, in December 1998 one estimate put more than 32 million Europeans on-line. By March 2000 the same survey reported more than 83 million

Europeans. Eventually European consumption of hardware and software will exceed that of the United States because the entire European market is much larger. The European Union (EU) with its current fifteen members — Austria, Belgium, Denmark, England, Finland, France, Germany, Greece, Ireland, Italy, Luxembourg, the Netherlands, Portugal, Spain, and Sweden — numbers about 310 million. With the addition in the future of Poland, the Czech Republic, Slovakia, and Hungary, that number will increase to 375 million. The combined population of Albania, Bulgaria, Romania, and of former Yugoslavia raises that number to over 425 million people. The Internet has not fully arrived on the Continent as yet, but the president of Microsoft Europe concluded in the spring of 1999 that there is no other choice but to close the technology divide between Europe and the United States:

> It's a must.... I think that we will see new approaches coming to market that will make it easy for small and medium businesses to embrace technology. I think that the prices will continue to go down, therefore driving better penetration of those technologies.

But is it a question of choice, or a question of how quickly Europe will catch up? In October 1999 the Gartner Group predicted that by 2001 approximately 30 percent of Europe's business enterprises would have established e-commerce strategies. What this could mean was well illustrated in Italy, where out of the country's 3.4 million companies, only 236,000 had more than ten employees: if information-technology companies, whether they are European or American, can design and market e-business solutions to small and medium-sized companies the growth will be enormous. The decisive point lies with human inventiveness, ingenuity, initiative, and imagination — and Europeans have just as much of that as Americans.

If borrowing from the ideas of others is a compliment, the Europeans are paying one in spades to the entrepreneurs of Silicon Valley. In June 1999, Bernard Arnault, chairman of the French luxury goods maker LVMH Moët Hennessy Louis Vuitton SA in Paris, announced formation of a 500 million Euro (equivalent to $500 million) venture capital fund to invest primarily in European Internet companies. His rationale was simple: "We're at the start of the Internet revolution."

The result has been to set the stage for imaginative ways to broaden the Internet's appeal, such as the introduction by the French postal service of a prepaid smart card to allow Internet access from terminals in post offices, or the initiative by British Internet service providers to allow free Internet access in order to undermine the impact of Europe's high telephone connection charges. The European Union is getting the message as well, as reflected in the European Commission's recommendation in December 1999 that initiatives be taken to create a digitally literate Continent

— to increase competition among telecommunications companies to lower the cost of Internet access, to bring the Internet and multimedia to educational and research institutions, to create a European infrastructure to encourage broad use of smart-card technology, to design a legal framework to promote the growth of e-commerce, and to permit private companies to bid on government contracts via the Internet.

The issue of access, addressed by the European Commission, was not just a matter of providing Internet service for a specific fee or for no fee at all. The real question was the cost of a local call. While in the United States a local call made from a computer modem costs a flat fee, in Europe the same call was billed by the minute. So, understandably, Internet users paid attention to how much time they stayed on-line. A communications analyst at the Organization for Economic Cooperation and Development in Paris, Sam Paltridge, explained the consequences in the spring of 2000:

> Where local calls are unmetered, users stay online for longer periods, listen to radio stations or follow stock prices or auctions or can respond immediately to e-mail.... They can surf, shop, and familiarize themselves with e-commerce in a way users are reluctant to do if they have a meter ticking.

Moreover, the longer a European user remained on-line the more taxes he paid, as Paltridge explained it: "For forty hours on-line, the average user in most European countries pays $9 in taxes, while in countries with unmetered local calls he would pay only $1." In April the European Commission announced that it would use its anti-trust powers against telephone companies that refused to end their monopoly on the cost of a local call, the so-called "unbundling of the local loop." The financial power of this monopoly was clear, and also expensive for the private consumer. Thus, in France for example, where France Telecom still held a monopoly on all local calling, the Ministry of Industry proposed legislation to open local calling to competition. But in April 2000 the proposal was withdrawn at the request of French communist party legislators. It is safe to say that the communist party position will not prevail, but the monopolistic attitude was a superb example of the barriers still to be overcome.

If e-commerce is to work in the European Union it has to be borderless. And it isn't, yet. Publishing cartels, for example, dictate retail prices to book shops, so that Dava Sobel's *Galileo's Daughter,* a best-seller in the autumn of 1999, was offered at Amazon.com for three different prices, depending on where it was ordered: $27 in Germany, $13.52 in Britain, and $16.20 in the U.S. European Union auto makers can still dictate retail prices and forbid dealers from competing with each other. On-line auctions are hindered by laws requiring the physical display of the items to be sold. Regulations exist as well limiting the time periods when consumer goods may be offered at a discount. German law fair trades most consumer products and forbids discounting prices to individual customers. Software shipped on CD-ROM discs to Europe from the United States are subject to customs duties, but if the order is paid for with a credit card on the Internet, the buyer in London can download it without paying any duty at all. In Germany lifetime product guarantees are illegal, and American clothing retailer Lands' End is forbidden by law to advertise its unconditional refund policy. In other European Union countries comparative advertising is not permitted. In Italy all forms of tobacco advertising are banned, in Greece toy advertising is illegal, and France forbids advertising in English.

Economists call such laws barriers to entry. I call them ridiculous and restrictive. But whatever their purpose, they will all be broken down as the competitive force of the Internet continues to gather momentum. And in parallel with it will move the developing power of networks used in e-business. If European bureaucrats and politicians believe that the freedom of marketplaces and communication will wrest economic, political, and social control from government, they are right. Those working for the public state have a lot to lose as their influence over the daily lives of the citizens they are supposed to serve diminishes. And, conversely, Europeans in private business have an enormous amount of economic, political, and social freedom to gain.

The winner will be European business — and that means private citizens — as European companies take competitive initiatives to lure well qualified employees from American companies such as Amazon.com and AOL. Salary packages are becoming more creative and lucrative, and pressure is mounting in Europe to grant stock options. Work habits are metamorphosing too, as European bricks-and-mortar companies adopt Internet-style casual dress codes, amenities like coffee bars, and even performance-based compensation systems. It is a process that may be slow, but it is going forward. The founder of the MIT Media Lab, Nicholas Negroponte, noted in 1999 that, for young people in France, Germany, and Italy, "it's hell" to go up against the entrenched state of regulation and control: "It takes them ten times the amount of energy to go through the bureaucratic nonsense to start a company, where kids who graduate from the Media Lab can almost do it in twenty-four hours."

But make no mistake: competition will force the replacement of the old orders with new ones. The story of Ana Patricia Botin, one of Spain's best-known bankers and a member of the country's oldest banking family, is one example. She resigned in 1999 as head of Spain's largest banking group, Banco Santander. By her own admission, she had never surfed the Web until after she left the bank. Following her resignation she traveled in Europe and the United States, looking for potential partners for Internet-related projects. She found both. In January 2000 she announced creation of a company with two young Spanish entrepreneurs called Coverlink, to design, select, finance, and support Internet projects in Europe and Latin America. At the same time, she also introduced her own multimillion-dollar private equity fund to invest in telecommunication projects, committed to raising up to a billion dollars over the next ten years.

5.

THE BUSINESS OF BUSINESS IS CHANGING

The truth of e-business is that it changes industries.
It merges industries, destroys industries and is unstoppable.
It is an epoch-making idea that is rapidly turning into
a fact of life.

{*Financial Times*, June 2, 1999}

On-line stock trading wasn't possible in the 1980s. And in France at that time, in the back rooms of investment houses in Paris, accounting was still being done with pencils. The electronic transformation of what portfolio managers call the equity market in the United States — and what I still call the stock market — preceded similar changes in Europe because there the real problem was attitude. Stocks were only owned by rich people, so ran the proverbial wisdom, and nobody liked them. Members of the middle class didn't want to own stock, because they didn't need to. The state took care of you while you worked and when you retired. Why spend your private money buying stock when public money was always there? Moreover, comparatively few Europeans understood how stock markets worked, and politicians knew it, so they declared stocks risky. Who could refute them, except the rich? Nobody believed them. Stock options were practically unheard of, and when some executive got some, both were called vulgar and exploitative.

In early March 2000 I discussed the question of attitude with Bertrand Jacquillat and Hubert Jousset during lunch at the Automobile Club on the Place de la Concorde. Bertrand told me the following story about the prevailing mood in France in 1977. At that time despair reigned among portfolio managers. Investors in France had been seeing low or negative returns for fifteen years. Transactions were small in number and there were few initial public offerings. Moreover, legislative elections were scheduled for 1978 and it was widely expected that the Socialists would win, which cast a further pall over the markets. Bertrand was in the process of preparing a conference of professional investment managers to be held at the famous HEC (Institut des Hautes Etudes Commerciales) in Paris. The conference advisory committee was headed by Yves Flornoy, chairman of one of the largest brokerage houses in Paris and also at the head of the Paris Bourse. At one of the committee meetings in 1977 Flornoy said that he wasn't sure if there would even be a French stock market in 1978, when the conference would be held.

Flornoy had reason for pessimism. European politicians promoted an image of capitalism as avarice and greed, because it enhanced their value as keepers of the commonweal. They had created the welfare state, so they asserted that financial security wasn't to be found in the stock market. It was provided by the state. Europe, in short, was not a society of free markets, risk taking, and economic reward. In Germany politicians had a name for it. They called it the social market economy; the primary responsibility of business was to produce socially acceptable results. And everywhere in Europe politicians were there to see to it that business didn't make "too much" money. So they created inefficient monopolies such as France Telecom or Deutsche Telekom, and refused to privatize them. Indeed, in France in 1979-80 the ratio of stock market value to gross domestic product was about 12, vis-a-vis about 80 in the United States. Free markets — and especially stock markets — were your enemy, and the state that took care of you was your friend ... until the Internet arrived.

The point was really made unforgettably clear to me in March 1997. I was having dinner with a distinguished German professor of history in Hamburg. The night before I had seen an interview on television with the German minister of finance in Berlin, during which he had been asked whether he owned stocks. He said yes, and was then asked what percentage of his wealth was in the stock market. He replied, "That's private and I'm not going to tell you." That short exchange really shocked me because that kind of private question would not have been asked several years earlier. It would have been considered rude, and besides, the answer would undoubtedly have been, "I don't own any!"

The next evening I told my host about the interview and asked if he owned any stocks. I am sure he considered it none of my business, but he is a gentleman and didn't bat an eyelash. He said, "Why should I? I don't need to. I have my pension." I am sure my good friend, who celebrated his sixty-fifth birthday in June 1999, still doesn't own any. And I'm sorry, because he believes in free enterprise yet doesn't know stock markets are for him, too. But an increasing number of Europeans do, and recently they have been flocking to the stock market in record numbers, as the consequence of a cultural economic revolution that began taking hold in the late 1990s.

In 1990 there were more than thirty stock exchanges in Europe; the largest ones were in London, Paris and Frankfurt. But they weren't connected. They had different trading hours, different pricing mechanisms, different settlement systems, and screen trading wasn't possible everywhere. Today, ten years later, the European Union is now a single market without tariffs, and with a single currency, the Euro, used in the stock markets. The days of back-room pencil accounting are over, and computer screens are a normal tool of brokerage houses everywhere.

The Internet brought about the decisive change. It made possible on-line trading, introduced in the United States in 1994, and opened stock markets to the common man. You didn't need to be rich, you just needed easy access. In turn, the ease of on-line access affected attitudes, and it didn't take long. By mid-1998 the directors of the Paris Bourse saw the use of information technologies as its European Union advantage. Bourse chairman Jean-François Theodore was quoted in 1998 as promoting Paris as "the most efficient gateway to the Europe of tomorrow."

Monsieur Theodore had good reason for optimism. He knew that 100,000 on-line accounts already existed in Europe at the end of 1997, and although these were primarily in Germany, growth throughout the European Union seemed inevitable. He didn't have long to wait. By the end of 1999 the number of on-line accounts in France and Germany together represented 7 percent of the number in the U.S., and the orders equaled 12.5 percent of those in America. Taken in comparison, these percentages, are small, but they're enormous in comparison to what existed in 1994 — namely, zero. Moreover, what's small can grow, and that led J.P. Morgan & Co. to predict in November 1999 that by the year 2002 there would be 8.3 million on-line accounts in Europe. In March 2000 an analyst with the French bank BNP Paribas estimated that 40 percent of French people doing business with on-line brokers had never owned stock before in their lives.

The promise of growth in France alone was astounding. In 1999 there were approximately 150,000 on-line accounts; that number was predicted to be 500,000 by 2001 and to grow to 2,000,000 by 2003. While Germany had the largest number of on-line traders in 1999, the French had a lot of money to spend, since on average they were saving 14 percent of their income (76 percent of the French older than fifteen had savings accounts in 1999). They had also become the most active on-line traders in Europe. While two Britons owned stock for every one Frenchman, French attitudes were still changing. It was becoming legitimate to talk about owning stocks, about the low cost of on-line trading, and about the dream of making money. And there was the nightmare of what might happen to guaranteed pensions from the

French welfare state, where there is wide debate concerning state-financed retirement programs versus private plans. In 1999 about eight million Frenchmen owned stocks, bonds, or mutual funds, and they represented just about 13 percent of the population (in comparison to 43 percent of the population in the United States, where the retirement plans of millions more were invested in stocks as well).

What would these numbers look like in the new century? One indication came from the announced merger in May 2000 of the London and Frankfurt stock exchanges, which would make it the fourth-largest in the world after the New York Stock Exchange, the NASDAQ, and Tokyo. It had been preceded in February 2000 by the announcement in London that a pan-European market for on-line traders would open in September. Another indication was the merger of the French, Dutch and Belgian stock exchanges in March. And yet another indication had preceded both. For the first time in the history of the Paris Bourse the capitalization of French stocks exceeded the value of France's gross domestic product. On January 27 the Paris Bourse registered trades totaling thirty-six billion francs, the first time that twenty billion francs had ever been exceeded in a single January day. Traders recalled the time, in 1994-95, when daily volume had been only three to five billion francs. The reason for the increase was due in part to the Euro. "But today the new fuel of the Bourse," wrote Michel Garibal in February 2000 in *Le Figaro* magazine, "is called the Internet."

Use of the Internet to expand customer bases, whether in Europe or the United States or elsewhere around the world, increases the size and number of marketplaces, thereby making them more profitable at the same time. How this was working in the United States began to attract real attention in 1997. At that time at Charles Schwab Corporation, half of all new accounts were opened on-line, giving Schwab 47 percent of the on-line trading market, with 712,000 accounts totaling $50 billion in cash and securities.

Why have on-line firms like Schwab proved so successful? The recent experience of two of my friends is a good example. In March 2000 one of them sold 500 shares of Qualcomm at $137 per share. The commission he paid to Schwab was $29.95, the same he would have paid if he had sold ten shares. His brother also sold 500 shares of Qualcomm in February, but he had to negotiate the amount of the commission with his broker at Morgan Stanley. They agreed on twenty-five cents per share, amounting to a commission of $125. There's a message here, and you don't have to be a mathematician to figure it out.

The saving in commissions is the principal reason why private traders of stocks and bonds began turning to the Internet. In 1996 on-line trading produced 1.5 million accounts. In 1997, on-line trading of retail stock was more than double the previous year's level. By the end of 1997, approximately three million on-line brokerage

186

accounts existed (about 5 percent of the total market of eighty million accounts with full-service houses or traditional discounting houses). By the end of 1998 that number had increased to approximately 5.3 million, and by April of 2000 to more than fifteen million. In May 2000 the amount of assets held in on-line brokerage accounts exceeded $1.1 trillion, and it was anybody's guess what would occur in the next five years.

The traditional stockbroker is becoming an increasingly rare commodity. Trading commissions, often between 1.5 and 2 percent of the value of the sale or purchase, are now negotiated, as the traditional broker competes with on-line investing. My three children are excellent examples. In their early thirties, all of them have brokerage accounts with Charles Schwab. My brokerage account is with a private investment manager, with whom I have been doing business for thirty years. I didn't switch to on-line trading because I felt loyalty to my broker, whose wisdom and judgment I respect. But in 1997, I began to negotiate the brokerage fees substantially downward — and he had no choice but to comply.

The competition is fierce (in August 1999 there were more than 150 on-line brokerages in the U.S.). In January 1998 Charles Schwab Corporation cut its average commission of about $65 for an on-line trade, to a flat $29.95 for trades up to 1,000 shares. Schwab candidly admitted that its new rate was designed "to lure customers from full-service brokerage firms" such as Merrill Lynch. In order for Schwab to keep its current revenues even, it would have to double its Internet trading, but what choice was there? Schwab estimated that about 70 percent of its 4.5 million customers had access to personal computers at work and/or at home, but only 15 percent of its customers had on-line accounts. By April 2000 the statistics had again changed. Schwab had 21.4 percent of the on-line market and was executing 244,000 trades daily. The two largest brokerages after Schwab were E*Trade in Menlo Park, California, with 15.7 percent of the market (214,000 daily trades), and TD Waterhouse with 13.3 percent of the market (182,000 trades per day).

Another change that cut into the monopoly held by traditional brokerage houses — until the Internet arrived — was seen in Schwab's announcement in the autumn of 1997 that it would offer analyst comments, research reports, and earnings estimates at its Web site at www.schwab.com. Shortly thereafter Schwab withdrew the offer because independent firms that wrote the reports objected to their free distribution on the Web. But this attitude didn't prevail long. Research reports today are part and parcel of on-line trading services, and on-line search engines and browsers like Yahoo! and Netscape provide real-time quotes and financial news. A short time ago Wall Street dismissed on-line trading as a novelty. In 2000 it can no longer afford to do so.

Who's trading on-line? To some extent it's exactly those you would expect, computer-savvy twenty-somethings and college-educated Baby Boomers, many of whom jumped on board in the first two years of on-line trading. But to leave it here isn't really fair. By 1998 mainstream investors were joining the pioneers in droves. The ability to buy and sell stocks on-line is technically just as easy in Berlin as it is in Palo Alto; that fact alone speaks volumes about the nature of trading places. If I can get company earnings reports, volume and pricing data, real-time stock quotes, and research information from the Web — and I can do it from my hotel room just as easily as from my kitchen — why do I need a full-service broker? Many people don't, prompting the man who pioneered touch-tone trading via telephone in 1988, J. Joe Ricketts, the CEO of Ameritrade located in Omaha, to say "I've never seen anything grow so fast."

Today, in 2000, traditional brokerage houses recognize they can't run away from technology. Morgan Stanley Dean Witter's 11,000 brokers provide full-service brokerage and negotiate commissions with their clients. In October 1999 the firm began providing on-line brokerage for its clients who wished to use it at a cost of $29.95 per trade. Why are they doing it? It's about finding a way for customers to trade inexpensively when they wish, and to call on the advice of an expert when they need help. It is about choices. The Internet is expanding choices everywhere.

The shape of things to come was put best at the beginning of this chapter, in the advertisement from Datek that appeared in the *Wine Spectator*. That ad concludes with "… and my broker wonders why I don't call him anymore." A similar unintended consequence of Internet trading is the effect on the value of a seat on the New York Stock Exchange or on the Chicago Board of Trade. A seat on the NYSE, priced at $2 million in February 1998, had dropped 32 percent by August 1998, and in Chicago the price was down 52 percent, to $410,000 from a high of $857,000 in 1997. The prices recovered in 1999, but during the year volume on the Chicago Board of Trade fell by more than 20 percent, and by April 2000 the price of a seat of the New York Stock Exchange had fallen again by one third. Is it only a matter of time until the NYSE is forced to abandon its famous trading floor, and replace it with an electronic trading system? Will the 207-year-old marketplace become a "bowling alley"? — a question asked in December 1999 by Lou Gorman, vice chairman and president of capital markets and trading at Charles Schwab.

Does the future rest with bricks-and-mortar stock exchanges and full-service brokerage houses, or with electronic communication networks? The inevitable conclusion is that mainline trading and investment houses must meet customer demand, offer on-line trading, and lower their commissions, or lose business. PaineWebber Inc., the fifth largest brokerage house in the United States, recognized what was coming and announced at the end of November 1998 that it would inaugurate on-line trading by mid-1999. Just one statistic was sufficient to explain why: on-line trading commissions have grown by a factor of five since 1996, to almost $1.3 billion.

By the end of the century one out of six stock trades in the U.S. was made through an on-line brokerage. Some estimates concluded that full-service brokers were losing $7 million a day in commissions. There are some traditionalists, of course, who call the phenomenon a fad and refuse to use the Internet, even if it means their customer lists dwindle to aging, conservative clients. These die-hard brokers cling to a belief that a serious bear market will send investors running back to traditional brokerages. This argument, alas, is an example of the wish being father to the thought. It will suffer the same fate as the horse and buggy.

Both business and government can draw a lesson from the horse and buggy analogy. In the case of government, the Internet's trading places provide a powerful incentive to do so, one that concerns the changing relationship between the taxpayer and the state. Unless governments figure out a way to monitor the Internet and further invade our privacy, they are going to have to change also, just as businesses are changing. As the Internet alters the way we do business, where we do our trading, and how we conduct commerce, it is also affecting how governments collect taxes. Will it become easier or more difficult? In mid-1997 *The Economist* published an article on the subject, addressing the fact that forces of globalization and new technology threaten to weaken the power of governments to tax their citizens. Nobel laureate in economics Milton Friedman agrees, because the Internet "makes it harder to collect taxes." And Alan Reynolds, director of economic research at the Hudson Institute, believes so as well, saying, "The declining cost of communication and decreasing importance of location mean that international tax competition will intensify. Governments, like companies, will have to compete in producing the most value for the lowest possible cost."

In cyberspace it is difficult to determine when and where a transaction takes place. In an *International Herald Tribune* story in 1998, Richard W. Stevenson quoted Milton Friedman:

> 'Governments can get funds fundamentally only from resources that find it difficult to move elsewhere … [T]he greater the freedom of movement of capital and people, the harder it is for governments. That's the kind of external force that is adding to what's coming from the intellectual tide of opinion.'

Thus far, governments in Europe and the United States have provided little imaginative leadership in this arena because they are at a loss for how to do so. Two striking examples are the sales tax in the United States and the value-added tax in Europe.

State and local governments are pressuring the U.S. Congress to impose sales taxes on Internet transactions and mail-order sales. On the one hand it's a political issue, and on the other a technology issue. Retailers in stores collect sales taxes, but retailers on the Internet don't. Traditional shop owners, therefore, are pressing politicians to impose taxes on e-commerce, and politicians react predictably, with such statements as, "We can't adopt a tax policy in America that assists in wiping out small-town Main Streets," or Michigan Governor John Engler's remark, "Government should not be in the business of picking favorites among competitive forces such as traditional retailers or emerging electronic retailers." The White House entered the debate in December 1999 when a spokesman declared that a tax-free Internet would "exacerbate the digital divide, requiring the less fortunate to subsidize the tax advantage of computer owners."

Politically this sells well to the owners of shopping malls, but technically it presents a problem. How does the government propose to collect sales taxes? By monitoring every business transaction on the Internet? One solution, reflecting the government's quandary and advanced by the nation's governors, is a multi-state agreement by which taxes would be collected voluntarily by Internet businesses from all shoppers.

What the argument is really about, according to Governor Jim Gilmore of Virginia, is government's desire "to tax anything that moves." It is also about something else, namely, that the existing system of collecting sales taxes isn't going to work in the twenty-first century. It will have to be changed. But the U.S. Congress was without a solution in October 1998 when it passed the Internet Tax Freedom Act, establishing a three-year moratorium on new Internet taxes, to expire in 2001. At the same time Congress also created the federal Advisory Commission on Electronic Commerce and charged it to submit a recommendation by April 2000. But the commission, at its final meeting in Dallas in March, adjourned without reaching consensus. A simple majority did recommend a ban on Internet access taxes, a repeal of the 3 percent telecommunications excise tax (a tax enacted in 1898 to finance the Spanish-American War), and a ban on Internet taxes until 2006. How Congress eventually will act is anybody's guess, and that includes the members of Congress themselves. Where the issue stood in the early spring of the year 2000 was summed up best by the commission's chairman, Governor Gilmore:

> The Internet changes everything — including government. Government at all levels must now begin to harness the efficiencies and productivity increases facilitated by information technology and the Internet. Free enterprise is doing it. Government must do it, too.

The Business of Business Is Changing

In an age in which information technology is transforming how business is conducted around the globe, nothing is left unaffected. More than a decade ago an astute observer of the world looked beyond the horizon. Today, in 2000, we can see that George Shultz's observation in 1987, published in a collection called *Thinking About America: The United States in the 1990s* (Annelise Anderson and Dennis L. Bark, editors), predicted a great deal:

> Manufacturing processes ... are becoming global in scale. I recently saw a snapshot of a shipping label for some integrated circuits produced by an American firm. It said, 'Made in one or more of the following countries: Korea, Hong Kong, Malaysia, Singapore, Taiwan, Mauritius, Thailand, Indonesia, Mexico, Philippines. The exact country of origin is unknown.' That label says a lot about where current trends are taking us.

A little more than a decade later current trends were reflected across industries, producing products, selling services, and creating strategic partnerships around the world. Part of the message was illustrated by on-line stock trading, as well as in the areas of banking and insurance. Another part was seen in a decision made in the spring of 1999 by the oldest business newspaper in the United States, *The Journal of Commerce,* founded by the inventor of Morse code, Samuel F.B. Morse. During the Civil War, when the paper published troop movements, it was temporarily shut down by President Lincoln. In the course of its 173-year history the daily paper has covered transportation, insurance, and global trade, including maritime and commodities reportage. Since 1995 its circulation has dropped by more than 12 percent. Its lines of advertising have also declined, and thanks to the World Wide Web, it no longer has a monopoly on the publication of shipping schedules. In mid-1999 the daily paper converted its broadsheet format to a tabloid, and opened a Web site, www.joc.com. The denouement arrived in mid-2000, when *The Journal of Commerce* announced replacement of its daily edition with a weekly magazine.

Current trends could also be found in the figures for newspaper circulation and classified advertising revenues, as well as in television network performance. Between 1994 and 1998 circulation for the five largest papers in the United States dropped in four cases: *The Wall Street Journal* (down 6.2 percent), the *Los Angeles Times* (down 3.4 percent), *The New York Times* (down 8.7 percent), and the *Washington Post* (down 10.9 percent). The exception was *USA Today,* whose circulation increased by 6.2 percent. During the same period, as the nation's gross domestic product increased, classified advertising revenue decreased (the three largest sectors are real estate, employment, and automobiles).

The effect of the Internet on the number of viewers of the nation's major networks (ABC, CBS, NBC, and FOX) has been equally dramatic. Between 1988 and 1998, as the cable audience increased, network market share declined from 62 percent to 45 percent. For major network news, current trends were summed up this way in March 1999 in a *Wall Street Journal* editorial:

> Not only is cable [and the Internet] where the analysis and debate is, increasingly it is where the news is — without millionaire anchors reading as though they were delivering a papal bull.... What this means is that Tom Brokaw, Dan Rather and Peter Jennings are increasingly addressing people who are either older or don't care that much about the news.

The trends of 1987 are passé in 2000, as the electronic world propels us forward faster and faster. The business of business is continuing to change, in the words of Intel's Andy Grove, "like a duck that looks calm on the surface and is paddling like heck underneath." By April 1999, Intel Corporation predicted that close to 90 percent of its revenue would come from e-business by 2002. New chips and systems were being designed to combine data and voice networks. NBC Internet was pursuing efforts to integrate on-line buyers with TV viewers and Web surfers. Mobile phones, wireless networks, and information streaming, using satellites and fiber optics, are writing the next chapter in the revolution of the Information Age, where information technologies are blending with telecommunications.

For those who "get it," the twenty-first century is going to be an exciting one. Exciting, for example, for the publishers of the oldest dictionary in the world, the thirty-volume *Oxford English Dictionary*, who put it on-line in the year 2000 at www.oed.com. For those who don't "get it," there is going to be little joy. Sadly for me, an example is that of "one of the oldest and finest consumer products ever sold: a veritable fount of knowledge." The *Encyclopedia Britannica* was founded in 1768 in Edinburgh, Scotland. When I was growing up my father contributed articles on the Middle Ages, and I still have the edition I inherited from my parents, published in 1969.

It was traditionally sold by door-to-door salesmen. Sales revenues of $650 million in 1989 were the highest in its history and the sales force numbered 2,300. When Microsoft produced an encyclopedia on CD-ROM in 1993, called Encarta, *Encyclopedia Britannica* followed suit. But the salesmen refused to sell it, sales collapsed, and by 2000 *Encyclopedia Britannica* had fewer than 350 employees. If there is a lesson to be drawn, it is that the Internet stands ready to topple any form of commerce, from pushcart to superstore.

The Internet, said Louis V. Gerstner Jr., chairman of IBM Corporation, in January 1999, has become the "ultimate medium of business." Gerstner estimated that IBM's Internet sales for that year would be between $10 billion and $15 billion, adding that the amount of money generated, not the number of Web site visitors, was the true measure of the Internet's growth.

6.

AND THE RETURN ON INVESTMENT?

One astonishing aspect of all this is that only five years ago,
the Internet was essentially a fringe tool,
the province of selected government officials,
university researchers and geeky hobbyists.
Executives mostly ignored it, and some called it a fad.
Politicians never mentioned the medium. Few declared it revolutionary.

{"Internet Builds Steam As Engine of Change,"
International Herald Tribune, June 21, 1999}

In ancient times, in 1996, Cisco Systems' annual report addressed the subject of networks:

> Prior to the 1990s, most people had little concept of what networks were and what they were capable of doing. But that was then. Today, however, everyone from business professionals to schoolchildren has some kind of opinion on the subject. Internet addresses are becoming almost as common as house addresses and telephone numbers. No longer the sole province of technical professionals, computer networks are everywhere. And the technology that connects many different kinds of networks — otherwise known as Internetworking — has created a market that is expanding at an astounding rate.... [T]oday's worldwide internetworking market ... [is] approximately $27 billion.

194

In 1998 the Semiconductor Industry Association, located in San Jose, California, announced that the most important "driver" of the U.S. economy was the computer chip industry. For many that translated into e-commerce and e-business. One of the leads was taken by Intel, which began conducting business transactions with its corporate customers on-line in July 1998. Within fifteen days more than one billion dollars of business had moved to the new system, therewith eliminating 45,000 faxes per quarter in the Asia-Pacific region alone. In September 1998 Intel's new chairman, Craig Barrett, who had recently succeeded Andy Grove, talked in London about what was happening. He spoke of a future world with a billion connected computers:

> This is like a seventh continent, it provides instant access to information and presents any organization with the ability to make informed and quick decisions.... It alters the 'economies of scale' equation to put the kind of resources that only used to be available to large companies, at everyone's disposal, twenty-five hours a day, seven days a week.

> It provides businesses, both large and small, with instant access to vendors, customers, manufacturers and customer information anywhere in the world. And it is fundamentally going to change the way we do business.

But not everyone agreed. Chris Stevens of the Aberdeen Group in Boston, Massachusetts, argued that "the current guesstimates of e-commerce are akin to trying to estimate the [gross domestic product] of a state based on the number of trucks passing by on a highway.... It's absurd." And Stevens has by no means remained alone. In January 2000 Robert J. Samuelson wrote that "sooner or later, the investment must pay a return, or it will stop." The message, of course, was that all the Internet euphoria hadn't yet produced profits for hundreds of dot-com companies, the "fireflies" of the Internet boom. He supported his point with a story told by a Tennessee farmer at a church meeting in the 1940s:

> 'Brothers and sisters, I want to tell you this.... The greatest thing on earth is to have the love of God in your heart, and the next greatest is to have electricity in your home.' Can the Internet [Samuelson asked] really top that?

Samuelson's question, for me, is rhetorical because five years after meeting the computer I appreciate the value of networks and, by extension, the value of the Internet. It is exponential, determined by the number of users. The more people using networks, the greater the connectivity, and the more valuable networks become. The broader the casting, the greater the geometrical growth in usage. Information technology has created an economic revolution made of knowledge, time, and money. Many of us call it e-commerce. But it is really a revolution about how we think about knowledge, time, and money, and what we do with all three. Those who know call this e-business, meaning this revolution is really about how we relate, connect, and communicate with each other.

Whether we call it an Internet ecosystem, as Cisco's 1999 annual report did, or increasingly expanding relationships, the point remains the same. Those who understand the value of relationships also understand why e-business is clearly bringing, and will continue to bring, enormous economic returns on investment — not just for a few, but for millions of people.

"Increasingly in the Information Age," wrote Bill Davidow in an article he sent me in 1999, "the success of one product is determined by how it interconnects with others." George Nation, who heads Microsoft's Internet and television operation for Europe, Africa, and the Middle East from his office in *La Defense* in Paris, expresses the same point this way: "The reason we invested in cable in Europe is because we want to make sure that our financial partner becomes our business partner and uses our technology." An example of what I think this means is a full page advertisement that appeared in *The Wall Street Journal* in February 2000:

The on-line shopper.

Is she an anomaly?

Only if you consider 3.2 trillion dollars an anomaly.

Welcome to the sale of the next century. By the year 2003, online sales are expected to reach 3.2 trillion dollars.
To compete in this new Internet economy, you'll need strategic partners. Partners who've implemented e-commerce solutions themselves. Cisco and Microsoft have that experience. And together we can help you create salable e-commerce solutions for your corporation based on Microsoft Windows 2000 and Cisco's intelligent network services. Today.

And the Return on Investment?

I wonder what the Tennessee farmer would say. Perhaps he wouldn't think so today, but at some point in the near future farmers are going to be connected too — many already are — as they trade information, and buy and sell everything from fertilizer, to pork bellies, to grain on the Internet. Will the expense in time and money they commit to being connected be worth it?

The answer was already in by early 2000, in the shape of partnerships, exchanges, infomediaries, and integrated value chains. Whatever fancy names the new economy gave them, they were all new forms of doing electronic business in electronic marketplaces. And they all added value by dramatically cutting the costs of purchasing goods and supplying services. General Motors Corporation, Ford Motor Company, and DaimlerChrysler AG have formed a marketplace for auto parts suppliers. Sears, Roebuck and Company, the second largest retailer in the U.S., has formed an on-line exchange for retailers and suppliers called GlobalNetXchange with the French company Carrefour SA, the world's second-largest retailer, with technical support from Oracle Corporation. In April 2000 a similar Web-based supply exchange was created by eleven more major retailers in the U.S. and Europe, including Kmart Corporation, Albertsons Inc., Safeway Inc., and Marks & Spencer PLC. Another was created early in the year by Chevron, Oracle, and Wal-Mart subsidiary McLane Company, where convenience stores can order, manage inventories, and centralize a whole range of operations. Electronic trading networks are also being created in industries from steel and chemicals, to oil and gas, as well as in the farming industry. Strategic partnerships are being formed between telephone companies and Internet companies such as that between Deutsche Telekom AG and Cisco Systems, and between Cisco Systems and the Paris technology consulting group Cap Gemini.

In a sense this could be described as an emerging law of relationships. The larger the exchanges, the more efficient they become. *The Economist* explains what is happening this way:

> The objective for large companies must be to become e-business hubs and for smaller ones to ensure that they are vital spokes....When a really large company moves some or all of its operations to the Web ... [a]ll the big company's trading partners come under intense pressure to turn into e-businesses too. The big firm, having invested a lot of money in e-business infrastructure, is determined to get a return on it. Customers and suppliers who want to trade the old-fashioned way will get frozen out, while those who 'get it' will simply win more business.

If there is an answer to what all this means, it was put best in the form of a rhetorical question by a man born in Hungary, András Gróf. He came to America from Europe as a teenager, following the Soviet invasion of Budapest in 1956. Today he is Andy Grove, considered the "person most responsible for the transformative power of microchips — the tiny silicon 'brains' of personal computers," in the words of two *San Francisco Examiner* writers. He retired as CEO of Intel Corporation in 1998, the year Intel was producing almost 90 percent of the planet's PC microprocessors. The company had a stock market value of $187 billion in November of that year (more than IBM at $152 billion), with $25 billion in annual revenues, and an annual return to investors of 44 percent between 1987 and 1997.

When Grove was named *Time* magazine's Man of the Year in December 1997, managing editor Walter Isaacson wrote: "The microchip has become — like the steam engine, electricity and the assembly line — an advance that propels a new economy.... The high-tech industry, which accounted for less than 10 percent of America's growth in 1990, accounts for 30 percent today." So when Grove responded in September 1997 to a question about the return on investment on Intel's Internet ventures, his observation was worth thinking about: "What's my ROI on e-commerce? Are you crazy? This is Christopher Columbus in the New World. What was his ROI?" Perhaps one answer could be found in Intel's market value in early April 2000. It was more than $437 billion.

And the Return on Investment?

CHAPTER FOUR

WHAT ARE WE BECOMING?

... [W]e the Priests of Clio's temple, would say a word for continuity.
All-seeing Time, with unrelenting, harsh acuity,
Imparts this truth: The oldest human code was once the newest change.
What makes old new, new old, is found in Clio's endless, questing range.
It ill behooves mere man to spurn his past, his History.
To treat of Change alone would change his History to Mystery.

{William Carroll Bark, 1908-1996}

True Patriotism is of no Party

{Tobias George Smollett, 1721-1771, from
The Adventures of Sir Launcelot Greaves}

1.

A New Age of Discovery

Cvm Gratia et Privilegio

*Following the invention of moveable type
the distribution of information in
fifteenth- and sixteenth-century Europe,
via the medium of the book,
was most carefully administered by government.*

Knowledge was published with permission of the King.

Auec Priuilege du Roy, pour dix ans

The Internet is a worldwide web of communication, not a cultural web (although the Internet is developing its own culture). This web represents a further shrinkage of the world's cultures that has been going on since the Age of Discovery, when the seeds of a global economy were sown for both goods and ideas. Since the 1500s the process of amalgamation of the world into one intellectual and commercial enterprise has been rapidly accelerating. This contraction has been made possible by physical and electronic travel via ships and navies, automobiles and airplanes, telegrams and telephones, radio waves and television broadcasting, fax machines and satellites, and today by the convergence of computers with telecommunication.

Before the Age of Discovery the first part of human history was expansion outward, from the original human homeland into every corner of the globe, where unique cultures developed to fit into local environments. Since then the increasingly sophisticated modes of transportation and communication that enable goods and ideas to move across the seas, earth, and sky, have been gradually redefining the human adventure. What is now changing is the speed with which ideas and commerce travel about the world, whether they concern astronomy or physics, fashion or food, engineering or computing, stock markets or financial markets. In the year 2000 ideas and wealth move in real time via the Internet. The Internet gives a quantum leap to this process of acceleration. This is nothing less than a revolutionary change.

As a historian, I consider that the postwar reconstruction of Europe ended with the unification of Germany in 1990. Since then a new construction has been under way, propelled forward by information and telecommunication technologies. This construction is being defined by new uses of information, communicated in creative ways. It is being shaped by a shift in economic, political, and social relationships, so that the timeworn image of a Cold War world of power blocs is today irrelevant. A new class is being produced — of political leaders, business entrepreneurs, and Internet users. The Information Age is weakening centralized and bureaucratic structures everywhere — including those in free and open societies. If it was true in Europe's communist dictatorships of the 1980s that "the fax shall set you free," we are now witnessing its corollary. Set free today are forces of change everywhere whose powers and purposes we do not yet fully understand.

The nature of these forces was addressed in a small book, *La Fin de la Démocratie,* published in 1993 by former French ambassador to the European Union Jean-Marie Guéhenno. How well his book was understood I cannot say. But it sold more than 10,000 copies in French. When his book appeared in 1995 in English, however, it was entitled *The End of the Nation-State,* and it met with mixed reviews. One on-line reviewer, A.J. Bacevich, writing for *First Things* (www.firstthings.com), called it "an exercise in Big Think … to divine the *zeitgeist* of the new age emerging from the political and cultural upheaval revealed by the end of the Cold War," but "for those not put off by a whiff of Continental affectation, this book merits careful reading." Guéhenno's basic argument was that power was no longer defined in terms of top-to-bottom hierarchy, and that "economic globalization and the rapid spread of information technologies … will subvert a political order that we have come to take for granted, ending the dominance of the nation-state just as the nation-state once superseded the authority of the Church." Another review culled from the Internet summarized Guéhenno's observations about governments and borders:

> … [S]trategic interests, economic interests and moral position no longer evenly overlap as they once did. Borders have suddenly

become not much more than meaningless lines drawn on maps by governments. Governments are out of touch with their own people. The borderlines depicting nations keep the governments in business but act as an impediment to the real business of human beings. In strategic terms the borders have become a very expensive ring of defenses against an enemy who is no longer as dangerous as the idea of government itself.

These thoughts were disturbing ones, irrespective of whether one agreed with all of them or not, which is why Guéhenno's book is intriguing. It was written at a time — 1993 — when the Internet was not yet an internationally recognized medium, and Netscape didn't yet exist. That was less than a decade ago, during the Middle Ages of the communication revolution. He wrote that the modern world is "at the inception of the fourth empire ... closer to Rome and to the ancient world than to Christianity ... created on the ruins of ideology, and of that Soviet empire that once claimed to be the third Rome." The image is provocative and strong, but it means little without elaboration. His conclusion, that we are at the beginning of the fourth empire, is based on the thesis that, "... 1989 marks the close of an era that began not in 1945 or 1917, but that was institutionalized thanks to the French Revolution, in 1789. It brings an end to the age of the nation-states." Is the logic of his argument compelling today?

The forces that flow from the idea of economic and political liberty and from new information and communication technologies are part and parcel of the Information Age — the determination, the commitment, the resolve to be free. It was these forces that defined the fax revolution and thus defined as well the transformation of European politics in 1989, two centuries after the French Revolution. If, on the one hand, the end of the nation-state is what we have to pay for the breakup of the Soviet empire, it seems cheap at the price. If, on the other hand, the dissolution of dictatorship, technological change, and Guéhenno's belief in the end of the age of the nation-state are inextricably entwined, do we know what the price is?

What has happened, Guéhenno explains, is that

> ... powerful economic, social, and cultural forces have disrupted the circumstances that permitted the formation of the nation-states. In a world frozen by the polarization of the Cold War, the effect of these forces on political institutions was checked. This effect will now be able to make itself fully felt. Radical questions will be asked, and the givens on which we have built our institutions since the eighteenth century will suffer a decisive jolt: the dis-

junction between our political order and the realities of today has become too great.

> We believed in institutions, in the force of laws to organize and control power. We persuaded ourselves that the best way of regulating the social clock was to limit power with power, to multiply the poles of force, taking care to avoid all collusion between them. These institutional constructions accompanied the diffusion of wealth and power that characterizes the modern era.... Because we have known nothing else, the words *democracy, politics, liberty* define our mental horizon, but we are no longer sure that we know them in a real sense, and our attachment to them has more to do with reflex than with reflection.

Is our attachment to democracy and liberty really so fragile, so very apt to break? Is the value we attach to freedom simply a reflex action? If it has bonds between generations — bonds of institutions, traditions, and customs, that hold the banks of the riverbed of history together, and keep the river from overflowing — are these bonds breaking down? Or are they changing shape and becoming stronger? Don't we still know democracy, politics, liberty?

These are troubling questions, because they are prompted by the often contradictory but powerful political, economic, social, and cultural forces that are affecting our lives now. These forces, which emanate from the communication revolution, also recall to life the memorable beginning to Charles Dickens's novel about the French Revolution, *A Tale of Two Cities*:

> It was the best of times, it was the worst of times, it was the age of wisdom, it was the age of foolishness, it was the epoch of belief, it was the epoch of incredulity, it was the season of Light, it was the season of Darkness, it was the spring of hope, it was the winter of despair, we had everything before us, we had nothing before us....

Any way we look at it, changes all around us suggest that to some it is the best of times, yet suggest to others that the Information Age is the Age of Foolishness. Where do the forces of change come from? Some come out of the vacuum created by the sudden and unexpected end of the Cold War. Others come from the birth of the interactive, technological world of the late 1980s and 1990s, with the attendant transformation of traditional social elites, of how information is gathered, distributed, and used. Still other forces come from changing demographics: the world's population will increase from today's six billion people to some eight billion to nine billion during the first half of our new century. And, as described in an October 1998 *International Herald Tribune* story, others are economic, coming from "the radically different world economy that is taking shape."

> At the heart of it, low-cost telecommunications and computer technologies are reshaping production and logistics across the globe, making services tradable over long distances and unleashing the full power of global finance.
>
> The ascent of electronic commerce and electronic money is not far behind.... This technological revolution — which goes deep because it is about time, distance and knowledge — is still amazingly young.

As the speed and volume of network communication grows, will power be measured in networks per capita? In "networks within companies, schools and entertainment sources, and then tied ... into the Internet and the World Wide Web" as an April 1998 *International Herald Tribune* article put it? Some argue that traditional institutional structures will not play the same dominant role in influencing societal behavior, in creating jobs and in stimulating economic growth. The *Tribune* article, for example, noted that

> [j]obs and economic power will gravitate to those societies with the most networks and bandwidth, because those countries will find it easiest to gather, tap, and deploy knowledge in order to design, invent, manufacture, communicate, educate, and entertain.

The head of Cisco Systems, John Chambers, draws the same conclusion, but in another way. He argues that the first phase of the Internet revolution was e-mail and e-commerce, and that we now find ourselves at the beginning of the second, namely, the incorporation of networks into business-to-business relationships. The third phase, however, will have even more far-reaching institutional consequences than the first two, since it will be education: "Education over the Internet is going to be so big it is going to make e-mail usage look like a rounding error." Chambers argues that "schools and countries that ignore this ... will suffer the same fate as big department stores that thought e-commerce was overrated." And indeed businesses are not ignoring it, as on-line academies are being started — by companies such as IBM,

AT&T, GE and Cisco Systems — to improve the skills of existing employees and train new ones. Says Chambers:

> ... [I]f universities do not reinvent their curriculums and how they deliver them, many people, particularly in information technology fields, 'will go to schools on-line'.... 'Unlike in the Industrial Revolution when you had to be in the right country or city to participate ... in this new era capital will flow to whichever countries and companies install the best Internet and educational capabilities.'

> Governments and unions will be powerless to stop this capital flow, which will affect the global balance of economic power.

If Chambers is right — and I don't think there is any question but that he is — his conclusions mean that a lot of institutional walls in education, business, and government are going to come tumbling down. Not all of them, by any means. For example, when hackers made their attack on a commercial Web site in February 2000, Yahoo!, Amazon.com and CNN.com turned immediately to an old government institution for help, the FBI. But the Internet Revolution isn't going to be so gentle to other old institutions, which will suffer the fate of transformation or disappearance.

If the age of the nation-state is coming to an end — as Guéhenno defines it — what will replace it, how, and when? The "when" is easy to answer. "When" will occur as a process, very hard to measure, and equally difficult to see. As former Secretary of State George Shultz so aptly put it, "history suggests that mankind rarely understands revolutionary change at the time it is coming about." The "what" and "how" will emerge as the result of a process as well, but not as specific dates in time.

At this point, at "the inception of the fourth empire," to quote Guéhenno, we do know that communication makes the world a freer place. The information monopoly, so coveted by dictators, is no more. But instant communication is no substitute for judgment, balance and experience, or for perspective, common sense and wisdom. To put it another way, the revolution in communication technology is changing the world, but it does not improve our intellectual capacity to analyze the significance of political threats, economic opportunities, classical values, or military alliance. The real worth of technological invention is directly related to the vision and values of those using the tools. The crux of the difficulty, Guéhenno writes, is that

> ... the populations continue to want to recognize each other as nations, but the nations — even the most powerful of them all, the United States — no longer have the capacity, in a global world, of protecting the peoples whose destiny they claim to embody from the uncertainties of the outside world that have irreversibly erupted into what used to be called their domestic affairs. Given competition from faraway countries, given the migration of poverty and terrorism, it has become as impossible to control the world that surrounds us as it is to ignore it. And the gulf between the nation as a locus of identity and the nation as a locus of power is formidable, for the natural temptation is to compensate with the complacent exaltation of one's identity what the nation has lost in effective power over the real.

> ... Infinitely more knowledgeable than Socrates, but keepers of a fragmented knowledge parceled out among innumerable specialists, we are capable of building all sorts of 'virtual communities' that will liberate us from the constraints of geography, and from the traditional political structures that have for so long framed our actions. But we are no more advanced than Socrates when it comes to exercising new powers and giving direction to our actions. More powerful than Socrates, we are neither freer, nor more just, than he.

No, we are not more just. But unlike Socrates' Greece, our world provides us with greater knowledge and broadens our choices. We can exchange ideas and interpret information in a way we never could in the past. That ability gives us a freedom that we had only in limited quantity before or, in many cases, not at all. But does this new freedom make the choices easier and the outcomes wiser?

We can see that the convergence of the computer with communication technology is changing how we conduct the business of government, the business of the marketplace, and the business of our private lives. We are, indeed, changing many of our social, economic, and political hierarchies — our conventional relationships, if you will — and replacing them with new networks that alter the structure, influence, and power of traditional institutions.

A case in point are chambers of commerce, which "are finding to their dismay that the fierce independent nature and self-sufficient style of many high-tech entrepreneurs make them hard to recruit." In an April 1999 *Wall Street*

Journal article, Alan Zaremberg, the president of the California Chamber of Commerce, concluded that

> ... soaring stock prices [of high-tech firms] make them less concerned than most Chamber members about immediate issues that affect profits. What's more, Internet companies so far haven't been heavily regulated. 'They're not used to looking over their shoulder at government the way, say, insurance companies do.'

Computer gurus, software writers, and Internet users are creating brand new social and economic interchanges. Stock markets are no longer the primary province of the socially prominent and wealthy elite. Electronic trading has eased access, opened the doors, lowered the cost, and changed the rules. Government has dealt with the issue of taxing e-commerce by placing a moratorium on it, but has proved incapable of providing a solution. The private lives and public positions of politicians can be tracked on the Internet, and their behavior is coming under closer scrutiny as a result.

The Internet is becoming a tool of communication and community in politics. The president of the United States held the first virtual town hall meeting in November 1999 at Georgetown University in Washington, D.C., and the French political group *Démocratie Libérale* created a Web site in October 1999 to debate proposed legislation, www.democratie-liberale.asso.fr (in France in the year 2000, no fewer than thirteen political parties maintained Web sites). Our twentieth-century pillars of community are multiplying, and "spontaneous communities" are blooming, "defined by common interests rather than by the accident of physical proximity," as *The Economist* put it in an October 1999 story. According to Nicholas Negroponte:

> [The Information Age is] really about how you're going to live.... What is community? What is family? And what does it mean to be part of a community?' The digital revolution is providing a new answer.... [C]ommunity today is defined less by physical proximity than by electronic proximity. Which means ... that today you're as likely to turn for information and fellowship to the Internet — that worldwide network of linked computers — as to a neighbor or colleague.... That's a change ... that has major implications for how all of us live.

It is a revolution, but not just gossip in electronic chat rooms. After all, my laptop is a machine, not a brain. It's not the machine that changes things, it's what I do with it that matters. Negroponte calls it *being digital*:

> As we interconnect ourselves, many of the values of a nation-state will give way to those of both larger and smaller electronic communities. We will socialize in digital neighborhoods in which physical space will be irrelevant and time will play a different role. Twenty years from now, when you look out a window, what you see may be five thousand miles and six time zones away. When you watch an hour of television, it may have been delivered to your home in less than a second. Reading about Patagonia can include the sensory experience of going there. A book by William Buckley can be a conversation with him.

How we make constructive use of information technologies, and how we give responsible direction to our actions, are in principle questions that have confronted every age. And, as in times past, we also are seeking answers. While we do so, we will live — and are already living — in an unpredictable and unstable world. If most of us do not yet know what we will become in the Information Age, we do know that the breakdown of the hierarchical discipline of the Cold War world and the introduction of Internet reflex are producing both certainties and uncertainties. New influences are being brought to bear on us as human beings, and on the institutions we have created to govern ourselves more reasonably and fairly and efficiently.

"The obituary of the nation-state is still unwritten," argues journalist William Pfaff, and it also "remains the most efficient and effective agency of self-government for a community of people united by a common history and culture." So far, so good. But Guéhenno is concerned about something different, about a weakening of traditional discipline and authority enforced by government. Who are the governor and the governed, and who is the caretaker? The traditional connection between the individual and the state is shifting, George Melloan observed in a January 2000 *Wall Street Journal* article, as "civil" institutions — "communities of interest," if you will — "often global in nature, are sprouting like daisies." The delights of such daisies, of course, are the social and business relationships that are developed and nurtured across continents and oceans, and the terrors are what we don't see, as organized crime and extremist groups coordinate their actions to prey on their victims. "Where does the nation-state fit in the world of global crime?" asks Peter Sommer of the London School of Economics: "There are no clear answers to it: civil rights of innocent people are involved, and politicians are concerned about national sovereignty."

What Are We Becoming?

These concerns are a reflection of Guéhenno's focus on "virtual communities" made up of electronic networks. That is why he writes about freedom from "the constraints of geography" — that is to say, instant communication via the Internet ignores geographical boundaries. That is why he writes about liberation "from the traditional political structures that have for so long framed our actions." That is to say, we are no longer dependent solely on government and parliamentary institutions to make us free, nor are we dependent on them to solve all our problems. Once important national political issues, as American sociologist Daniel Bell predicted, are becoming both global and local. But if the fabric of the nation-state is changing, it has not disappeared yet, nor is it going to vanish soon. By the same token, no country in the twenty-first century can stop the technological clock and survive if it cuts itself off from the wired and wireless world.

In the Information Age, in the absence of structured knowledge monopolies, governments are no longer the primary arbiters of the social, economic, and political commonweal. Since centralization and control of information, to differing degrees in both open and closed societies, have defined government, it is not surprising that its nature is affected by the operation of communication networks, whether they are worldwide or local. Our own sense of identity is being affected by the Information Age as well, and so are our loyalties. It is no longer axiomatic that we will seek and find our identity in a government whose actions we consider intrusive, any more than Netizens will be loyal patriots. On the contrary, identity is now being found on the Internet, on Web pages, in chat rooms, in news groups, in cybersalons, in addition to the traditional realms of religious belief, political loyalty, cultural heritage, economic position, and social elites.

As my colleague in Copenhagen, David Gress, put it in an e-mail, "1989-91 was simply the last in a long series of changes in Western societies that have undermined old-style loyalty and defense, the kind that made millions of Germans, Frenchmen, Russians, and British happily march to war in 1914." And, one should add, those changes prompted thousands of Americans to fight and die in both European wars of the twentieth century. The state itself, however, is still very much with us. A June 1998 *International Herald Tribune* article headlined "The Nation-State Is Still Alive and Well" observed that our parliaments, legislatures, government ministries, and international agencies such as the World Trade Organization and the International Monetary Fund still provide "the main framework for political expression and the passage and enforcement of laws." If the power of the nation-state is on the wane, government bureaucrats will not relinquish authority happily or without a fight. Gress goes to the heart of the matter: "Ask yourself if you as a citizen or businessman feel that the federal or state government is LESS rather than MORE intrusive than twenty years ago. What can you do with your land, your employees, even the layout of your office (disabled ramps, no smoking, etc.). This is the END of the state? Please!"

Indeed, had Gress been aware of a little-known government agency called the U.S. Access Board, he probably would have added it to his list. The board, created in 1990, has in the meantime become charged with making Web sites accessible to the disabled, and in 1999 designed standards for all sites purchasing from or selling to government agencies. Sites offering wild graphics, for example, would have to make sure they are useable by people with visual impairments, and sites that offer audio would have to provide supplemental text for those with hearing impairments.

Is it a laudable objective? Jenifer Simpson, manager of technology initiatives for President Clinton's Committee on Employment of People with Disabilities, explained in April 1999 that the federal government has the right to regulate form and content of on-line information as opposed to print: "The Internet is subject to market forces, but it didn't start through market forces, it was started by the federal government." My wife's cousin, Peter Thieriot, would say in response to Simpson, "So what?" And he would have a point.

Following the logic of Simpson's convolution, the argument could be made that government should regulate what kind of jobs we perform because the amount of money it collects in taxes is dependent on what we earn. So in what kind of age are we living? Is government becoming more powerful, or less so? Is it true that greater freedom and ease of communication are undermining the power of centralized authority? If so, where does that leave us? Guéhenno expresses his concern with the following question: "How can we prepare human communities for the new global world while preserving liberty and the values that, for a few centuries have inspired the best of our past?" Guéhenno doesn't have an answer. So he makes it clear that one of the consequences of the end of the Cold War is that

> ... the precariousness of institutions that have for two centuries been our reference points — the state, the nation, democracy — is not a fact that one can treat lightly. The extreme difficulty with which human beings build compromises and consolidate institutions renders their disappearance all the more disturbing, at the very moment at which those compromises and institutions seem to have achieved a sort of equilibrium.

Is there sufficient evidence to excuse what one book reviewer called Guéhenno's "whiffs of Continental affectation"? Is it possible that Europeans may know something the rest of us don't? They, after all, have been trying to figure out the riddles of civilization and its discontents for a long time. As one of my French friends in

Montigny-sur-Aube reminds me, "Europeans see things, Americans do things!" Guéhenno concludes that we do not yet know what we have inherited from the destruction of the two great totalitarian regimes of the twentieth century: Nazism and communism. New institutions have not arisen to take the place of the centralized political and military machines of the Cold War. And the legitimacy of those that remain is being challenged by the forces of decentralization, unleashed by the Information Age. Is the outcome of the challenge in sight, or is the world adrift, bobbing like a plastic sphere on the ocean?

Until the emergence of the wired world, the basic framework of statist institutions had remained unchanged for centuries. On all continents institutions were hierarchical in structure. But in the 2000s the credibility and legitimate authority of the hierarchy is being called into question — irrespective of whether legitimate authority has been freely elected. New interest groups are already forming. The nature and power of the classes are beginning to be defined by degrees of connectivity — that is to say, by the new relationships and the influence they build. Guéhenno illustrates this point by looking at Russia:

> On the periphery of the power struggles at the apex of the state, struggles in which analysis of the 'private' interests of each actor often entails as many explanations as a classical political analysis, another Russia is in the process of emerging, one that increasingly eludes the influence of the central power.... Thousands of local actors obliged to 'make do' — company functionaries, municipal or regional officials — have begun to construct a parallel society, not against the state, but alongside it.... [W]hat will become of the disjunction between economic structures that acquire their own dynamic and political structures that do not manage to produce the monetary and regulatory foundations indispensable to the development of an economy?

The relevance of selected institutions, historically vested with tremendous powers to regulate, is being bypassed by technology. As digital communication increases, as electronic commerce and business become global, as radio stations broadcast over the Internet on more than 6,000 Web sites on seven continents, as television sets become Internet screens, as e-business explodes in dimension, what new roles will traditional government agencies play? At home or in the office we will have a stream of hundreds of television channels from around the world to choose from on the Internet. Web sites will offer financial, commercial, cultural, educational, and scientific services that have heretofore been the province of the institutions of nation-states, determined by cultural mores, and confined within territorial borders. The armies of the Information Age will be global capital markets and electronic commerce, moving in the Internet.

Guéhenno's treatise on the nation-state sends a simple and powerful message of concern. Ours is a season of darkness, just as it is a season of light:

> ... [S]ocial invention is never completed, and the development of technology, by multiplying contacts and networks, by changing the rules of power, multiplies possibilities, thus increasing the human capacity for evil as well as good.

2.

HENDRIK FULDA AND THE CHAOS COMPUTER CLUB

*Conversation is still the most efficient
networking protocol that exists.*

{Bob Muglia, group vice president of Microsoft's Business Productivity Group}

The German village of Hammoor lies at the edge of the Lüneberger Heide. South of Lübeck and north of Hamburg, its weather in mid-November is misty, gray, and cold. It was like that on a Friday morning at 9:30, as I left to go to my last appointment. I was coming to the end of almost three weeks in Germany in the autumn of 1997, talking with business people, politicians, and government officials about the Internet. I had crisscrossed the country, from Bonn to Berlin and from Munich to Hamburg. I had visited Siemens Communications Networks and the Bayerische Vereinsbank, spoken with officials of Egon Zehnder International (a headhunting firm) and at BMW, and finally taken a tour of the German National Research Center for Information Technology, headquartered in a baroque castle in Birlinghoven, in the Rhineland.

I had listened to all kinds of people, from computer whizzes to egotistical politicians. The computer experts, with few exceptions, had been under the age of thirty-five. The two brightest "youngsters" I had met in some time were twenty-eight and thirty years old. In Munich they were in charge of guarding the computer security of one of the largest banks in Germany. They knew what they were talking about, and it was impressive. It was, for me, another encounter with the Internet Generation; they talked and I listened.

I met a well-known politician, in his mid-fifties, at his office in Prenzlauer Berg in what used to be the Soviet Sector of Berlin. He was charming, engaging, and, so it seemed to me, a born preacher. I should also add he was very generous with his time, because it was a Saturday morning and he spent most of it with me. He talked to me about Karl Marx's importance for the new Germany. I told him I thought Marx and the Information Age had little in common, and that information technology would be more helpful in rebuilding eastern Germany than Marx's political philosophy. Further, I explained that I was interested in talking about the Internet and the communication revolution it represents, because I thought both would profoundly affect how governments and free markets operate. I asked him what he thought. He didn't hesitate a minute before replying, "There's so much garbage on the Internet I just don't have time to use it. Anyway my assistant tells me if there's anything important. I'm still drowning in paper. I can dictate the letters. I have secretaries. There's no respect for others on the Internet, it's too undisciplined, and it's a pain in the neck. I much prefer a personal meeting where you can look someone in the eye and have a glass of beer at the local tavern. So I will be interested to see how the Internet changes politics." One year later, my host became president of the German *Bundestag.*

The conviction and the certainty with which he spoke surprised me, because I knew he was wrong. But he obviously believed what he was saying, and it continued to bother me.

When I returned to Stanford I talked to Gaku about it. He thought the politician's views pointed out "a common misconception."

"To those who don't use it," Gaku said, "who only hear about it by media and rumor, the Internet is a vast, undifferentiated, undisciplined, messy, dirty, dangerous place. But you never use the whole Internet, just as you don't wander the whole bookstore. You pick sections, and pick subjects, and pick authors, and ignore the rest."

Gaku was right. It was ignorance that was reflected in the comments of my German host. To be honest, he was mirroring my own B.C. (Before Computer) sentiments, and I couldn't fault him for that. Moreover, his view of the Internet in early November 1997 was the same one I had encountered in the Senior Commons of the Hoover Institution just two years earlier, when one of my colleagues had said to me, "the Internet's fine, but it has no future."

When I left Hammoor for my last appointment, on November 14, I wasn't really sure what to expect. I only knew where I was going.

Christian Hacke, a professor of international relations at the University of the Bundeswehr, dropped me off at the station in Ahrensburg, a small town about twenty kilometers outside of Hamburg. I was taking the train into the city to meet a member of the Chaos Computer Club. The appointment had been made for me by Frau

Heibey of *Internationes* in Hamburg, an office of the German government that helps official guests with their appointment arrangements.

I wasn't at all convinced that the person I was to meet, about whom I knew absolutely nothing, would even keep the appointment. I was sure he had never heard of *Internationes*. "Was he wondering," I thought, "whether it was a front for an intelligence operation?" This wasn't idle speculation, because I knew that intelligence agents from at least two European countries had tried to become members of the club. If I had been in his position I would have asked myself the same thing. But I'm jaded and suspicious, and older, and he, as it turned out, was quite the contrary.

Since my arrival in Germany on October 29 I had been looking forward to this visit, because I had read about the club in Cliff Stoll's book *The Cuckoo's Egg*. And I had told the very efficient people at *Internationes* that I placed a good deal of importance on this particular meeting. What was it, this club? From *The Cuckoo's Egg* I knew it was a group of hackers who had achieved notoriety in the mid-1980s by allegedly breaking into computers in Germany and France, at NASA, at the European Laboratory for Particle Physics in Cern, Switzerland, and into American physics labs in Illinois, at Stanford, and at Caltech. "They were said," according to Stoll, "to have stolen passwords, destroyed software, and crashed experimental systems.... [They] created headaches for network folks — they were thumbing their noses at hundreds of system managers and thousands of scientists." Stoll continued:

> [In 1988] the Chaos Club triumphantly announced their break-ins to the press, painting themselves as brilliant pro-grammers.... Chaos Club members justify their actions with a peculiar set of ethics. They claim that it's perfectly all right for them to roam through others' databases, so long as they don't destroy any information.... [T]hey believe their technicians' curiosity should take precedence over personal privacy...."

That was all pretty intriguing stuff to me, and I wanted to meet these people. As it turned out, what had been reported in the press about the club was not accurate. The real story, I was to learn about two hours later, was much more interesting.

Outside the main train station in Hamburg, I told the taxi driver where I wanted to go. I couldn't see him very well, but he certainly was younger than I, so I asked him if he'd ever heard of the Chaos Computer Club. He said, "I've never heard of it, but I know something about computers." In fact, when I had

Hendrik Fulda and the Chaos Computer Club

gotten into the taxi I had noticed several computer manuals lying on the front seat next to him, so I asked what he knew about them.

"Two years ago," he replied, "I decided I would teach myself how to use a computer, so I bought a book and started to read it while I was waiting for customers. Last month I bought a brand new Dell with a Pentium chip operating at 266 megahertz and 64 RAM."

I said, "You've got to be kidding. It's the first time I've heard this kind of story. In fact, I find it fascinating because I'm writing a book about the Internet for my friends. Do you mind if I ask you hold old you are?"

He said, "I'm seventy-two!" You could have knocked me over with a feather.

The CCC, as the club is known, is at 85 Schwenckestrasse, located in a residential neighborhood of one of Germany's most cosmopolitan cities. The club is in an old building that has been converted into apartments. You enter it by walking down five or six concrete steps, so that you are sort of halfway below ground.

I rang the bell at 11 A.M. I am almost six feet tall, but the man who answered the door was well over that. I looked up to introduce myself to Hendrik H. Fulda. We went down a narrow hallway to an office that opened off to the right. The walls were painted green, and the room was about ten feet square. It was piled high with computers and was strewn with papers and notes. It also smelled of tobacco, with the expected ashtrays full of cigarette butts. Herr Fulda offered me one of the few better chairs in the dark room, and I started our conversation by asking him about "the future of the world" while he brewed some fresh coffee. In fact, Herr Fulda did much more than that for me. He was open, frank, and perceptive as he answered my questions.

I asked him several months later to describe us both at the beginning of that meeting:

> It may sound a bit pathetic: 'the future of the world, the Internet and everything,' but we're discussing things like that in the CCC … when we meet for lengthy breakfasts on Sunday mornings in some café. Most of the time you can't really discuss this with strangers because if you do talk about this a lot, you come to some strange theories, observations and stories — which are not easy to understand when confronted with them for the first time. So, normally I would have a head start, but this time was different because Mr. Bark had his own share of theories, observations and stories to tell (and I didn't say strange, notice it? :-).
> So there we were, I — grown up with computers, connected since the first affordable acoustic couplers were available in Germany,

having done the transformation from stand-alone mailboxes to networked mailboxes to Internet systems, and the only paper-based mail I do is invoices, government-required stuff and letters to my girlfriend — and Mr. Bark, grown up in a paper-based world, just recently transformed into the world of reusable, non-bleached electrons of e-mail and the Internet.

At our meeting, I told Herr Fulda I had read about the club in *The Cuckoo's Egg*, and that I was writing a book for people my age about why they need to know how the Internet works — why they need to catch that silicon train. Partly in an attempt to make him feel less suspicious, but also because it was true, I explained that I really wasn't concerned about the club's capers in the1980s, but much more interested in how he and his friends think about computers. I wasn't sure whether he believed me or not, but he certainly could not have been more patient. I attempted to add to my credibility by saying I was trying to learn as much as possible about this new world, which for me had been foreign until 1995. "If one thing is becoming clearly evident," I said, "it is that this new, virtual world belongs to your generation, not mine. Will you tell me about it?" So, he poured me the first of three cups of coffee, and began to answer my questions. I spent almost two hours with him.

The Chaos Computer Club was legally established as a nonprofit organization in 1986, but existed before that time as an informal group of men and women, fewer than 100, interested in computers and new media. Keep in mind that during the early 1980s there were basically only two kinds of people interested in computers: (1) those who were using them to develop networks and conduct research, and who therefore weren't afraid of computers, and (2) those in their late teens and early twenties, who were curious about them and wanted to know how it all worked. They called themselves "hackers" (a term which in those days didn't necessarily carry sinister connotations). Herr Fulda defined the word for me this way: "Someone who is driven by curiosity and the urge to gather knowledge (well, sometimes about things he isn't supposed to know), thus learning the way things work — which is sometimes very different from how things are supposed to work."

The hackers in the CCC were interested in cyberspace and its impact on our society in general, and in computer security in particular — and therefore in hacking — seeing what you can do with computers and their systems. Individually or among friends, several club members — probably a group of four — broke into computers in the early 1980s to test their security.

What really got the club members in trouble was a break-in during 1983-84 into something called the BTX on-line service. This is where the "real story," as Herr Fulda recounted it, becomes much more interesting than the version recounted in

The Cuckoo's Egg. Various members used BTX to exchange e-mail and to talk about things of mutual interest. While they were happily discovering the joys of computer technology, some among them were also figuring out that you could, with a little creative ingenuity, change the content of an already-sent but not-yet-read e-mail message in someone else's in-box on the BTX service (in those days you could send and receive e-mail, but you could only download it and print it out with great difficulty). In the process, they had also discovered that the BTX service would spit out other people's passwords under certain circumstances. What this meant, of course, was that the password system was poorly designed, or the security wasn't strong enough, or the BTX system managers were not concerned.

In any event, one of the passwords was for the BTX computer account of the *Hamburger Sparkasse*. This was an old and respected savings bank in Germany which maintained accounts on-line, any of which could be accessed directly if one knew the password. The CCC hackers found this security hole outrageous, and decided to make a point. It was a breach of major importance, they reasoned, and it never should have happened. So, using the password garnered from the computer, some club members accessed the *Sparkasse's* BTX account, presumably told the computer to withdraw funds, and then dozed off to sleep. (In explaining this to me Fulda asked, tongue in cheek, "what are computers for anyway?")

When one of the members woke up in the middle of the night, a dial on the screen indicated that 135,000 German marks had been electronically withdrawn from various accounts. The group thought that a princely sum of more than 100,000 marks was enough to make their point, so they credited the amount to the CCC's BTX account, and shut down the computer. No one noticed. The next day the club informed the *Hamburger Sparkasse*, the BTX on-line service, and finally, the press. The club has been well known ever since! It should be added, as a kind of postscript, that there were no laws against computer-based crime in Germany at that time, and that the money was returned.

In November 1997, when Fulda and I met, the CCC had about 500 members, primarily in Germany, but also elsewhere in Europe and throughout the world, including the United States. The club publishes a quarterly magazine, in a mixture of German and English, called *Die Datenschleuder: Das wissenschaftliche Fachblatt für Datenreisende* (*The Data Sling: The Scientific Journal for Data Travelers*). The September 1997 issue, by way of illustration, dealt with short news updates on all kinds of computer-related issues, a new bug in Microsoft's Internet Explorer 4.0, regional and local meetings of computer clubs in Germany, the encryption debate, the death of Princess Diana, hacking digital TV, virtual women, and the forthcoming Chaos Communication Congress '97 to be held in Hamburg at the end of December.

A primary concern of the club was, and remains, security and freedom from government control — an interest which is shared by millions of computer users all over the world, of every ethnicity and political persuasion. It is true that in the early 1980s, various club members did access other computer systems, and not always for honorable reasons nor with defensible results. But it is also true that club members have demonstrated dramatically that computers cannot be considered secure merely because they are sophisticated technological devices. Fulda made that clear when he said, "You can create new worlds, but it is still people who make them work." I couldn't argue with his logic. He said, "Herr Bark, security is a question of attitude, not of science. We hack people's minds to make them aware of issues like the importance of security, and of the threats like people trying to steal your password."

CCC members don't sit around agreeing with each other any more than my colleagues do at the Hoover Institution. Nor do they spend a great deal of time congratulating themselves on how "neat" the Internet is. "We do," Fulda emphasized, "discuss computer problems and successes in order to keep going forward. If we have any kind of purpose, it is that we view ourselves as an information platform, as a turntable, as a springboard for the hacker community."

Close to one o'clock I thanked him for his time and told him sincerely, "This has been an enlightening morning for me. By the way, do you mind if I ask how old you are?" He said, "Not at all. I just turned 26." He is thirty years younger than I am; in fact, he is younger than my children. But it was he who had the knowledge, and it was he who did the talking. As I listened I thought, and still believe, that the really interesting history of the Internet lies in the distant future. It's going to be written in large part by people like Hendrik Fulda in Hamburg.

We left the club together, he for the U-Bahn station and I for a taxi. As we were walking he told me the following story. It's worth repeating, because the truth in it will make anybody laugh who's tried to learn how to use a computer (my Hamburg taxi driver would appreciate this story, too): "A friend," he said, "sent me installation instructions for some imaginary software. They read like this":

> You can choose different ways for installing our software. We recommend that you start with procedure (a) and, if not suitable, move on to the other options.
>
> a) Give the CD-ROM to a twelve-year-old and tell her, 'Please install this software on my computer.'
>
> b) Put the CD-ROM into your CD-ROM drive, change to the appropriate drive letter and run SETUP.EXE. Follow the instructions.

Hendrik Fulda and the Chaos Computer Club

c) If you still do not have the software installed on your computer, please call our customer help line. One of our representatives will gladly help you through the process of how to adopt a twelve-year-old.

Fulda is an IBM-certified Warp Server Engineer and member of Team OS/2, an international group of knowledgeable users of IBM's OS/2 operating system. His e-mail messages all carry this slogan at the end: "Team OS/2: Bother, we will. Fight, we must. And win, we shall." It's reminiscent of the conviction voiced by the Founding Fathers of the United States. Tom Paine and Patrick Henry spoke in the same way. It is the kind of language that makes me feel a lot better when I read that Orwell's predictions may only have been premature, "but not wrong."

Writing in *The Washington Post* in 1996, Jim Hoagland said:

> The struggle over the course of the information revolution is only beginning. The bureaucracies that are most threatened still have powerful hands to play. There is no guarantee that cyberspace will provide the world with the era of new freedoms that now seem likely. That battle is still to be fought, and won.

If the battle was just beginning in 1996, it was continuing, and much more intensely, in 2000. Arguments over encryption and the security of e-commerce were framed by the question, "Who will govern the Internet?" I know where Fulda stands, and I find that reassuring. But there can be no mistake that the situation at hand — the end of the knowledge monopoly — has enemies who live in the houses of government everywhere.

Governments want "to plunge their flagpoles into cyberspace," in the words of Andrea Petersen, writing for *The Wall Street Journal,* to collect taxes on e-commerce, to invade the privacy of communication, to monitor who is communicating with whom, about what, and how. These concerns are why, in January 1999, seventeen companies from France, Germany, Japan, and the United States — including America Online, France Telecom SA, Bertelsmann AG, Toshiba Corp., and IBM — established the Global Business Dialogue on E-Commerce. The group will look at nine areas: (1) taxation, (2) data security, (3) on-line privacy, (4) liability for on-line content, (5) intellectual property-rights protection, (6) technical concerns about the Internet, (7) controversial content such as pornography, (8) who has jurisdiction over Internet transactions, and (9) consumer confidence in e-commerce transactions.

The basic issue is straightforward. According to Graham Smith, writing for the

Financial Times, if "net content is not invasive and ... is as diverse as human thought," it must be protected from those who would censor, regulate, and govern it. Smith continues:

> The real need is to free the Internet and other digital networks from the threat of censorship by licensing and discretionary regulation, and to establish them as subject only to settled laws protecting free speech, enforced by independent judges. Achieving this in a world replete with countries whose governments do not value freedom of speech should be the important task for international lawmakers.

What kind of balance will be found is still an open question. I am not convinced there is a role for international lawmakers — why should they be any more responsible than national lawmakers? But I certainly agree with the conclusion reached by Kenneth Neil Cukier in *The Wall Street Journal* in 1998:

> ... [T]he Internet would never have come into being had it been forced to wait for bureaucrats to make decisions. Indeed, the Internet was created by privately owned data networks that voluntarily agreed to interconnect for mutual benefit.

Hendrik Fulda and certainly many of his friends understand this, just as they appreciate the value of freedom. CCC's Web page, "Welcome to the Club," begins as follows:

> Dear Hacker,
> The Chaos Computer Club is a galactic community of human beings including all ages, genders, races, and social positions. We demand unlimited freedom and flow of information without censorship. For more than a decade, the Chaos Computer Club has been a voice for all the hackers in this world. Confronted with an exploding use of information technology we will broaden our efforts to address the issues of our time, which is more than just the Internet.

I haven't seen Herr Fulda since November 1997, but I remember that morning well and with a great deal of pleasure. After I had returned to California at the end of that month, I began to wonder what he would say in response to a question I had not raised. I sent him an e-mail asking him, "When you think of this technological/computer/communication world we are living in, what does it mean?"

"Communication," he wrote to me,

> is the nature of human beings. 'I think, therefore I am' is nice, but most of the time it's, 'I communicate, therefore I am' for most of us. Communication networks do offer us a choice in how we can communicate with whom, and when. Thus, it changes the interaction of human beings and thus it changes everything.
>
> ... Knowledge [information] is ... one of the most important assets a human being can hold. And the transport of knowledge is becoming cheaper and easier with the new technologies at hand. Other important assets, such as wisdom and love, are perhaps not transferable at all; but I believe knowledge alone will help us all a great deal.
>
> ... [T]he Information Age holds many challenges and dangers. Most of them are our own fears.... The Information Age is supposed to feed on information. Information is supposed to be processed by our brains eventually. So, we'll have to use our brains even more.... It is important to care, to bother. Important to fight for the things you think are right and to fight to win. And of course it is even more important to have fun along the way, to have friends to be with and talk with and fight with. If you can join a group like the CCC to talk with and to fight with ...

Hamburg isn't very far away anymore. Distance is just a touch of my finger on my laptop. It's closer than it used to be when the only way I could get there was by boat, plane, train, and taxi. Today it's not a question of distance and borders, because I am "connected" in a mobile world.

3.

MOBILE CERTAINTIES

*It seems to me that I would never like
to have a telephone at home.
Once the initial amusement is over it's going to be a real pain in the neck.*

{Marcel Proust}

*By 2004/2005 there will be
one billion fixed-line telephone subscribers,
one billion Internet subscribers, and
one billion mobile subscribers worldwide.*

{*International Herald Tribune*, December 9, 1999}

For breakfast I went to the bistro next to Bertrand Jacquillat's office, in the rue Saint Honoré. It was Monday morning on March 6, 2000. I was looking forward to reading my newspapers in peace and quiet, before returning to Marina's apartment. I hadn't anticipated what was going to happen as I ordered a café au lait and a croissant, and opened up the *International Herald Tribune*. Several minutes later a young man came in. He sat down next to me and ordered a café au lait and a croissant too, and also an orange pressée. "How civilized," I thought. "That's why I love Paris." He had no newspaper to read. Instead he put his hand in his pocket, took out a mobile phone, dialed, and started his morning analysis of the stock market. I rattled my newspaper. He didn't bat an eyelash. He just kept on talking three feet away from my ear, louder than if he had been speaking to me directly.

It made me think of my friend Hubert Jousset's introduction to *les branchés* when we had lunch in the garden courtyard of the Hôtel Costes in September 1997. The difference on this March morning, two and a half years later, was that in Paris mobile phones were now everywhere. At least 30 percent of the French were using them — on the streets and boulevards, in the parks, in train stations and on trains, in restaurants, in shops, in private cars, in taxis, and in bistros — which leads to the conclusion that the simple act of peacefully walking through public places is now a kind of relic of the *ancièn regime*. When I returned to the apartment, in the rue Royale, I immediately looked for an article in my briefcase that I had cut out of the December 3, 1999 issue of *Le Figaro*. The headline said that there would be 450 million mobile telephones in use throughout the world in four more weeks, by the New Year 2000. Further, the article announced that the mobile telephone had become the primary symbol of globalization.

Signed by a one C.H., the article pointed out that in France (the writer could have mentioned other countries as well) "the mobile telephone remains victim of an image of the frivolous, and of the numerous journalists who present it as an object of luxury and of the mundane." But if at least 450 million cell phones are in use worldwide, the logical conclusion is they either serve a useful purpose or 450 million people are dilettantes. So which is it? And why is it important?

The answer, I think, is self-evident. Just like the Internet, mobile communication via the wireless telephone gives us a new kind of freedom. I now have four mobile phones, two in France and two in the United States. And each of them is there for a different reason. One is for the old house in the French countryside — we've been robbed twice since 1994 — so if burglars cut the telephone lines the guardians can still call the police. The second is for the property manager, so he can make a call if he's going to be late, and his family won't worry. The third, in the United States, is for making calls if I'm stuck in a traffic jam so I don't waste my time, and the fourth is for emergencies if my wife's car breaks down on the highway. It may be difficult to remember all the numbers, so they're all written down on a piece of paper. That greatly simplifies things. All of us can be always connected, as long as we remember where we put the piece of paper. But it's even easier if I program the different numbers into the memory of each telephone, then I don't need the piece of paper at all.

An even more powerful example was given in a full page advertisement by Siemens Corporation in a March 2000 issue of the *International Herald Tribune*. At the top of the page there is a picture of a wheel, and underneath is written "10,000 years ago: Man becomes mobile on the ground." The next picture is of Icarus' wing, followed by the words "100 years ago: Man becomes mobile in the air." The last image is of an *m* with a circle around it, and below, "Today: Man becomes mobile everywhere." This last conclusion is the whole point, which is why Finnish mobile-phone maker Nokia describes its vision of the future as "the mobile information society" — the convergence of wireless communication with the Internet. And this is why Forrester Research Inc. predicts that one-third of all Europeans will use the Internet via mobile phones by 2004 — for banking, stock trading, auctions, shopping, and for news reports on all kinds of things, from sporting events to the weather.

The chairman of Nokia predicts that by 2004 there will be one billion mobile telephones in use — just about as many as there are land-line phones. And Bill Gates has revised his vision of a personal computer in every home and on every desk, to having Internet access any time, any place, via a range of devices. Is this sovereignty *writ large*, in the form of a little device that weighs four and a half ounces? The answer is yes. And that sovereignty frees me from both home and office, and gives me an independence that I control. It means I can be anywhere and everywhere. It also means an irony for Bell Labs, which in the United States invented cellular telephony technology. Bell followed the recommendation contained in a market-research study it commissioned in the late 1970s that predicted a subscriber base of 800,000 by the year 2000, and concluded there would be "no market at any price." AT&T thus didn't go into the business and left cellular development to others — never imagining that by the year 2000 there would be more than 100 million mobile phone users in the United States, generating more than $45 billion in annual revenues. Nor did anyone foresee that by the year 2004-2005 predictions would estimate cellular revenue in the U.S. to be $100 billion, and a $200 billion market in Europe.

Europe has been, and remains, ahead of the United States in the use of mobile telephones. The principal reason is that the Europeans adopted a single digital standard a decade ago, called GSM (global system for mobile communications). It was, as a December 1999 *International Herald Tribune* article pointed out,

> ... a rare instance in which Europe's love of bureaucratic rule-setting and centralized economic planning has been of enormous benefit. It gave the Europeans a uniform standard, which allowed wireless operators and manufacturers there to build out the technology quickly.... [B]ecause European companies can produce for a single standard, 'they have economies of scale of four to one or five to one' over companies producing for the U.S. market.

The use of just one standard meant that Europeans, in whatever country they lived, could call anywhere in Europe. Phones made by Nokia in Finland or by Ericsson in Sweden worked just as well in Germany as they did in France or Spain, which explains in part why Nokia sells more mobile phones today than any other company in the world (Motorola is second). As noted in a February 2000 *Tribune* story, the explanation is simple: "... standardization has a tendency to snowball — wide adoption increases a standard's value, triggering even wider adoption. This is the case in computing, telecommunications and consumer electronics." In the United States, meanwhile, the unbridled power of competition in a free market produced competing standards, first with analog cellular phones, then with the second-generation digital mobile phone.

The result is that usage has grown at a slower rate, and depending on who is giving the opinion, the mobile phone is still considered by many to be a status symbol rather than what it really is, namely, a very handy communication device. But it obviously serves more constructive purposes if more than 450 million of them are in use, and that number is growing. By 2002, predicts the Strategis Group (which monitors the industry), mobile phone usage will reach 71 percent in Europe, and 40 percent in the United States. This latter estimate is too low in my view. The reason is that you can't do without it once you start to use it, and its use is going to grow like wildfire as prices continue to drop. As reported in a story distributed by Reuters on March 24, 2000:

> Robert Silvestri huddled over his wireless phone to chat in a bitter Manhattan wind, then straightened and proclaimed his love for the slim black device. Praising the phone's use-any-where convenience, Silvestri, a twenty-five-year-old tobacco company salesman from Fairlawn, N.J., said, 'I always carry it. I feel naked without it. I need it.' More and more Americans feel the same way. [I am one of them!]

Mr. Silvestri isn't alone in his addiction to the wireless world. Large companies such as Intel, Salomon Smith Barney, and Credit Suisse First Boston are giving hundreds of their employees wireless e-mail devices, with brand names such as Blackberry and Chatboard. "This is crack for investment bankers," said Tim Smith of Credit Suisse in April 2000. "It's the best gadget I've ever had." And not far behind is a wireless technology called Bluetooth, named after a tenth-century Viking king.

More than 1,800 companies in the telecommunications, computing, and network industries, including 3Com, Toshiba, Motorola, Nokia, Microsoft, IBM, Lucent, and Ericsson, are supporting use of a technology that allows computers, printers, televisions, VCRs, and mobile phones to communicate with each other without wires or cables if they are within thirty feet of each other. As Microsoft executive Brian Shafer told the *Financial Times* in April 2000,

"Bluetooth will revolutionize the electronic and communications device market ... because for the first time, all devices can become connected to each other and therefore to the Internet." By 2005, so predicts one market research firm, more than 670 million Bluetooth-enabled devices will be on the market.

But Bluetooth's taste of things to come will be preceded by the arrival of third-generation technology, called 3G, and the introduction of a new set of standards known as UMTS (universal mobile telecommunications system). There is already a new standard called WAP (wireless application protocol), which allows mobile phones to access the Internet. WAP will do for wireless telecommunication what GSM did for the mobile phone itself, and other 3G standards will certainly follow. Nokia's chairman, Jorma Ollila, predicted in October 1999 that 600,000 of the estimated one billion mobile phones in use by 2004-05 would use WAP, and the head of Oracle Corporation, Larry Ellison, agreed with the probable result: "This new generation of wireless Internet device will allow more Europeans to have access to the Internet than Americans." Whether or not Ellison's prediction comes true, it is a certainty that wireless technology is producing a marriage between mobile communication and the Internet. That's why WAP is called the "personalized Internet."

This marriage, as that between the computer and communication technology, will also have unexpected and unintended consequences. Telecommunication and banking are already converging as European banks and telecoms form partnerships, such as the Deutsche Bank with Mannesmann in Germany and the Bank of Scotland with British Telecom's BT Cellnet. Traditional fixed-line telephone infrastructures don't have to be in place because mobile telephony has leapfrogged over telephone poles, introducing the possibility that there may be a generation that won't get on the PC. In Finland wireless phones outnumber traditional ones, which is why the mobile e-services revolution is happening in Scandinavia and not in Silicon Valley. What will happen to phone booths? And even though the price of using mobile phones in the U.S. has dropped by 38 percent since 1996, it's even cheaper in Europe where the purchase of prepaid cards, with a specific number of minutes of usage, replaces expensive monthly service charges. Indeed, cellular prices fell between 15 and 25 percent in Europe during 1999. And it is also a certainty that the use of voice, mobile, and Internet communications, still converging, will introduce a new kind of enterprise to the worlds of e-commerce and e-business, called m-commerce.

How soon will all this occur? And how will it affect the use of our hard-wired personal computer, if we can connect with our mobile phone anywhere in cyberspace, from everywhere? I don't know the answers. But I do know that

Mobile Certainties

elementary school children being educated today will consider the wired and the wireless world to be one and the same, as they conduct their private lives and professional careers in a mobile society from anywhere, any time, any how. What we are becoming is being decisively influenced by networks both wired and wireless, and by the Principle of Now.

4.

THE PRINCIPLE OF NOW

Now is the Watchword of the Wise.

{Old proverb; author unknown}

*The distinction between past, present and
future is only an illusion, however persistent.*

{Albert Einstein}

The song "White Christmas," written by Irving Berlin, was featured in the film *Holiday Inn* in 1942, the same year that Hedy Lamarr's patent for a "Secret Communication System" was registered in Washington, D.C. Twelve years later, in 1954, Bing Crosby, Danny Kaye, Rosemary Clooney, and Vera-Ellen starred in a movie that has become a classic, *White Christmas*. It is the story of an American Army general, Tom Waverly, who in his retirement following World War II runs an inn in Vermont.

It is mid-December. Crosby and Kaye have become famous entertainers and unexpectedly find themselves on their way to the inn. On arriving they discover that the former general, under whom they served in the 151st division in Europe, is the owner. Things are not going well. It has not snowed, there are no guests, and General Waverly is about to go broke. Crosby and Kaye decide the only way to save the retired general's investment is to have all the men who served under him come with their families to spend the holiday in Vermont. But there is a problem: Crosby needs to contact all of them at once. So he goes to New York City, appears on the nationally televised *Ed Harrison Show,* and appeals to all the men of the 151st division "to give the nicest Christmas gift he'll ever get, to the nicest guy we'll ever know." Of course, thanks to the television network, the appeal is heard. The men arrive with their families on Christmas Eve. The inn is filled with guests. General Waverly gives some warm and generous words of thanks. And the movie ends with the song "White Christmas," as new snow falls in Pinetree, Vermont.

There are several parts to the message here. Real-time networks are not as new as we sometimes may believe and, of course, Bing Crosby used the only one available half a century ago. It wasn't fast but it was live, and it connected thousands of people. Like the Internet, the television network's speed was defined by real time. Also like the Internet, its value was enhanced by how many people were "connected." In this case, in 1954, most of the men from the 151st division happened to be watching TV. Today, millions of people "watch" the Internet. On December 25, 1999, the AltaVista search engine listed 7,000 Web pages for "White Christmas."

The use of today's vast and intertwined world of nets doesn't differ very much from Crosby's use of *The Ed Harrison Show.* The networks of the Information Age are computers connected with computers, but the principle is the same. Real people operate them, just as real secretaries once wrote business letters on Underwood typewriters. But here the similarities stop, and the unintended consequences begin. In the past, if we wanted to keep a copy of a typewritten letter, we took two sheets of paper and used a carbon sheet between them. Just try buying a piece of carbon paper in a stationery store now! You can still find it everywhere in Europe, but we have to look hard in the United States.

We have moved beyond carbon sets to the mimeograph machine, to the photocopier, to making electronic duplicates of our letters. The real difference here, though, is that typewriters couldn't talk to each other, and computers can. Bing Crosby's appeal to the 151st division, while live, wasn't interactive, but the Internet is. That's the gist of the revolution.

Like the older network of television, the Internet is changing our habits and how we use our time as more and more people are connected. According to a report in the *Financial Times* in December 1999, "[T]he internet might have brought some changes, particularly in the world of business. But history shows that it is unlikely to make any difference to the lives of ordinary people."

"Don't ask me anything about it 'cause I ain't interested," as Richard Tomkins quotes Derek Smith, a truck driver coming out of the Pea Bung fish-and-chip shop in Grimsby, England. "I get sick of hearing about it. Web-site this, dot-com that — it drives you up the bloody wall." I don't want to pick an argument with Mr. Smith, but he doesn't know what he's talking about — and neither is he ordinary. But he is a member, in good standing, of an increasingly shrinking minority in Europe.

Critics of the Internet, and more specifically of the World Wide Web, often refer to it derisively as "the world wide wait," and sometimes, if a lot of people are trying to use limited bandwidth at the same time, the critics have a legitimate point. It isn't always possible to access a Web site immediately. But cynics shouldn't be too smug about it, because the present isn't standing still. As my friend Michael Raoul-Duval pointed out to me, "By the time you finish your book, the speed of the Internet and the number of people using it will have increased many times over." And in fact, that is what's happening. The IBM 600 E I purchased in January 2000 is infinitely faster than the computer in my office, purchased in 1998, which in turn was almost three times as fast as the laptop I ordered at the Stanford bookstore in 1995. By the time this book goes to press, all of the user statistics in it will have changed as well.

Interwoven with mobile communication and the Internet is speed. The forward motion, driven by new information technology, and the constantly expanding reach of the Internet, acquires an energy of its own. This momentum accelerates the rate of change. As the Internet grows in size and use, it becomes more powerful as a medium. When the electronic transmission of information is commonplace and the mystery surrounding the operation of computers has disappeared, the Internet will be essential. There exists tremendous commercial competition to improve access and speed, and pressure also mounts to expand bandwidth, to bring hardware up to date, and to make software state-of-the-art. Some people call it "convenience in a box." I call it the Law of Relationships.

For the "connected," access to information and speed of transmission have values all their own. What does speed mean? That's difficult to answer, because speed has different applications. For Qwest Communications, one of the nation's largest long-distance telephone carriers headquartered in Denver, speed means building the highest-capacity fiber-optic network in Europe, the United States, and Mexico, and expanding into the Pacific Rim as well. It means sending data, images, video, and voice at hyperspeed. It means participating in ventures, alliances, and partnerships with Hewlett-Packard, SAP America, Siebel Systems, Netscape, and Microsoft. It means creating a network that can transmit the entire Library of Congress from the Atlantic to the Pacific coast of the United States in twenty seconds.

Between 1999 and 2001, in partnership with the Dutch telephone carrier Royal KPN, Qwest will commit almost $1.5 billion to construct a high-speed telecommunications network among twenty-eight cities across Europe and connecting to the U.S.

For a wide variety of reasons the advantages of speed are many. It's an invaluable tool for architects, designers, and engineers, because it allows Internet-based collaboration. For example, to design and construct Hong Kong's new airport, dozens of

The Principle of Now

architects and construction companies were able to electronically exchange more than 100,000 two- and three-dimensional computerized models.

Consider, too, the transformation of medical education and research. Alan Millman, an assistant professor at the University of Illinois in Chicago, designed a three-dimensional computer model of the human ear in 1997. When he tried to show it to his class on the Internet, however, the model froze on the screen. The Net was too slow. But that same year the world's fastest supercomputer at that time, called Janus and built by Intel Corporation, was installed in Albuquerque, New Mexico, at Sandia National Laboratories. Named after the Roman god of beginnings (or portals), it performed one trillion mathematical operations per second, using 9,072 Pentium Pro processors. According to a report in the *International Herald Tribune*:

> Janus is so fast and has so much memory that it can simulate complex events — like explosions, nuclear fusion reactions, missile impacts of the crash of a comet into the Earth — with detail that was impossible before....

> While two-dimensional simulations are now commonplace, adding the third dimension takes an enormous amount of additional computer power. Rendering a three-dimensional process in fine detail, and then having it unfold along the fourth dimension, time, strains even the most powerful computers.... It is called Janus because, like the Roman god, it has two faces; one side of the computer can be used for classified research while the other is solving unclassified problems.

What was significant about this, from a scientist's viewpoint, was that Janus represented a "qualitative change," according to William Camp, director of computational science, computer science, and mathematics at the laboratory. "For the first time," Camp explained in the late summer of 1997, "we can do full four-dimensional simulations.... Until recently, scientists have described themselves as either experimentalists or theorists ... but computational science is rapidly establishing itself as a third branch of inquiry, and the one that is the most likely to lead to the next major breakthroughs in many areas of research.'"

If Alan Millman is to use his three-dimensional ear as a teaching tool in a virtual classroom he needs greater speed. So do business men and women who want to hold real-time, three-dimensional meetings — thereby saving on travel days, airfares, and hotel bills. To this end, research efforts are under way to develop faster architectures for global networks. One of them, Internet2 — www.internet2.edu — is a collaborative effort among academia, industry, and the National Science Foundation, initiated in the autumn of 1996. By early 1998, its members had invested more than $50 million in the five-year, $300 million project. This was followed in April 1998 by the donation of $500 million in fiber-optic capacity and equipment from Qwest Communications in Denver, Cisco Systems of San Jose, and Northern Telecom of Ontario, Canada, to create a private, experimental network. On leave from the University of Michigan as vice provost for information and technology, Douglas Van Houweling is president of the project, officially called the University Corporation for Advanced Internet Development (UCAID). UCAID's purpose is to lead the way for development of many more advanced networking technologies.

It is hoped the project will develop the means to send and receive data at speeds from 100 to 1,000 times faster than today's Internet allows. If Internet2 develops still faster ways to send data, one envisioned result is a three-dimensional version of teleconferencing: a virtual-reality encounter whereby scientists and others anywhere in the world can collaborate in manipulating the same information simultaneously. Greater speed will allow a proliferation of Januses in smaller and less expensive form. As computers approach the speed of *now,* the Internet's electronic skeleton will change as well, so that backbones which run at forty-five million bits per second today will be running at 2.5 billion bits per second in Internet2. And if the history of the ARPANET is any guide, there is an Internet3 somewhere in the future that will transform our networks once again; in fact, a project with this title is already under way in Sweden.

The California portion of the UCAID project involves a multi-campus network, including Stanford University, the University of California at Berkeley, and UCLA. It should eventually operate at speeds so fast that experiments can be conducted to create, for example, a simulated global environment, a virtual sky, the library delivery of a thirty-volume encyclopedia in less than two seconds, or for the medical profession, a map of electrical pathways traversing the virtual brain. Tomorrow's Internet will see a new generation of advanced education and research applications that will include digital libraries, telecollaboration, telemedicine, and remote laboratories. In 2000, more than 170 universities are participating in the effort, as well as information-technology and telecommunication companies from around the world, including Siemens, Sun Microsystems, GTE Corp., Microsoft, Deutsche Telekom, Cable & Wireless, IBM, Ericsson, Cisco Systems, Alcatel, British Telecom, Qwest, and Nortel Networks. One of the likely results of Internet2 will be the emergence on a global scale of real-time multicasting.

But there is, as Douglas Van Houweling explained to the *Detroit Free Press,* a

234

more important aspect of this work. There does not yet exist a mechanism that allows two different procedures, such as video conferencing and ordinary e-mail, to receive different priorities on the Internet. "… [T]he most important innovation we're focused on for Internet2," said Houweling, "is to add additional protocol capabilities to the Internet so that applications can request and be guaranteed the kinds of quality of service they need to do their job."

For speed and technology's relentless movement forward, there is no stopping point. When Internet2 arrives, the speed it brings with it will represent another quantum leap. The only certainty is that Internet2 will not be the last word. A research project at IBM called "quantum mirage," for example, demonstrates that information can travel through solid substances without the benefit of wires. This work, called nanotechnology processing, represents a dramatic and critical departure from the microprocessors of today, one that may eventually afford computers millions or even billions of times as much processing power using a fraction of the electrical power. Another project, conducted by Hewlett-Packard Co., involves research into a microscopic world where computing components no larger than a single molecule can be produced. HP's scientists conclude that at some point computers may operate 100 billion times faster than today, creating a universe in which supercomputing power is inexpensive and pervasive enough to be incorporated into everyday objects of all types.

The logical consequence of all this is that in another generation the Internet will no longer be considered a miracle of technology; being connected will be taken for granted. It will allow us to conduct much of our lives — personal and cultural, business and professional — on different kinds of screens, in different sizes and shapes, using devices large and small, wired and wireless, in all kinds of locations we aren't yet accustomed to using.

Imagine wired kitchens and wired coffee pots, electronic walls for writing, and remote-controlled heating. Products that interact with the environment. Or clothes that "refresh" themselves, made from fabrics that "know" how to restore creases and remove stains. "Smart" homes, too, will be able to adjust lighting and climate. Already, houses built in Silicon Valley in 2000 were being wired with networks for e-mail and video conferences, and with the means to link television sets, computers, and printers.

In 1997 the City Council in Palo Alto, California, proposed the creation of a Silicon Valley Communications Authority to issue revenue bonds and upgrade the city's cable system. The idea was to install fiber-optic lines to allow high-speed transmission of data and Internet access as well as more television channels. The city even hired its own telecommunications manager, with the goal of

What Are We Becoming?

connecting every citizen to the Internet. As plans developed in 1998, the expense involved became significant, so the city initiated plans to privatize management of access and usage of the network, and announced a pilot program in April 1999. In early 2000 the project was moving forward, although slowly. But the idea here is the message: access and speed entice. Fiber-optic cable was laid along the town's El Camino Real in the spring of 2000.

It is not surprising that Palo Alto, located in the heart of Silicon Valley, would take steps toward citywide connection. It was merely the reflection of a decision of greater significance, taken in Washington, D.C., one year earlier. The Telecommunications Act of 1996 included a $2.25 billion program to wire every public school and library throughout the United States; by February 2000 an estimated 95 percent of American schools were Internet-connected, and the same thing was happening, albeit more slowly, in Europe. This continuing pace of change — the real pressure of the Principle of Now — foretells that by the end of the first decade of the twenty-first century, an entire generation of Americans will be communicating via the Internet. That, in turn, will give new definition and enhanced meaning to the term Internet Generation. Bruce Sterling, author of the article "A Short History of the Internet," put the same conclusion another way, a long time ago in 1993. I wonder if he really knew how right he would be:

> Learning the Internet now, or at least learning about it, is wise. By
> the turn of the century, 'network literacy,' like 'computer literacy'
> before it, will be forcing itself into the very texture of your life.

If "network literacy" is becoming part of the texture of our lives — and it is — what do we become? How do we keep our balance as we seek to manage our use of information technologies, so that the Principle of Now doesn't become simply overwhelming? Thomas Gerrity, dean of the Wharton School of Business at the University of Pennsylvania, points out that information technology is not only time-saving but can also be time-strangling. In a story in the *Financial Times*, he said:

> It's tempting to spend less and less time thinking about the mes-
> sage. There is a tendency not to prioritize. But how do you keep a
> balance, a judgment, when all the stimulus around you tells you to
> react, react, react? Managing that balance is important. It's like
> balancing the wide-angled lens and the telephoto lens.

Gerrity's concern, expressed in December of 1998, was preceded two years earlier, in December 1996, by another voice urging caution: "I understand and have always understood," wrote Mark Helprin in *Forbes ASAP*, "that the heart of western civilization is not the abdication of powers but rather meeting the challenge of their use." Helprin continued, addressing those who embrace without reservation the Information Age:

> You have been too enthusiastic in your welcome of it, and not wary enough. Some of you have become arrogant and careless, and, quite frankly, too many of you at the forefront of this revolution lack any guiding principles whatsoever or even the urge to seek them out. In this, of course, you are not alone. Nor are you the first. But you must. You must fit this revolution to the needs and limitations of man, with his delicacy, dignity, and mortality always in mind. Having accelerated tranquility, you must now find a way to slow it down.

I can't argue with Helprin's admonishment to be wary, nor with Gerrity's concern with balance. The acceleration of tranquility and the pressure to react make it tempting to forget that man is not the measure of all things, and that the Principle of Now is not a moral imperative. On the contrary, the electronic tools of the Information Age are just that, tools. Our creation of them gives us the responsibility to meet "the challenge of their use," and prompts some to ask, "Are the tools in charge?"

It's a fair question, and some argue that they may become so. A study released in early 2000 argued that "the Internet was creating a broad new wave of social isolation in the United States, raising the specter of an atomized world without human contact or emotion." Two professors, at Stanford and the Free University of Berlin, conducted the study. The results were billed as reflecting the unintended social consequences of using the Internet. One of the effects, reported the authors, is that every hour spent on-line reduces television viewing by the same amount of time, and therefore makes us more lonely and isolated than we already are. An alternative interpretation, however, might say that social networks are expanding. Take the case of clinical social worker Janna Malamud Smith, who said in an article in the *International Herald Tribune* on February 22, 2000:

> On-line, in the last couple of weeks I've kept in touch with busy friends, some of whom live halfway around the world, and tracked temperatures in Seville, which we will visit next month. I have easily located and purchased out-of-print books from small, secondhand dealers and looked up some useful exercises for a knee I had hurt. Each of these little solitary outings made me shamefully happy.

Others speculate that the question "what we are becoming?" isn't answered yet, but that the future may hold some unpleasant surprises. This concern was found in the writings of Ray Kurzweil and Hans Moravec, who published, respectively, two books in 1999, entitled *The Age of Spiritual Machines* and *Robot: Mere Machine to Transcendent Mind*. The disquiet was reflected again in an article by Bill Joy, co-founder and chief scientist at Sun Microsystems, published in the April 2000 issue of *Wired*, headlined "Why the Future Doesn't Need Us." All three participated in a symposium held at Stanford University on April 1, 2000, whose subject was "Will Spiritual Robots Replace Humanity by 2100?"

George Gilder, editor of the "Gilder Technology Report" co-published by *Forbes*, called Kurzweil's book "[one] that makes all other roads to the computer future look like goat paths in Patagonia," and Bill Gates described it as "a thought-provoking analysis of human and artificial intelligence and a unique look at the future in which the capabilities of the computer and the species that invented it grow ever closer." Joy's argument in *Wired* is less encouraging; he asks whether "our most powerful twenty-first century technologies — robotics, genetic engineering, and nanotech — are threatening to make humans an endangered species." The symposium at Stanford addressed the following, disturbing proposition:

> ... [T]oday's human researchers, drawing on emerging research areas such as artificial life, artificial intelligence, nanotechnology, virtual reality, genetic algorithms, genetic programming, ... DNA, and quantum computing ... are striving, perhaps unwittingly, to render themselves obsolete — and in this strange endeavor, they are being aided and abetted by the very entities that would replace them (and you and me): super-powerful computers that are relentlessly becoming tinier and tinier and faster and faster, month after month after month.

> ... Will we soon pass the spiritual baton to software minds that will swim in virtual realities of a thousand sorts that we cannot even begin to imagine?...Will thinking take place at silicon speeds, millions of times greater than carbon speeds? Will our children — or perhaps our grandchildren — be the last generation to experience 'the human condition'? Will immortality take over from mortality? Will personalities blur and merge and interpenetrate as the need for biological bodies and brains recedes into the past? What is to come?

I recognize that the challenges are real, and that technology in irresponsible hands poses serious dangers; but I don't believe in spiritual machines nor do I believe that my grandchildren will be the last generation to experience "the human condition." I found it reassuring that the symposium was held at all, though, with the issues being discussed by thoughtful people. And I feel certain that questions will continue to be asked and that debate will flourish. While the debate interests me, it's not the object of my attention as I think about what we are becoming now. I'm much more concerned with machines that can't be programmed with common sense and wisdom, and with old-fashioned concepts of loyalty and patriotism that for some seem to be changing in the wired world.

There is a tremendous difference between sending and receiving data on networks, and applying wisdom to the interpretation of what information means and how it is used. "The Internet is exposing all of us to oceans of data," said my friend Jim Gidwitz. "Making sense of it requires a framework of values and ethics that are not universally shared." So, how will we proceed? We can see that part of the Internet story visible to us today, but we don't know yet how the story's going to end.

The Internet does make the world of communication closer and faster. But it is also a neutral force. It's a new "language," in a sense, that more and more people are learning to speak. How it is spoken determines its meaning. Instant messages and "the death of distance" do not, ipso facto, improve either behavior or the quality of analysis. The Internet is not a substitute for reflection, and it does, unfortunately, encourage reaction by reflex in the pressure cooker ruled by the Principle of Now. The Internet does not endow its users with the ability and courage to tell the difference between right and wrong. Neither does it provide the user with a set of values and ethics. On the Internet, in chat rooms and via e-mail, people have been known to talk to each other in a rude, vulgar, and insulting manner that they wouldn't presume to use if they were addressing each other face to face. This kind of behavior was never expected or anticipated by those who created the Internet. Will it, too, have long-term and unintended consequences for what we are becoming? Are we placing false confidence in the positive power of faceless communication?

We know that the control of information, and the means to hide it, censor it, distort it, and distribute it, can be weapons in evil hands. The communist regimes of Europe proved this point beyond a shadow of a doubt between 1945 and 1989. Today we read a great deal about the importance of protecting freedom on the Internet from the intrusive burdens of government control and regulation. But, thus far, we read much less about how the freedom of the Internet will influence our concepts of nationalism and sovereignty, our social mores and cultural traditions, our political judgment and management of our governmental institutions, our conduct of foreign policy and warfare, our promotion of peace, and our practice of tolerance and civility. And what of one of the greatest unknowns, the future of privacy and freedom of speech? Will governments successfully assert a right to violate the privacy of our communication by reading our messages if there is a so-called "legitimate reason"? The encryption controversy is a serious debate about freedom of speech. Those who use encryption on the Internet understand its importance, yet much of the general public is unaware that the debate is taking place.

At the beginning of the new millennium there is less government control over information than there has ever been. Will this new freedom to transmit knowledge over oceans and across continents ultimately — and ironically — produce more government control? And how ironic it would be, as well, if the freedom of the Internet lulls us into the erroneous conclusion that government has no role to play at all. There is evidence to suggest this may be occurring; what is not clear is how widespread it is and how it may progress. The following observation comes from an article in *The New York Times* in April 1998, headlined "Techno-Nothings":

> ... [W]hat is so striking about Silicon Valley is that it has become so enamored of its innovative and profit-making prowess that it has completely lost sight of the overall context within which this is taking place. There is a disturbing complacency here toward Washington, government, and even the nation. There is no geography in Silicon Valley, or geopolitics. There are only stock options....

> People here [Silicon Valley] are not involved in Washington policy because they think the future will be set by technology and market forces alone and eventually there will be a new world order based on electrons and information.

Can the Principle of Now influence our feelings of loyalty? The Internet may be altering our traditional image of the patriot. Our time-tested loyalties to the state are being redefined. If we use the Internet, many of us become Netizens of the world, whether we like it or not. The structures of our national and international social, economic, and political communities are being taken apart. How will they be put back together, and by whom? Will traditional concepts of loyalty and patriotism be essential parts of new structures, held together by national patriotism and political loyalty to governments which are no longer sovereign in the conventional sense of the word? Is the traditional partnership between the private citizen and the public state changing too?

In a *New York Times* article from April 18, 1998, one Silicon Valley business executive described the relationship between citizen and government in an alarming way. In response to a question about how often he discussed Iraq or Russia or foreign wars, he replied:

> Not more than once a year. We don't even care about Washington. Money is extracted from Silicon Valley and then wasted by Washington. I want to talk about people who create wealth and jobs. I don't want to talk about unhealthy and unproductive people. If I don't care enough about the wealth-destroyers in my own country, why would I care about the wealth-destroyers in another country?

The article's author, Thomas Friedman, points out that, "because of the intense competition here among companies, and the continuous flood of new products, there is a saying in Silicon Valley that 'loyalty is just one mouse-click away.'" There is no way of knowing how typical a response this really is, but the implications are significant. Will the Internet make our world, and the relationship between citizen and government, more or less stable? In the same article, Robert Kagan of the Carnegie Endowment for International Peace in Washington, D.C., argues that "the people in Silicon Valley think it's a virtue not to think about history because everything for them is about the future.... But their ignorance of history leads them to ignore that this explosion of commerce and trade rests on a secure international system, which rests on those who have the power and the desire to see that system preserved."

My own view, although I sympathize with Kagan's predilection, is that this argument is too simple. Part of a secure international system is undoubtedly "the hidden fist" of military power that maintains a safe environment for Silicon Valley's technologies to thrive — in other words, we still need armies, navies, and air forces, as well as the FBI. But another, equally important part is the obituary of the knowledge monopoly written by one communication revolution. Most people experience freedom as personal autonomy, which means personal sovereignty. Once they have tasted it, they don't want to give it up. Users of the Internet are experiencing the same sovereignty when they locate information and exchange knowledge. It isn't surprising that they don't want it taken away from them.

As more and more people use the tools of the wired and mobile world, the sovereignty conferred by freedom of communication becomes more influential. It is a force completely different from an organized, institutional defense of sovereignty, such as a nation going to war. If we wish to survive and prosper in the global marketplace of goods and ideas, our governments must treat this force carefully.

Governments, after all, have not conferred the freedom of the Internet on us. We have conferred it on ourselves. Its influence is already being felt. Pressure is mounting on government officials to tell the truth rather than obfuscate and dissemble. They can only serve us well if they are credible. Since information is mutually accessible to both citizens and government officials on the Internet, the primary ingredient for doing business in the future, whether it is private, political, or commercial, will be credibility. If credibility is in doubt, loyalties will change, and the partnership between the private citizen and the public state will very likely be replaced with at least ridicule and contempt, if not outright conflict. In Washington, D.C., William Jefferson Clinton's failure to conceal the truth from inquiring media is an example of "chapter and verse" on the subject.

In times of old we had loyalties to our government, to our flag, and to our country. We were generally proud of our politicians. We didn't always agree with them, but we respected them. In more recent times the Internet has generated a healthy respect for the freedom of our new communication networks that in some cases seems to be more important than respect for our political leaders. Once, when we had comparatively little control over what information was available to us via the newspaper, radio, or television, we depended on the information provider. So we read our newspapers, we listened to the radio, and we watched the evening news. But if the individual becomes the information searcher, the information gatherer, and the information transmitter, how independent do we become? To what and to whom do we have loyalty? One answer is: to ourselves and to our networks.

No one is immune from the lure of this kind of loyalty, new to all of us who use the Internet. This changes the political loyalty conundrum in a fundamental way. If we have unlimited access to information — whether we buy it from satellite companies, download it from the World Wide Web, exchange it via electronic mail, deposit it via electronic money transfers, trade it via on-line stock transactions, fax it from laptop computers, or discuss it on mobile telephones — we become sovereign. And some of us become loyal to our sovereignty. We become patriots of no party, rather than embracing patriotism born of philosophical commitment and of the need to protect territorial borders. We don't yet know how new definitions of loyalty and patriotism may affect how we behave. Are we loyal to our country? Which country?

The Internet is now part of the information infrastructure of the globe. A separation is no longer possible. For those countries with access to it — well over 200 in the year 2000 — the Internet is creating a global industrial and economic infrastructure shared by 300 million people throughout the world. What will the number be in January 2001? Living in the Information Age, they are becoming members of a new Age of Informational Man. James Dale Davidson and Lord William Rees-Mogg, in *The Sovereign Individual,* put it this way:

Information technology makes possible a dramatic extension of
markets by the way assets are created and protected.... Leading
nation-states, with their predatory, redistributive tax regimes and
heavy-handed regulations, will no longer be jurisdictions of
choice.... [Welfare states] will lose their most talented citizens
through desertion.

Is the stifling embrace of welfare paternalism compatible with the freedom of the
Information Age? If governments maintain policies of class warfare, reflected in con-
fiscatory taxes on wealth and in legislation mandating equality at the expense of free
choice, one wonders how the members of the global marketplace will react. Netizens
might choose to use the Internet to avoid taxation and to circumvent political
authority. And if electronic mobility is available as an alternative to government regulation of communication and commerce, there is potential for the relationship
between the individual and the state to change. If government no longer controls
access to and acquisition of information, will traditional respect for the public state
grow stronger? Or will private citizens increasingly assert their private interests vis-
à-vis loyalty to the public state?

There are some who point to the European continent, saying these questions are
already being asked and answered there. In 2000 more than 100,000 Europeans
were working in Silicon Valley; they had become frustrated with bureaucracy, with
punitive taxes on private income, capital gains and corporate earnings, with market
regulations serving social ends, and with political attitudes that stifle free enterprise
and choke individual initiative. Political leaders, and politicians — whether they are
in Europe, Asia, or in the United States — are reacting to the challenges of information technology as though their constituencies are merely domestic, as though the
Internet and the Information Age are changing nothing. We must face the possibility that the credibility of politicians and the merits of statist societies are being judged
today, to an increasing degree, by international electronic constituencies whose loyalties are global.

What Are We Becoming?

5.

THE MAN IN THE WHITE SUIT

*How many things served us yesterday as articles of faith,
which today are fables to us!*

{Montaigne, 1533-1592}

*Not chaos-like together crush'd and bruis'd,
But, as the world, harmoniously confus'd:
Where order in variety we see,
And where, though all things differ, all agree*

{Alexander Pope, "Windsor Forest," 1688-1744}

*Late in 1999 the Queen of England invested 100,000 pounds
in an Internet start-up that was mapping her British realm.
When www.Getmapping.uk was scheduled to go public,
in April 2000, her stock would be worth
approximately 1.2 million pounds.*

In 1951 the English actor Alec Guinness starred in a film called *The Man in the White Suit*. He played the role of a scientist whose invention of a remarkable cloth ignited a revolution in the textile industry. The synthetic fabric was indestructible, made by a new machine. The invention promised to transform the world of apparel, to change the nature of weaving and the creativity of design, and to redefine the role of the textile industry in society. By extension, it promised to leave nothing unaffected, including where people worked and how they exercised their taste in everything from food to wardrobe. Moreover, the cloth never got dirty. Its revolutionary nature was so overwhelming that analysts were ecstatic in praise of its global implications.

What did such an invention promise? The daughter of the textile mill owner said, "Don't you understand what this means? Millions of people all over the world, leading lives of drudgery. Fighting an endless losing battle against shabbiness and dirt. You've won that battle for them. You've set them free. The whole world's going to bless you." But, as it turned out, opinion was divided on this point.

Invention of an indestructible cloth which never soiled represented a major threat to professions of all kinds. The invention would shut down the cotton industry and make cotton plantations obsolete. There would be no more need for cotton pickers or for truckers to haul cotton to market. There would be no more need for cotton mills, or even for new clothes. So a conspiracy was hatched by government officials and competing industrialists to destroy the fiber. But, quite by accident, a flaw in the fabric emerged. The inventor got caught in a rain shower, the white suit got wet, and it fell apart. That was the end of the revolution, and of euphoric touters of the invention's revolutionary character.

Will the communication revolution end the same way? Is its alleged increased productivity all a fraud? Is "the world wide wait" a euphemism for a worldwide sham? Are Internet companies nothing more than buggy-whip stocks?

It is not certain what kind of fabric the Internet is made out of, nor do we know yet if the Information Age has created an Informational Man. But the analogy with *The Man in the White Suit* is worth considering. If the whole cloth had not soon gotten wet and disintegrated, astute investors everywhere would have been purchasing stock in companies with strange names like Whiteazon, FabricSystems, Cottonscape, and Suitsoft, all of which had gambled that the fabric would create a brave new world. In our example, none of these companies would have had any real, hard assets, but were worth billions of dollars on the stock market. And although the companies weren't paying any dividends, their stocks were owned by new millionaires who sang the praises of the Textile Age. On paper, the return on investment would have been enormous. Some called this the Goldilocks Economy.

The analogy is obvious, and so are the risks. During 1999 in the United States, the value of stocks traded on the NASDAQ increased by 85 percent. By the end of January 2000 the top ten stocks on the exchange were all Internet stocks: Microsoft, Cisco, Intel, Oracle, Sun Microsystems, MCI WorldCom, Ericsson, Dell, Qualcomm, and Yahoo!, with a combined stock market value of more than two trillion dollars. There existed a frenzy to buy, expressed in a cartoon depicting a suspendered businessman at his desk, holding his head in one hand and the telephone in the other. The caption read, "I don't care what it is — if it's got 'dot com' in the title, buy it!"

The investment frenzy was motivated by a desire to make easy money, and by a genuine belief in the power of computing and the Internet to improve our lives. Speculation in the future financial profitability of the information technology revolution changed the stock market, leading Mitchell Martin, writing in the *International Herald Tribune* in January 2000, to express some concerns:

> Investors obviously think Internet-related companies are going to earn a lot more than movie studios, car makers, newspaper publishers and everything else, which is why they are willing to accord stratospheric price-to-earning ratios to those technology stocks that bother to have profits at all. Many of the dot-coms do not have any earnings. Instead they have what are called burn rates, or the pace at which their losses will eat up their capital. Amazon.com Inc., the on-line retailer that is worth $23 billion, essentially takes investors' money and gives it to its customers, raising sales but creating a business model that puzzles conservative stock market observers.

The chief executive officers of the Internet companies themselves, sometimes described as "on-line pioneers," believe the risk justifies the cost — of course, they are using other people's money. A good example is the attitude of Kevin O'Connor, the thirty-eight-year-old CEO of DoubleClick, an Internet advertising network company founded in 1996 that creates and sells database technology and information to help advertisers reach specific groups of consumers. At a business roundtable discussion held in New York in November 1999, O'Connor was asked how long he thought DoubleClick could continue to exist without making any money. He replied:

> It's clear what the market's telling us. They want to give us a lot of money, so we take it and we invest. Why? We look back, and what was the biggest mistake that we made? We should have invested more money. We should have lost more money. Why? Because this is the biggest thing that's ever hit. Market share is everything.

> But it depends on what stage the company is in. People are going to start expecting profits from us in the next one to two years.

246

What O'Connor didn't say is that while some will succeed in making a profit beyond their wildest dreams, others (the majority) will fail. The trick is to pick the winners. Which of the Internet fabric makers are creating products and providing services that will add value, and which aren't? There is also another question, voiced by Alan Greenspan, chairman of the Federal Reserve Board, as quoted in Martin's *International Herald Tribune* story. Ten years from now, Greenspan wondered, will we look back and conclude that "the American economy was experiencing a once-in-a-century acceleration of innovation, which propelled forward productivity, output, corporate profits and stock prices at a pace not seen in generations, if ever"? Or will we conclude "that a good deal of what we are currently experiencing was just one of the many euphoric speculative bubbles that have dotted human history"?

No one knows the answer yet. But some writing on the wall appeared in October 1999, when the composition of companies comprising the Dow Jones industrial average was changed. The Dow is the world's most closely watched blue-chip stock index of thirty industrial companies. The substitution in October was made by the editors of *The Wall Street Journal,* Dow Jones & Company's flagship publication. They removed two bricks-and-mortar companies, Union Carbide and Goodyear Tire & Rubber, replacing them with Microsoft, the world's number-one computer operating system maker, and Intel, the world's number-one computer chip maker. The only other technology companies in the index were IBM and Hewlett-Packard. Did this represent the growing importance of technology in the economy? Or was it just inflating what skeptics call the Internet bubble?

This speculation deals with two different questions, and each has a different answer. Franco Modigliani, who received the Nobel prize in economics in 1985, said to Floyd Norris for an April 2000 article in the *International Herald Tribune,*

> [T]he bubble is rational in a certain sense. [The expectation of growth] produces the growth which confirms the expectation.... People will buy it because [the stock price] went up. But once you are convinced it is not growing anymore, nobody wants to hold a stock because it is overvalued.... Everybody wants to get out, and it collapses.

The inflated-value bubble did burst for many of the so-called dot-coms in the spring of 2000. We must ask, then, which Internet companies are "fireflies" and which aren't — and why not. My own answer is based on what I've learned since meeting the computer. Information technology represents a revolution begun in the twentieth century that will increase the productivity and enrich the lives of millions of ordinary men and women in the twenty-first. While stock prices and market indices will go up and down, some of the revolution's products and the processes they make possible are going to be very profitable for the customers, employees, and stockholders of those corporations that "get it."

It will not be a smooth ride, and no one with any sense claims that it will be. Jeremy Siegel, a professor of finance at the Wharton School of Business in Philadelphia, put this idea in an unusual way in *The Wall Street Journal* in April 1999:

> No one can deny that the Internet is a communications revolution. But the very accessibility that has made it spread like wildfire limits its ability to create premium profits....
>
> One of the fundamental tenets of economics is that value is created by scarcity, not by usefulness, need or desire. Water, necessary for the sustenance of life, costs pennies, but diamonds, used solely for adornment, fetch astronomical prices. I have no doubt that the Web will revolutionize the way goods and services are marketed. The Internet will deliver many billions of dollars of savings to consumers. But this in no way guarantees those billions will be handed over to the suppliers of this new form of communication.

One of the unknown factors that will affect financial outcomes is the role still to be played by governments that want to tax and control the marketplace. Bill Gates, the head of one of the largest corporations in the world, Microsoft, learned in 1998 that the iron hand of Uncle Sam is very much alive. His company was accused of predatory pricing of its Windows operating system and of monopolizing access to the World Wide Web by combining its Web browser, Internet Explorer, with its Windows programs in a way that made it very difficult to use competing browsers like Netscape. Gates, not known for his philanthropic commitment to think tanks whose scholars support free markets, endured trial by fire when he began testifying before the U.S. Congress in March 1998. He discovered that not even then-Vice President Albert Gore, renowned technophile, would come to his defense. Mr. Gates's "wealth and wit" offered him little protection before the Senate Judiciary Committee where he was attacked by Democrats Ted Kennedy, Herb Kohl, and Dianne Feinstein, all millionaires. The significance of the lesson was summed up best in March 1998 by Washington, D.C., columnist Paul Gigot in *The Wall Street Journal*:

> Mr. Gates, the country's most visible capitalist, is finally speaking

as if he isn't embarrassed by capitalism. You still won't mistake him for Ronald Reagan, or the invaluable T.J. Rodgers of Cypress Semiconductor. But he's at least warning that America's software success 'has not been driven by government regulation, but by freedom' and individual ingenuity.... Gates is like many CEOs who think that if they leave Washington alone, Washington will return the favor. Washington never does. Mr. Gates and Microsoft will find more allies if, while defending themselves, they also defend the liberty that allowed them to get rich.

During the remaining nine months of 1998 Gates discovered that, despite the new powers of the Information Age, the government in Washington, D.C., still had the will and legal authority to prosecute, in the national interest, alleged monopolistic business practices. Whether or not the lawsuit was the brainchild of individuals who understood the Internet and how it works is beside the point, because the lawsuit attacked the commercial use of information technologies that was changing faster than the lawsuit progressed. Indeed, the change was so rapid that what constituted alleged monopoly practices in March appeared to some to be obsolete in December as Sun Microsystems, AOL, and Netscape joined forces in the late autumn to challenge Microsoft's role in the use of computer technologies.

Sun's chief executive officer, Scott McNealy, predicted that Microsoft would have less than 50 percent of the market by 2002. And software developers were successfully writing and selling applications for Linux, a competing operating system. It's worth recalling the Department of Justice's antitrust suit in the 1970s against IBM, which allegedly had a monopoly on mainframe computers — a suit that cost millions of dollars until it was dropped in 1982, when IBM was in the throes of remaking itself as a competitive force in the industry. In November 1999, however, U.S. District Judge Thomas Penfield Jackson issued a finding of fact which concluded, in essence, "that Microsoft was a monopoly whose bullying tactics had hurt consumers and the economy by stifling innovation in the computer industry." And thus an arm of the government had succeeded, for the moment, in setting "the stage for an eventual ruling against the software giant and for remedies that could be as extreme as a breakup of the company."

On April 3, 2000, Microsoft was found guilty of breaking federal and state antitrust laws — many of them enacted at the beginning of the twentieth century — to protect its alleged monopoly. That left the company open to hundreds of private lawsuits filed by people looking for money, not government supervision. Almost immediately, the NASDAQ, where most high-tech stocks are traded (including Microsoft), and the Dow Jones Industrial Average both suffered large drops. And the "winners,"

Microsoft's competitors, who are supposed to benefit from the successful government prosecution — their stock prices too were sent reeling on April 3.

Whatever the merits of the case, the lawsuit was a case of government control versus freedom of the marketplace.

Unlike the fabric of the White Suit, the fabric of the Internet is getting stronger and more resilient. Part of the reason is competition, and part of the reason is found in the nature of networks, a point which the U.S. government in its case against Microsoft failed to understand. George Priest, a professor of law and economics at Yale Law School, wrote this opinion for *The Wall Street Journal* in September 1999:

> Neither Judge Jackson nor any court has seriously worked out the implications of competition in the context of a network. A network is different from traditional markets. In a network, the more connections, the more all participants gain. In a typical market, to tie one product to another may reduce consumer choice; in a network, it may expand choice.

The Internet does expand choice, and the freedom that goes with it. That's why the traditional historical relationship between the distribution of information and the exercise of power is breaking down. Centralism, welfare states, collectivism, hierarchical structures, old-boy networks, statist societies are all, in different ways, fossilized animals unwelcome in a wired world. The Information Age makes no distinctions between them or between the institutions that run them. It doesn't have to, because the force and freedom of the Internet is not dependent on any of these forms of institution or government. The best illustration is the question that has been raised in different ways throughout this book, namely, who controls the Internet and access to it? The University of Michigan's Douglas Van Houweling puts it this way:

> Who should be the traffic cop for the Internet — the federal government or private industry?

> As this ultimately works out, the traffic cop will be the marketplace. One of the things we've got to preserve when we do this is [the certainty] there is no central organization that manages the Internet.... The extraordinary thing about the Internet today is if somebody wants to use the Internet, you make arrangements to get connected to the Internet with some provider.

> ... You don't need to ask somebody's permission.

The Man in the White Suit

Whether it is certain that we are going to be connected is a moot question. In the United States, national policy is to connect the entire country — but before it became national policy, the Internet was already expanding, by itself. And in the United States, as elsewhere in the world, enthusiastic national policies of "connection," hailed by politicians who recognize the inevitable, is in conflict with expensive political policies of "control." If the Department of Justice's lawsuit against Microsoft demonstrated one thing clearly, it is that politicians are still trying to have it both ways.

As economic and financial boundaries become more porous — the common currency of the Euro is one example — new communities emerge connected to each other electronically, not politically. The meeting on the town square of the past is now taking place on the World Wide Web. In some ways we have just as much in common with the people we are communicating with across the globe as we do with our next door neighbors. Isolated communities now have the means to end their isolation if they wish, as George Melloan wrote in the January 18, 2000, *Wall Street Journal*:

> The idea that we are moving toward a dehumanized world in which technology rules our lives is rather the opposite of the truth. Information technology places greater importance than ever on the quality of human thought and its civilizing influence.... AOL Time Warner is indeed a big story, but not because some new corporate colossus is taking over the world. Rather, it's because two corporations are maneuvering to try to stay in business by better serving the public. That is the message, and it is not especially important what medium is used to carry it.

Countries that formerly had little to say in the global marketplace are now playing larger roles in the creation and manufacture of information technologies, from Ireland to India and from Singapore to Scotland. Interests in common, shared on the Internet, allow the exchange of ideas among people whose social classes and racial backgrounds once made such contact improbable, if not impossible. The name given these Netizens by David Farber, professor of telecommunication systems at the University of Pennsylvania, is "Interesting People." And that's what my friend Hodge said also, when I asked him how he thought the Internet had affected me. He said, "You have become friends with interesting people you never would have given the time of day to before, nor they to you. It's opened up worlds of common interests and communication for you all. And, in your case, it's made you more tolerant."

To paraphrase Gaku, the revelation of revolutions is that *the new*, replacing *the old*, often becomes institutionalized itself. A good example is the French Revolution. Many of the results it produced — described by Ben Franklin's phrase *liberté, égalité, fraternité* — are the statist institutions of today's France that replaced the royal networks of pre-1789. It should be expected that some of the results of the Communication Revolution will become institutionalized as well. Governments will, sooner or later, try to construct new tax structures for e-commerce. Governments will seek to impose federal regulation of software products and their use. Governments will attempt to institutionalize new ways to monopolize information, control its distribution, and invade privacy. Governments will seek to control access to and use of the Internet. But governments will also encounter new obstacles, because rules and relationships have changed. There is not a new dimension of real time, but information technology gives us new ways to use it. That development alone is challenging the operation of government as it challenges the conduct of our lives. Information technologies have compressed the time it takes to traverse distance, have reconfigured the clockwork of our marketplaces, and have also raised our social, economic, and political expectations. The Internet, in short, has created what disciples of Friedrich Hayek, Nobel laureate in economics, call "spontaneous social order without centralized control."

The outcome of the struggle between spontaneous social order without centralized control will have major social, economic, and political repercussions in every society around the globe in which the freedom of the individual is subservient to the state. It is not surprising, for example, that convergence of the computer with telecommunication technology vexes China's leaders, because they recognize that a "spontaneous social order" is incompatible with rigid government diagramming of social, economic, and political life. Chinese leaders are facing a specious choice. They are seeking to suppress dissent at the same time they are encouraging the growth of the information technologies that make the electronic expression of dissent possible. Do they believe that the global marketplace of the twenty-first century will really allow them to choose just one, or just the other?

And what of the Europeans, whose creation of a single currency, the Euro, is a welcome attempt to make the European Union a dominant force in the global marketplace? Do Europe's leaders recognize that the Euro alone will not be sufficient to meet the challenges of the Information Age? Thanks to the Internet and telecommunication, the physical location of a corporation in Europe is becoming less important than the tax jurisdiction. The Euro gives German corporations, for example, greater freedom to make capital investment in Ireland if Germany's corporate tax rates are not competitive. Do Europe's leaders now understand that the viability of their respective economies will be decisively affected by their tax policies? In this case, among the European governments caught in the conflict between free market competition and control, France is a notable example. The centralized control of free markets so coveted by French political leaders and the zealousness with which that authority is exercised stand in stark contrast to the commitment to personal freedom by French citizens. It's known as "capitalism of connivance" between government and business. It allows government to rule royally and to tax punitively. And it permits private enterprise to survive marginally.

The irony, explained Nobel laureate Milton Friedman in a March 1999 interview with *Le Figaro* magazine's Guy Sorman, is that France will find a way out: "I think that fraud and the black market are well enough developed to compensate for your stupid laws." When my assistant Elisabeth read this she said, "That's the story of the rooster!" She told me the following riddle, asked for decades in France: Why did France choose the rooster as its national symbol? Because it's the only animal that sings when its feet are in shit!

The grand reluctance of the French government to give up control is an irony par excellence in a country whose political philosophers authored the concept of laissez-faire. In Paris, government leaders laud the French economic and social model, as they derisively compare it to "Anglo-Saxon capitalism." But thousands of French men and women working in Silicon Valley look at the model differently. Darius Sanai elicited the following comments for a story in *The European* the first week of June, 1998:

> 'In France the whole system is paralyzed, from the bottom up.... It is a gigantic pyramid which sucks the best people into public service or careers where they become intrinsically part of the system, with no incentive to change anything and every incentive not to do anything at all. The system of elite *grandes écoles* ... dates from times when the military was fundamental [to the economy], nearly 200 years ago, yet it still forms the structure of our country.'

> 'In French companies, if you're not from the *grandes écoles* then you'll never make senior management.... You know you can be extremely good and never get to the top....'

What is occurring in France can properly be called the French Paradox. In contrast to the government in Paris, individual French citizens are embracing the Information Age with creativity, imagination, and style, as they are in Republic Alley in Paris. So also are people like Luc Perron, who lives in a manor house with the beautiful name of *Chante Alouette*, near the Loire river, where he designs furniture by computer for shops as far away as Japan, Mexico, and South Africa, and as close as Paris. He communicates with his clients around the globe using e-mail service provided by Wanadoo (Luc.Perron@wanadoo.fr), and via his Web site: www.luc-perron.com. Or, marvel at an illustration in the Auvergne. Located there is one of the oldest continually operating businesses in France, founded in 1463. It is in an ancient mill next to a stream, in the hills above a town called Ambert, famous for its cheese. The company has customers on almost every continent, including Queen Elizabeth in England and Bark Frameworks in New York City. The company's most famous product is paper, still made by hand. Today, the company recognizes that using pen and ink is not the only way to communicate. If you're interested in doing business with Richard de Bas you can write the company a letter, call on the telephone, or send a fax. And if you know how to use the Internet, you can find Richard de Bas on the World Wide Web.

If it can't be said with certainty how the French Paradox will be resolved, it can nonetheless be concluded with virtual certainty that France's "Bourbon Bureaucrats" of the *grandes écoles* face a formidable challenge in their efforts to orchestrate the "spontaneous social order" the Internet has created. In turn, the future struggle between the private French citizen and the public French state is likely to be both revolutionary and profound. Is the significance of the consequences beyond the vision of those controlling the centralized institutions of France?

The answer is anyone's guess. But one approach was taken by French prime minister Lionel Jospin in May 2000 when he announced creation in Marseille of an Internet *grande école*. Was this another example of the French maxim "the more things change, the more they remain the same"? If there is going to be a French renaissance, said French Parliament member Pierre Lellouche in the spring, it is going to come "from outside the political debate and independently of the political class.... What the political class is doing is foreign to the real world and basically irrelevant." And the outside catalyst will be, according to French communication specialist Patrick d'Humières, "the young generations who embrace the values of liberty, of risk, of challenge, and of profit, all of which are essential aspects of economic creation."

Has history, in the Information Age, lost its compass? Well, as a historian it seems to me history has never had one. History records revolutions, it doesn't choreograph them. Those of us who are part of them, for good or ill, seldom recognize the moment and can never be certain of the reality of the result to follow. So wrote Albert Einstein in 1938:

In our endeavor to understand reality we are somewhat like a man

trying to understand the mechanism of a closed watch. He sees the
face and the moving hands, even hears its ticking, but he has no
way of opening the case. If he is ingenious he may form some picture of a mechanism which could be responsible for all the things
he observes, but he may never be quite sure his picture is the only
one which could explain his observations. He will never be able to
compare his picture with the real mechanism and he cannot even
imagine the possibility of the meaning of such a comparison.

Father Time, on the other hand, has always known the real mechanism, long
before hypertext mark-up language was invented. That doesn't help us very much,
because we don't know him. But we do have something in common. Neither he, nor
we, could anticipate what we would do with webs and nets, once we discovered we
could use them, nor that they would take us on an amazing adventure. But if we
think we've changed something fundamental in the nature of man, we've gone one
step too far. Alexander Pope was right that "the proper study of mankind is man."
The Internet doesn't change that; man after all, created it. Indeed, the Internet makes
the proper study of mankind more compelling, because the Internet's fabric is real
and so is man's fragility. For some it may seem that the world is too much with us.
But for others, such as Italian industrialist Carlo de Benedetti, "we are living in a veritable revolution never seen before in economics."

Apropos of something real, when this book goes to the publisher, I'm going to sit
down with Hodge and have a visit with one of the oldest technologies in existence.
It's called Jack Daniel's technology. And it's not a virtual reality. It is certain. And I
like to think I control it. All I have to do is pull the cork, pour a little sour mash in
a highball glass, add ice, and listen to Glenn Miller play "A String of Pearls." That's
getting wired the old-fashioned way; and, if nothing else, I understand the music
playing. In the meantime, I will also continue communicating with wonder and
excitement on the Internet. If my use of real time hadn't changed my life, I wouldn't
have written this book. Nor could I say that, among the things I've learned, is to use
my time more carefully. It may not travel, but it's in limited supply. Once it's gone,
it's gone. It's history. I'll never get it back. Father Time knows that. I trust I'll remember it, too!

Do we need a compass pointing to the future? If we had one, would we use it?
History tells us we probably wouldn't recognize it, and we wouldn't follow its true
direction if we did. So where does that leave us? I'm not sure. But I know that the
final word on the Information Age will not be written by wireless networks, or by
the Internet. "What we are becoming" will be determined by ourselves. I also am

convinced that Christopher Columbus, if he were with us, would agree that the return on this investment in time and technology will be measured in ways we can't yet imagine. That measurement will be taken in the future, not the present. He would also applaud the exploration of the Information Age, whose vehicle is not a ship but the Internet, taking us on a voyage to a new Age of Discovery. And, I suspect, if we expressed doubt about the wisdom of the journey, he would say, "Don't you think I had doubts? Don't you think I was tempted to turn around halfway? And what if I had? The answer is simple. The adventure was inevitable, and someone would have made it."

AN AFTERWORD FOR THE CAST

When you sell a man a book
you don't just sell him twelve ounces of paper and ink and glue
— you sell him a whole new life.

{Christopher Morley, 1890-1957}

I wasn't entirely confident, when I began writing this book, that I knew what I was doing. I had a Ph.D. degree in history, not in computer science. But I wanted to write it.

Meeting the computer was changing my behavior. I could see it first in little ways. I began to turn on the computer as soon as I arrived at my office, rather than looking at my phone messages. Then in bigger ways: I started sending e-mails instead of writing letters on the typewriter. It astonished me, as I thought about it — and I couldn't help thinking about it — because my life was changing. My friends weren't using computers, at least most of them weren't, and their lives seemed to be just fine. That's what they thought, and they were so sure of it they told me so. It was a little disconcerting. But as I learned more about the wired world, the clearer it became to me that some of my friends weren't living on the same planet I was. So I started writing it all down.

The bits and pieces, first scribbled on scraps of paper in airplanes and hotel rooms, became the introduction, written on my laptop. As I wrote, I remember saying to myself with real conviction that the Internet was also affecting how I thought about things. And it hit home when, as I started telling my children about it, they told me that I was becoming more liberal. They hastened to add, as they saw the horror-stricken expression on my face, that they meant to say, "You're becoming more reasonable since you decided to enter the twentieth century."

I chose to consider their observation a compliment, but accurate or not, it didn't help me find a title for my book. Throughout 1999 I had tried to find a brilliantly inspired one that would roll off my tongue. Even though I had a list of more than one hundred, none of them worked. One, for example, was *Virtual Certainties* — that was dreamed up in a seafood restaurant in Seattle, influenced by prawns, French bread and chardonnay. Another was *The Connected* — a friend unintentionally gave me that one in a restaurant in Paris as we watched Parisians talking on their mobile phones during lunch. A third was *I'm Wired*. It seemed like sheer genius at the time, but it was really a bad idea that occurred to me about midnight on New Year' s Eve 1999, when I was undoubtedly wired the old-fashioned way. But all of the titles had one thing in common. They were tired, trite, and boring.

On the evening of January 14, fourteen days into the new millennium, I went to a dinner of my wife's book group to hear a discussion led by Bill Davidow, chairman of the board of a Silicon Valley company called Rambus. We talked about isolation, instability, and the Internet. The gist of the discussion was that the Communication Revolution, for better or worse, is producing a lot of unintended consequences.

As we were leaving that evening, I saw a member of the group, Suzanne Roth, at the door. I told her that my book was also about unintended consequences, and asked her if she thought that would be a good title. She smiled and said, "What you really want to call it is *What the Hell Happened?*" I started to laugh because I know what has happened to me and I wouldn't change a thing! And that is when it occurred to me, for the first time, that my Internet travels have really been about *Professor Bark's Amazing Digital Adventure*.

What you have just read — from Hedy Lamarr in Hollywood to *Les Branchés* in Paris to Henrik Fulda at the Chaos Computer Club in Hamburg — is what has altered, profoundly, my view of our world. I am, five years after that chance encounter in an airplane in 1995, still embarked on an amazing digital adventure, but now as a Wired Man living in a networked world in which the convergence of computer technology with telecommunication introduces all of us to perplexing perspectives.

These are for me, however, not questions of isolation and instability, or whether we are living in an age of spiritual machines. On the contrary, I am living in an elegant universe in which my electronic affair with my laptop and the Internet continues to change everything I do, the way I think, and what I think about, as I send my e-mails flying across continents and over oceans.

I now think about time and knowledge as a digital dimension to which I am connected. How I use information has set my mind free in a way I could never have imagined before I met the computer. I hope and trust that what has happened to me will happen to you, also. If it does, the wired world will change your life too.

ACKNOWLEDGMENTS

Writing this book has been the most challenging, exhilarating, and vexing thing I've ever done. And I loved doing it. I don't know how reviewers will judge what's here — that's obviously their call — but that's not the point. I do hope my friends have enjoyed reading this book as much as I have enjoyed writing it. This story is really for you, as well as for me. Many of us grew up in a world vastly different from what we call today the Information Age. We thought about taking flowers to our sweethearts on Valentine's Day and then summoning up the courage to ask them for a date. We never dreamed of sending them an *e-vite*. We never thought of a wired world, where our freedom would be made of webs and nets — never, that is, until our vertical world of success, defined by clubs, class, and comfort, was changed forever by the communication revolution of the 1990s.

How ironic it is — but not surprising — that after all my efforts to understand the Internet, a wired world full of new choices, I am left with only one: to publish this manuscript before I decide that the Internet was a great invention but, like *The Man in the White Suit,* it wasn't made of real fabric after all. Yet that's a decision I will never make, any more than I can make the hands of the grandfather clock tick yesterday's time. Real time, even as I write these words, continues to move inexorably forward. The Internet's unintended consequences are changing the world forever. There's no going back!

For my friends, also, the only direction to go is forward. Many of them helped me do that, which is why this book has a cast of characters. They, both old friends and new ones, have all ventured with me along the way. The following words are my grateful acknowledgment to them:

Annelise G. Anderson. The first person at the Hoover Institution to take real time, when she didn't have much to spare, to help me meet my new laptop.
Gwendolyn Barnes. She gave to me consistently, continually, and constantly her faithful encouragement, with smiles, laughter and wit. I can't thank her enough.
Eleanor Carlton Bark. At the age of eighty-five, my mother read the introduction and said, "You know, I like it!" Do mothers always say that?
William Carroll Bark. My father, who died before this manuscript was finished, was a classical man who had great respect for Clio, the Greek muse of

history. I wonder what he would say about this new Age of Discovery.

Jared C. Bark. *The New York Times* calls him "the Tiffany of picture framers." I call him my brother in New York City.

France de Sugny Bark. It took a little doing to persuade my wife, but she's wired now too. During the writing of this book she gave real meaning to the word "patience," because I was really difficult to live with.

Gilles and Séverine Béal. They learned about the fax revolution firsthand in 1997, and about the telecommunication revolution in 1999. They haven't been the same since, but their joie de vivre hasn't changed one whit.

Jean-Luc Béal. He became a mobile man in October 1999 and a wired man two months later; but to give credit where it is due, he was already *un homme moderne.*

Peter B. Bedford. In a parking lot across from the Mark Hopkins Hotel in San Francisco, Peter told me about Nicholas Negroponte's book *being digital.* It was spring 1997, and I'd never heard of the author or the book.

Carolyn Billheimer. She is the business data analyst at the *San Jose Mercury News.* If you want to know what's going on in Silicon Valley don't read the *Washington Post.* Read the *Mercury.* Then call Carolyn!

G.R. Blank. He modestly refers to himself as a "Senior Program Manager, Marketing" for IBM Corporation. He finds the Internet, as he wrote to me on December 8, 1998, "indispensable" in his daily life too.

William Bonnett. He is the Hoover Institution's Chief Computer Guru. You have to get in line to talk to him.

Thomas J. Bray. A distinguished journalist for the *Detroit News* with a quick wit, he knows how to write.

Sheryl J. Brown. She is a Renaissance woman, and director of the Office of Communications at the United States Institute of Peace.

Elisabeth Burgess. She read the entire manuscript, and when I asked for her ideas on the title, she wrote them down on a sheet of letterhead, asking "What the Devil is this About?" But ... she knows!

Thierry Burgess. In between and during airplane flights to New York and Europe, he took the time to read the entire manuscript, and then the time to write to me. *Merci, beaucoup!*

Ursula Morris Carter. To my irreplaceable, implacable, and unflappable research assistant of more than fourteen years' standing, I owe a debt of gratitude, which if I e-mailed the whole world, wouldn't do her justice.

A. Michael Casey. He is a very smart lawyer related to our family who always goes right to the point, even if I don't like it.

Samuel Adams Cochran. He's the twin who asked, "Hedy Whooo?"

Dwight M. Cochran III. Dwight is Sam's brother, who thinks he knows who Hedy was, and will tell you early and often.

Matthew John Cochran. Matthew is the Twin who knows who Hedy is ... as well as a number of other things.

William H. Davidow. He understands. He wrote a book in 1992, with Michael S. Malone, called *The Virtual Corporation*, when only a very few had thought about it.

Audrey Decherd. Audrey!

Maureen Decherd. Audrey's mother.

Robert W. Decherd. Audrey's father. He is also president and chief executive officer of A.H. Belo Corporation.

William Decherd. He took his sister's photograph, which appears in Chapter One.

Marie Fitzgerald Dion. She married Sam Cochran. At first, I thought that's all the recommendation she needed. But then she created her own Web site. "Wow" is the only word that will do. She's a peach, and also my daughter-in-law.

Bruce P. Dohrmann. He is the most thoughtful investment banker I know, and I've known him a very long time! But most important, he is a good friend.

Wilson D. Donohoe. He is an extraordinarily creative and resilient cousin who knows the difference between quality and mediocrity.

Janet R. Dutra. She kept the wolves at bay for twenty-two years. That's no small accomplishment. She also knows where they all live! But don't call her; she'll never tell you.

Lester D. Earnest. He was the executive officer of Stanford University's Artificial Intelligence Laboratory from 1965 to 1980.

Marina Eloy. Perceptive and wise, she also knows how to laugh. She gave me a bedroom and a limitless supply of grapefruit juice in her Paris apartment in December, and again in January, March and June 1999-2000, as I was frantically trying to finish this manuscript. *Merci, mille fois, Marina!*

eMarketer, Inc. Based in New York City, eMarketer has a statsmaster named Geoff Ramsey, whose colleague, Robert Janes, provided me with a wealth of up-to-date information about e-commerce and advertising on the Internet. Both were exceedingly helpful.

Forrester Research, Inc. This is one of the leading research firms that analyzes information technology and its impact on businesses, consumers, and society. Public relations manager Mike Shirer provided me with statistical information on short notice.

Hendrik H. Fulda. He is an IBM-certified Warp Server Engineer & Team OS/2 in Hamburg. If the truth be known, Tom Paine and Patrick Henry would have been his friends in the eighteenth century.

William S. Geisler. He is an Episcopal minister with whom I can discuss both God and the Internet — and I do!

Barbara Geisler. William's wife, she laughs, cooks, writes novels, and has an extraordinary sense of savoir faire. Her company, if you are fortunate enough to enjoy it, is delightful.

James G. Gidwitz. He explained to me, patiently, why I shouldn't use the phrase "Mr. Real Time," citing as reasons his three daughters. I never challenged him on that point.

David Green. On New Year's Eve 1999 he introduced me to Einstein's perspective on reality.

Michèle Griotteray. She doesn't know it, because I've never told her, but she incomparably enriched my world of virtual reality on a Paris evening shortly before Christmas 1999, then redefined my concept of e-mail flying over the ocean. *Merci*, and that is the only word that will do.

Moira Gunn. Moira goes right to the point, and took the time in August 1997 to help me "get it" also.

Vipin Gupta. Not only did Vipin actually read my manuscript, he patiently gave me the benefit of his insight, and continues to do so.

Christian Hacke. I've known Christian since I was a graduate student at the *Freie Universität Berlin*. We have a special friendship, not only because we enjoy each other's company, but because both of us love life.

Cathy Haibach. She is a representative of Tribune Media Services, the company that syndicates *Dick Tracy*.

Marie-Caroline Hammerer. A practicing physician and the mother of my goddaughter in Hamburg, Sophie Charlotte, M-C is an extraordinary lady — one who obviously used superb judgment in the selection of her parents.

Judd Hanna. After I told him what I call "The Nalini and Gaku Story," he got a laptop too. He hasn't been the same since.

Earl I. Heenan III. He is a sensitive and perceptive man who leads a double life of business and unceasing intellectual curiosity. In both roles he has plied me with articles about the Information Age for four years. He is Sheryl Brown's counterpart, a Renaissance man.

Anne Heenan. I call her "Mrs. Wrong Time" — what else can I say except that I'm very fond of her (and of her sharp tongue!), and equally respectful of her ability to combine her professional and private commitments in a unique fashion.

James W. Hodgen. There is and will always be only one Hodge. By choice and not by birth, he is also a member of our family. God broke the mold when he was born.

Eberhard Hoene. He is the father of Matthias, and one of my oldest friends in Berlin.

Matthias Moritz Hoene. The very intelligent, eldest son of Eberhard, he understands electronic "trees" and *Baumkuchen*.

Victoria Sophie Hoene. She is my goddaughter in Berlin, with whom I am always connected, thanks to the marvel of e-mail.

Bertrand Jacquillat. He thought he understood the Internet, but needed other people to answer his e-mail because he didn't know how it worked. Until, that is, he became wired himself in March 2000. You owe me *un déjeuner*, Bertrand!

Hubert Jousset. He is *branché* in Paris, and "connected" with us in California.

Max Kampelman. He is a "diplomat" of the United States, for whom I have a great deal of respect.

Nalini C. Indorf Kaplan. Nalini gets credit for changing my life. Nothing less.

David B. Kennedy. He read the introduction to this manuscript, but he never told me what he thought of it. He would say he's very sensitive, too! Having said that, I do consider his company both pleasure and privilege.

Burkhard and Erika Koch. They both lived the significance of the Berlin Wall, and its relationship with control, information, and freedom. Burkhard had an e-mail address before I did.

Henry N. Kuechler III. If it weren't for Henry, I wouldn't have ridden off into the computer sunset. But more than that, Hank is a friend who has ridden with me on this entire, amazing journey.

Connie Loarie. When she sent me her comments on the introduction, she signed her name in real ink! And added a footnote to that effect, to make sure I didn't miss it.

Stephen J. Lukasik. He was the director of ARPA in the early 1970s. When I called him out of the blue for help, he gave it, in spades.

John McCarthy. He is much more than merely a professor of computer science at Stanford University.

Carol MacCorkle. She had the presence of mind to give the draft introduction to her husband.

Mac MacCorkle. He had the good sense to read it, and then called me to discuss "Father Time."

Thomas Gale Moore. He is a Hoover colleague whose eyes never glazed over, although he probably wondered from time to time what I was trying to talk about.

John H. Moore. A goodly part of Chapter Three is thanks to John's reflection.

Mike Nelson. He is at Pretty Good Privacy, and believes in the right to privacy.

Lucile Oliphant. In addition to my mother, she is the best-read lady I've ever met, and she actually liked this book.

Jeanne Poett. She sat in front of the fireplace in our kitchen at Stanford while I read her excerpts of this book during a three-year period. She was never impatient and she always laughed. Then she said, "Don't you think it might be better if you said it this way, Dennis?" I can't thank her enough.

Robert L. Queller. The spell-check on his computer didn't recognize the word "Internet."

John Raisian. The director of the Hoover Institution, he generously, patiently, and consistently supported this enterprise.

Michael Raoul-Duval. Michael understands the concept of time better than anyone else I know.

Alexander Rühland. He is my godson in Hannover, whose late father was one of my closest friends.

Gaku Sato. Gaku, whom you have met in this book, is and will always be *The Professor*. He also is a gourmet cook.

Amity Shlaes. She is a writer and journalist of the finest caliber, formerly at *The Wall Street Journal* and today a columnist for the *Financial Times*. I have been the beneficiary of her judgment, perception, and wit for more than fifteen years.

Thomas Simmons. He is a unique investment advisor who understands the meaning of change and its consequences, and meets both with integrity.

Richard H. Solomon. He introduced me to Stephen Lukasik, but also to the value of real audio and virtual diplomacy.

Terry Su. He is the former Webmaster at the Hoover Institution.

Jim Taylor. He is associated with KCBS News and Programming. He has done us all, in Silicon Valley, a real service with his superb reporting on the communication revolution.

Peter E. Thieriot. I call him "The Whittler." We're still "whittling" together.

Joshua P. Thieriot. He is The Whittler's highly literate, spread-spectrum-hopping, on-line-trading son. I've never understood why he named his dog Calvin K.

Ferdinand M. Thieriot. He doesn't know it, but when I want a refreshing outlook on life, I can always count on him.

Bert D. Thomas. We exchange e-mail — Bert, at age ninety-eight, in Montecito, and I, at age fifty-eight, in Stanford.

Darrell M. Trent. After he changed his e-mail address for the seventh time, I gave up! His wife and I discuss that from time to time.

Rachael Trinder. A very quick and sharp-witted Washington attorney, she was the first person to laugh when I read her Hodge's description of Mr. Real Time.

Richard A. Ware. He is a gentleman of intellect and wisdom whose friendship I have been privileged to enjoy for almost forty years.

Donald Alford Weadon, Jr. Perceptive and patient, he explained to me the history and importance of encryption. My gratitude to him is herewith encrypted: "*vkdklalr44laldkdk220alaldk33ka d3ka e77*." I think that's my digital signature, Don!

Dan Wilhelmi. He is the Other Computer Guru at the Hoover Institution. He and Bill Bonnett are irreplaceable.

Matthew F. Wilson. The *San Francisco Chronicle*'s executive editor, he never failed to return my telephone calls.

Woodford Press. In Emeryville, California, there is an outstanding group of professionals who have contributed their unequalled expertise to the creation of this book — Richard Defendorf as the editor, Debby Morse as the copy editor, Jim Santore as the designer, and Ann Lewis as the director of marketing. Their patience in listening to the explanation of my concerns and then showing me the right direction is why they are a unique group I hold in the highest regard. Thank you, each and every one!

Sunia Yang. She is an indispensable computer-systems manager who knows just as much about flora and fauna as she does about the Internet, and can explain why.

BIBLIOGRAPHY

Ashbrook, Tom. *The Leap. A Memoir of Love and Madness in the Internet Goldrush*. San Francisco: Houghton Mifflin, 2000.

Berners-Lee, Tim. *Weaving the Web. The Original Design and Ultimate Destiny of the World Wide Web by Its Inventor*. New York: Harper Collins, 1999.

Bronson, Po. *The Nudist on the Late Shift and Other True Tales of Silicon Valley*. New York: Random House, 1999.

Borsook, Paulina. *Cyberselfish: A Critical Romp Through the Terribly Libertarian Culture of High-Tech*. Washington/San Francisco: Public Affairs, 2000.

Cairncross, Frances. *The Death of Distance*. Boston: Harvard Business School Press, 1997.

Cringely, Robert X. *Accidental Empires: How the Boys of Silicon Valley Make Their Millions, Battle Foreign Competition, and Still Can't Get a Date*. New York: Harper Collins, 1993 and 1996. Originally published by Addison-Wesley Publishing Company, 1992.

Davidow, William H. *The Virtual Corporation*. New York: Edward Burlingame Books/Harper Business, 1992.

Davidson, James Dale and Rees-Mogg, Lord William. *The Sovereign Individual. How to Survive and Thrive During the Collapse of the Welfare State*. New York: Simon & Schuster, 1997.

Dertouzos, Michael. *What Will Be: How the New World of Information Will Change Our Lives*. New York: Harper Collins, 1997.

Dorn, James A., ed. *The Future of Money in the Information Age*. Washington, D.C.: Cato Institute, 1997.

Drexler, Eric. *Engines of Creation*. London: Fourth Estate Ltd., 1996.

Dyson, Esther. *Release 2.0. A Design for Living in the Digital Age*. New York: Broadway Books, 1997.

Dyson, George. *Darwin Among the Machines*. Reading, Mass: Addison Wesley Publication, 1997.

Etzioni, Amitai. *The Limits of Privacy*. New York: Basic Books, 1999.

Evans, Philip and Wurster, Thomas. *Blown to Bits: How the New Economics of Information Transforms Strategy.* Boston: Harvard Business School Press, 2000.

Fortey, Richard. *Life: A Natural History of the First Four Billion Years of Life on Earth.* New York: Vintage Books, 1999.

Freedman, David H. and Mann, Charles C. *At Large. The Strange Case of the World's Biggest Internet Invasion.* New York: Simon & Schuster, 1997.

Freiberger, Paul and Swaine, Michael. *Fire in the Valley: The Making of the Personal Computer.* New York: McGraw Hill, 2000.

Gates, Bill. *The Road Ahead.* London and New York: Penguin Group, 1995; revised paperback edition 1996.

Gelernter, David. *Machine Beauty: Elegance and the Heart of Technology.* New York: Basic Books, 1998.

Greene, Brian. *The Elegant Universe.* New York: W. W. Norton & Company, 1999.

Guéhenno, Jean-Marie. *The End of the Nation State.* Minneapolis: University of Minnesota Press, 1995.

Hafner, Katie and Lyon, Matthew. *Where Wizards Stay Up Late. The Origins of the Internet.* New York: Simon & Schuster, 1996.

Hagel III, John and Armstrong, Arthur G. *Net Gain: Expanding Markets Through Virtual Communities.* Boston: Harvard Business School Press, 1997.

Hauben, Michael, and Hauben, Ronda. *Netizens: On the History and Impact of Usenet and the Internet.* Los Alamitos, California: IEEE Computer Society Press, 1997.

Henderson, Bill, editor. *Minutes of the Lead Pencil Club.* New York: Pushcart Press, 1997 (1996).

Huntington, Samuel P. *The Clash of Civilizations and the Remaking of World Order.* New York: Simon & Schuster, 1996.

Jonscher, Charles. *The Evolution of Wired Life.* New York: John Wiley, 1999.

Katz, Jon. *Geeks: How Two Lost Boys Rode the Internet out of Idaho.* New York: Villard Books, 2000.

Kelly, Kevin. *New Rules for the New Economy. 10 Radical Strategies for a Connected World.* New York: Viking, 1998.

Komisar, Randy. *The Monk and the Riddle: The Education of a Silicon Valley Entrepreneur.* Boston: Harvard Business School Press, 2000.

Kurzweil, Ray. *The Age of Spiritual Machines: When Computers Exceed Human Intelligence*. New York: Viking, 1999.

Lewis, Michael. *The New New Thing*. New York: W.W. Norton, 1999.

Liebowitz, Stan J. and Margolis, Stephen E. *Winners, Losers & Microsoft*. Oakland, California: Independent Institute, 1999.

McKenzie, Richard B. *Trust on Trial. How the Microsoft Case is Reframing the Rules of* Competition. Cambridge, Mass.: Perseus Publishing, 2000.

McRae, Hamish. *The World in 2020. Power, Culture and Prosperity: A Vision of the Future*. London: HarperCollins Publishers, 1995.

Micklethwait, John and Woolridge, Adrian. *A Future Perfect: The Challenge and Hidden Promise of Globalization*. San Francisco: Jossey-Bass, 2000.

Moravec, Hans. *Robot: Mere Machine to Transcendent Mind*. New York: Oxford University Press, 1999.

Negroponte, Nicholas. *Being Digital*. New York: Vintage Books, 1996.

Nelson, Theodor Holm. *Literary Machines*. Published simultaneously by the author in a massmarket edition by the distributors, of South Bend, Indiana; and as hypertext on disc for Macintosh by Owl International, Inc., of Bellevue, Washington, 1987.

Packard, David. *The HP Way: How Bill Hewlett and I Built Our Company*. New York: Harper Collins, 1995.

Perkins, Anthony and Michael. *The Internet Bubble*. New York: HarperBusiness, 1999.

Pottruck, David S. and Pearce, Terry. *Clicks and Mortar: Passion Driven Growth in an Internet Driven World*. San Francisco: Jossey-Bass, 2000.

Reid, Robert H. *Architects of the Web. 1,000 Days that Built the Future of Business*. New York: John Wiley & Sons, 1997.

Rifkin, Jeremy, *The Age of Access*. New York: Jeremy P. Tarcher/Putnam, 2000.

Rivlin, Gary. *The Plot to Get Bill Gates: An Irreverent Investigation of the World's Richest Man and the People Who Hate Him*. New York: Times Books, 1999.

Rushkoff, Douglas. *Ecstasy Club*. New York: Harper Collins, 1997.

Schneier, Bruce. *Applied Cryptography*. New York: John Wiley & Sons, 1996.

Scully, Arthur B. and Woods, William W. *B2B Exchanges: The Killer Application in the Business-to-Business Internet Revolution*. Humble, Texas: ISI Publications, 1999.

268

Seabrook, John. *Deeper: My Two-Year Odyssey in Cyberspace*. New York: Simon & Schuster, 1997.

Seabrook, John. *Nobrow*. New York, A. A. Knopf; distributed by Random House, 2000.

Segaller, Stephen. *Nerds: A Brief History of the Internet*. New York: TV Books, 1998.

Shapiro, Andrew. *The Control Revolution*. New York: PublicAffairs, 1999.

Shiller, Robert J. *Irrational Exuberance*. Princeton: Princeton University Press, 2000.

Spector, Robert. *Amazon.Com*. New York: HarperBusiness, 2000.

Standage, Tom. *The Victorian Internet. The Remarkable Story of the Telegraph and the Nineteenth Century's On-Line Pioneers*. New York: Walker Publishing, 1998.

Stoll, Cliff. *Silicon Snake Oil*. New York: Doubleday, 1995.

_____. *The Cuckoo's Egg: Tracking a Spy Through the Maze of Computer Espionage*. New York: Pocket Books, 1990.

Strauss, William and Howe, Neil. *The Fourth Turning. What the Cycles of History Tell Us About America's Next Rendezvous with Destiny*. New York: Broadway Books, 1997.

Stross, Randall E. *eBoys: The First Inside Account of Venture Capitalists at Work*. New York: Crown Publishing, 2000.

Toffler, Alvin. *The Third Wave*. New York: Morrow, 1980.

Turkle, Sherry. *Life on the Screen: Identity in the Age of the Internet*. New York: Simon & Schuster, 1995.

Waugh, Alexander. *Time*. New York: Carroll & Graf Publishing, Inc., 1999.

Whitaker, Reg. *The End of Privacy: How Total Surveillance Is Becoming a Reality*. New York: New Press, 1999.

Wriston, Walter B. *The Twilight of Sovereignty*. New York: Baker & Taylor, 1997.

Yergin, Daniel and Stanislaw, Joseph. *The Commanding Heights. The Battle Between Government and the Marketplace That Is Remaking the Modern World*. New York: Simon & Schuster, 1998.

INDEX